I0817545

PROFILE DRAFTING *for* HANDWEAVERS

Designs, Projects & Expert Tips for Turning Your Ideas Into Weave Structures

DEB ESSEN

Other Schiffer Craft Books by the Author:

Easy Weaving with Supplemental Warps: Overshot, Velvet, Shibori, and More, ISBN 978-0-7643-6470-9

Swatch Critters from the Pin Loom: Step-by-Step Instructions for Making 30 Cuddly Animals from Woven Squares, ISBN 978-0-7643-6810-3

Other Schiffer Craft Books on Related Subjects:

The Enigma of Shadow Weave Illuminated: Understanding Classic Drafts for Inspired Weaving Today, Rebecca Winter, ISBN 978-0-7643-6204-0

The Techniques and Art of Weaving: A Basic Guide, Marylène Brahic, ISBN 978-0-7643-4413-8

Pick-Up Bandweaving Designs: 288 Charts for 13 Pattern Ends and Techniques for Arranging Color, Heather Torgenrud, ISBN 978-0-7643-6813-4

Library of Congress Control Number: 2025930673

Designed by Lori Malkin Ehrlich
Cover design by Lindsay Hess
Type set in Brother 1816, Dax Pro Condensed
All photos by Marty Essen

ISBN: 978-0-7643-7000-7
ePub: 978-1-5073-0628-4
Printed in China

10 9 8 7 6 5 4 3 2 1

Published by Schiffer Craft
An imprint of Schiffer Publishing, Ltd.
4880 Lower Valley Road
Atglen, PA 19310
Phone: (610) 593-1777; Fax: (610) 593-2002
Email: Info@schifferbooks.com
Web: www.schifferbooks.com

CONTENTS

INTRODUCTION

WELCOME TO PROFILE DRAFTING—a powerful weaving tool that lets us create one fabric design and translate it into many weave structures! Whether you are a beginning weaver or have been weaving for years, my intent is to open this wonderfully versatile design toolbox for you and explain how to use the tools inside.

I consider profile drafts as weaving "shorthand," where I can quickly see the overall fabric design and then plug in the treading, treadling, and tie-up for the block weave structure I want to use.

I've taught profile drafting for many years, and there are three big questions everyone has that I will answer in this book:

Question 1: Why use a profile draft?
Question 2: How do profile drafts work?
Question 3: How do the squares on a profile draft translate into the threading, the treadling, and especially the tie-ups for different weave structures?

This book is a sampler platter of block weave structures using profile drafts. I could literally write an entire book on each weave structure, but my intention is to answer those big questions above for each weave structure and whet your appetite for using profile drafting when designing fabrics. In the "Resources" section at the end of the book, I have listed other books that are dedicated to deeper dives into the different weave structures.

All the projects can be woven on 4 or 8 shafts. If you have more shafts available on your loom, you can weave more blocks of pattern in your fabric. At the end of chapter 2, I have a Block Weaves Threading Chart for the threading units for the weave structures in the book that shows how many shafts you may need to weave more blocks of pattern.

Handweavers tend to fall into two different, but related, camps—Color-and-Texture weavers and Technical/Structural weavers. Color-and-Texture weavers are all about the yarn—playing with color combinations and textured yarns to create patterns in pieces that make their hearts sing. Technical/Structural weavers love yarn and color but are fascinated with creating fabric designs using various weave structures.

I learned very early in my weaving life that I fall firmly into the Technical/Structural Camp. If you have picked up this book, you likely fall into the same camp. And I'm very happy to see you! We are going to have some fun together!

As a Structural weaver, you likely own some sort of weaving software. I was introduced to Fiberworks back in 2002. If you don't own weaving software, it's a wonderful tool to add to your weaving toolbox. There are several weaving programs available online, and I encourage you to try them out (usually for free!) before deciding which program works best for you.

Weaving software is great for thread-by-thread drafts but also works really well for profile drafting. You can create a profile draft, and, using the "Block Substitution" (usually under "Tools" on the main menu), you can select from multiple weave structures to convert your profile draft into a thread-by-thread draft.

But be aware; not every weave structure is available in every weaving program! Thus, it's good to know how to work with profile drafts without software conversions.

Moreover, you do not need to convert a profile draft into a thread-by-thread draft to weave! With a bit of key information, you can weave using just the profile draft! No thread-by-thread conversion to a new draft is necessary. No software is needed. No coloring (and erasing) all those little squares in a full drawdown thread-by-thread draft. How? That's what this book will teach you and much more. Let's get started!

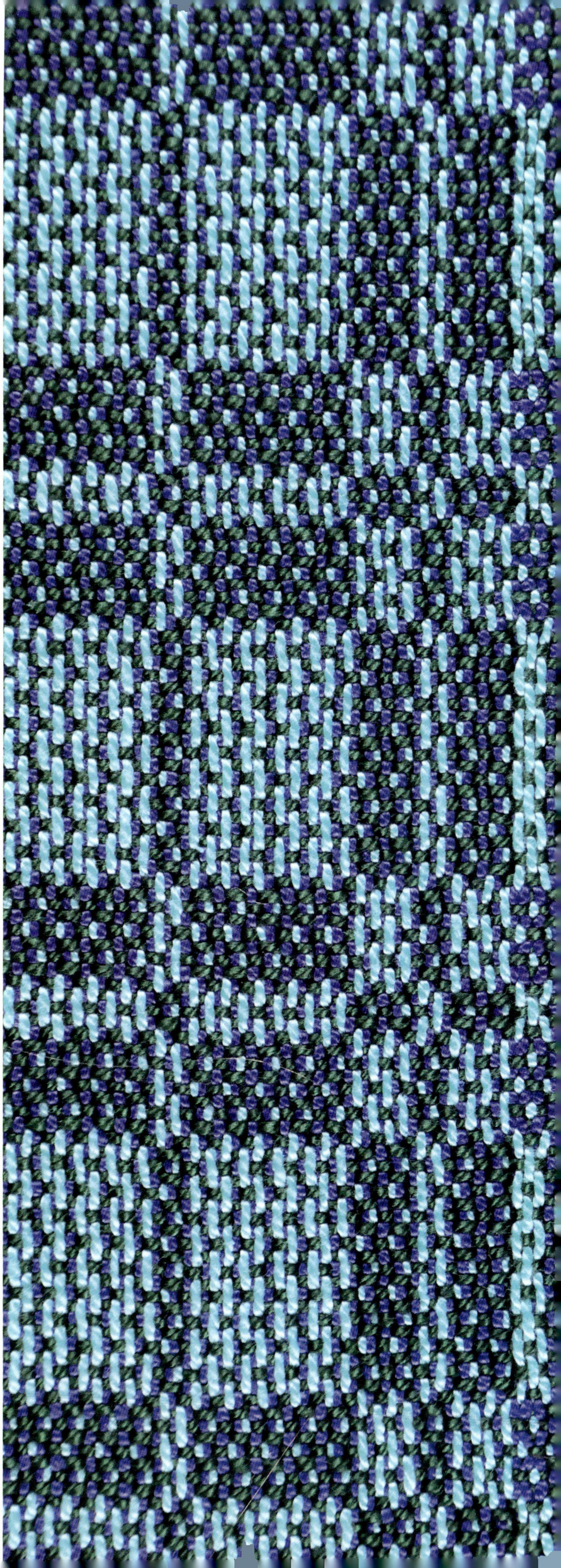

PROFILE DRAFTING TERMS

THE FOLLOWING TERMS will be used frequently in the book. I'm putting these definitions front and center so they are easy to refer to later.

PROFILE DRAFTS: Profile drafts are graphed illustrations showing the placement of blocks of woven pattern for the threading, treadling, tie-up, and drawdown.

In the threading, treadling, and tie-up portions of the profile draft, each colored-in square represents threading units, treadling sequences, and which blocks of pattern are tied up for the weaving pattern.

The profile drawdown shows the weaver how the blocks will interact in the fabric to create the overall design.

Using a profile draft allows a weaver to use the same profile draft design with many weave structures by simply inserting the threading, treadling, and tie-up for different block weave structures. No matter which block weave structure is used, the overall fabric design will look similar.

***Important!** Each colored-in square for threading and treadling of a profile draft represents groups of warp threads and picks of weft. This means each square can represent two or more threads, depending on the weave structure. This is different than a thread-by-thread draft, where each colored-in square on the draft is a single thread/pick of weft.*

BLOCKS: Blocks are what build your design in a fabric. Groups of warp and weft threads that interlace in the same way to create a specific pattern in an area of your fabric are considered the same block no matter where the block is placed in the fabric. Any groups of warp and weft threads that interlace differently and independently from the other block are in different blocks. Depending on the weave structure and number of shafts on your loom, you can have many different blocks in your project.

COMBINED BLOCKS: Two or more blocks are woven at the same time, combining them into one large block of pattern. This is accomplished by either pressing the treadles tied up for the different blocks at the same time (possible only on a rising shed / jack loom) or having treadles tied up that engage both blocks at the same time (countermarche looms).

BLOCK WEAVE: Block weaves are weave structures where the warp and weft interlace in one way on the pattern side of the fabric and interlace differently on the background side. When the warp and weft interlace in the same way, whether for the pattern or background, these sections are in the same block. Overshot is a good example of a block weave where a supplemental weft creates floats across a base of a plain weave fabric. The pattern weft floats move from the top side of the fabric, where you see the pattern weft, to the backside of the fabric, so you see the plain weave background / base cloth. Looking across Overshot fabric, when you see pattern wefts on the surface of the fabric in the same configuration, you know those sections are in the same block.

PATTERN vs. BACKGROUND IN THE BLOCKS: These terms are used to indicate that the warp/wefts interlace in one way for the pattern and interlace in a different way for the background. Summer and Winter or Overshot are good examples. When the supplemental pattern wefts are on a surface, you are weaving pattern in that block of threading. At the same time, the other blocks of pattern that are threaded differently will weave the background, where you can see only the plain weave base cloth. This is easy to overthink, because technically the other blocks have pattern floats, but the floats are on the other side of the fabric. Stick with looking at one side of the fabric to determine pattern vs. background to keep from overthinking this. (Believe me, I've been there!)

DESIGN: This term is used for the overall design of the fabric created by combining blocks of pattern floats with base cloth / background areas (examples are Overshot or Summer and Winter) or by combining blocks by using different interlacements of the warp and weft threads, such as in Turned Twill.

UNIT WEAVE: Unit weaves are structurally the same in each block of pattern and are threaded and treadled in units (groups) of warp thread / treadle repeats. Changing the threading unit creates different blocks because it changes the interlacement of the warp and weft and creates pattern vs. background blocks that look different but are still structurally the same as the other blocks in the design. A familiar example of a unit weave is Summer and Winter. Each block of threading assigns a set of warp threads in each threading group to tie down the pattern wefts at the same intervals in each block. When weaving for a specific block, the pattern weft shows on top, while in the other blocks the pattern weft is on the other side of the fabric. The tie-down warp threads create a plain weave with little dots of color where the warps are catching the pattern weft. All unit weaves are block weaves, but not all block weaves are unit weaves.

PROFILE TIE-UP: The colored-in squares in the tie-up grid represent a weaving pattern in a specific block. Blocks are designated A, B, C, D, and up if you have enough shafts on your loom. See chapter 1 for a more in-depth discussion.

PROFILE THREADING DRAFT: This is the horizontal threading section of the draft where each colored square represents threading groups/units for the different blocks. Always read the threading from the tie-up grid out. See chapter 1 for a more in-depth discussion.

PROFILE TREADLING DRAFT: The vertical treadling section of the draft where each colored square represents a *treadling sequence* for creating a pattern in a block. Always read the treadling from the tie-up out. See chapter 1 for a more in-depth discussion.

PROFILE DRAWDOWN: This is the area of the draft between the threading and treadling that shows the overall fabric design when pattern vs. background is produced in the various blocks.

"AS DRAWN IN" or "TROMP AS WRIT": The treadling sequence is the same as the threading order. For example, if the first four squares on the threading are for the "A" block, then you treadle for the pattern in Block A the equivalent number of picks, so the pattern is woven wherever you have threading for the Block A pattern. See chapter 1 for more threading and treadling discussion.

SETT: Sett indicates the number of warp threads per inch of warp width—also called "ends per inch" or "e.p.i." for short.

PICKS PER INCH: This indicates the number of weft threads in a woven inch. In plain/balanced weave, the number of ends per inch (e.p.i.) and the number of picks per inch (p.p.i) should be the same number. For example, if the warp is threaded at 16 e.p.i., then a balanced plain weave would have 16 picks of weft per inch.

WARP FLOATS: When the warp and weft threads intersect, the warp threads go over or under (float) two or more weft threads.

WEFT FLOATS: When the warp and weft threads intersect, the weft threads go over or under two or more warp threads.

FLOATING SELVEDGES: Floating selvedges are extra warp threads, one on each selvedge, that are not threaded through a heddle but are sleyed in the reed. These warp threads float in the middle of the shed when treadling. Floating selvedges are necessary for tidy selvedges when weaving structures like Summer and Winter or Overshot that use a supplemental pattern weft or twill structures that have warp and weft floats by ensuring the outermost warp threads are always caught by the weft. When weaving, your shuttle enters over the floating selvedges and exits under the floating selvedge on the opposite side. On the return, again the shuttle goes over the floating selvedge and exits under.

GETTING STARTED

I vividly remember taking my first "Introduction to Multi-shaft Weaving" class way back in the 1990s. We followed written step-by-step instructions (no drafts involved yet) on how to thread the loom and which treadle(s) to press in sequence. And we wove cloth! It was magic! I was hooked!

I learned a very important lesson in that class: Read the instructions, and you are set up for success in weaving.

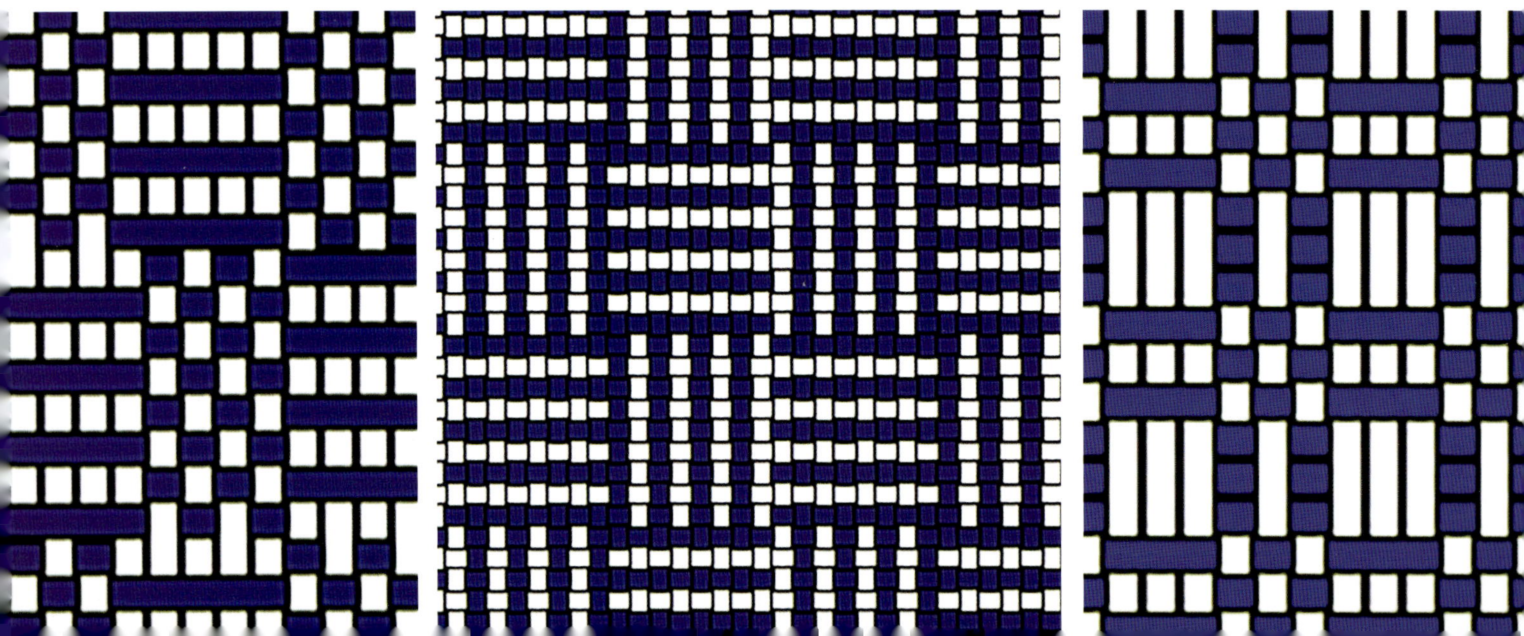

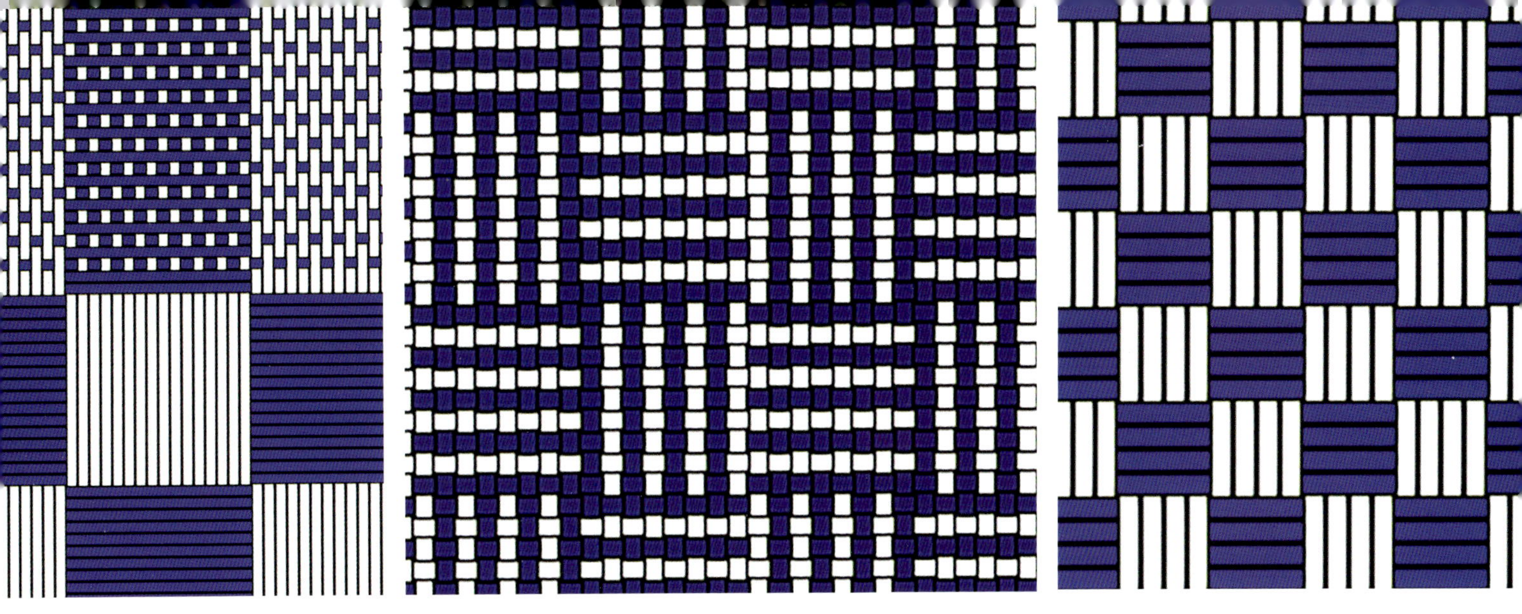

I MENTION THIS TO GENTLY ENCOURAGE YOU to read the first two chapters—"What Are Profile Drafts?" and "Designing with Profile Drafts"—and the definitions of terms before you dive into the projects.

Like many weavers, I am always eager to jump right to the projects and weave! However, this book is not your typical weaving book, with the threading, treadling, and tie-up all written out for each project. In other words, the drafts are not thread-by-thread drafts.

Instead, each of the 15 projects has a unique profile draft and instructions on how to translate the profile draft into the weave structure threading, treadling, and tie-up. Once you know the threading/treading/tie-up for a weave structure, you don't need to write out the entire thread-by-thread draft! You can simply create a threading/treadling key and use it whenever that block of pattern is being woven.

And you can use the same profile draft with projects in other weave structures. Intrigued?

The weave structures in this book are block weaves (read those definitions), so the profile drafts can be used interchangeably with multiple weave structures/projects. It all depends on the number of shafts required for each block of pattern in the profile draft and how many shafts you have on your loom(s). Because many weavers have 4- or 8-shaft looms, I have restricted the projects to 8 shafts or fewer for your first "run" at translating a weave structure. However, don't let that restrict your design explorations if you have more shafts on your loom. More shafts on your loom can mean more blocks of pattern! Consider the projects in the book to be a jumping-off point for more exploration.

Oh, the fun you will have!

chapter 1

WHAT ARE PROFILE DRAFTS?

What is a profile draft? The short answer is that profile drafts are a quick, easy way to draw out an overall design for a fabric without having to decide on a weave structure first! Think of it as designing "shorthand."

Before we can create and use a profile draft, we need to talk about what makes up a weave structure. Woven fabric is created by the interlacement of the warp and weft. By changing how the warp and weft interlace, designs are created in the fabric.

CALCULATING SETT

Sett is the number of warp threads per inch. The number of warp threads per inch can vary depending on the weave structure, the purpose of the textile (a scarf with soft drape vs. placemats), the fiber content of the yarn being used, and even the manufacturer of the yarn. Because of all these variables, I strongly advise calculating the sett for the yarn that you are using instead of using "sett charts." Sett charts were developed to give a general range of setts for a particular yarn. Using the sett charts blindly can lead to frustrating results!

To properly calculate the sett for the yarn you are using, wrap the yarn around a ruler or sett gauge for 1 inch. Make sure you have the yarn wraps lying nicely next to each other—not squished together or with space between the wraps. Don't pull on the yarn so it stretches when wrapping. Stretching the yarn makes it thinner, so your wrap count will be off.

Now count the number of yarn wraps in the inch. Divide the number of wraps by 2. This gives you the plain weave sett for that particular yarn. If you are weaving twill, the general rule of thumb is to add 4 more warp ends per inch vs. the plain weave sett. If you are weaving a weft-faced weave, such as a rug or runner, you need fewer warp ends per inch, and a good place to start is to divide the plain weave sett by 2. If you are weaving a structure using a supplemental pattern weft, you need the space between the base cloth warp/weft intersections to be large enough to accommodate the supplemental pattern weft. Now the "squish-ability factor" (yes, I made that term up) becomes important. If you are using a yarn that easily compresses (squishes) into that space between warp and weft, such as wool, you can use a larger pattern weft yarn without changing the sett. If you are using a pattern weft that does not easily

Calculating sett of a warp by wrapping the warp yarn around a ruler for 1 inch. Divide the number of wraps by 2 = warp sett for plain weave. With fabrics that have a base cloth and pattern weft, the base cloth yarn determines the sett for the fabric.

Sett gauges come in all sorts of sizes and shapes. Sett gauges have a 1-inch-wide notch cut into them to make it easy to wrap the yarn to determine sett.

compress, such as perle cotton, you may need a slightly more open sett to accommodate the pattern weft. The only way to be 100% sure of your yarns playing well together is to weave a sample.

Let's start with plain weave. Plain weave is also called "balanced weave" or "tabby." *When* you learned how to weave can change *which* term you likely use. The different names all mean the same thing. When weaving, every other warp thread is lifted, one pick of weft is thrown, and the weft is pressed/beat to the fell line. The weft thread alternates going over one warp thread then under the next warp thread all the way across the fabric. For the next pick of weft, you lift the warp threads that were down on the previous pick, lower the warp threads that were up on the previous pick, and throw another pick of weft. You continue this sequence for the length of your piece.

When I learned to weave, this was called balanced weave, a term I like because there should be the same number of weft picks as there are warp ends in 1 inch of woven cloth. However, plain weave is the current preferred term, so I will be using this term in the book.

When you see the phrase "use tabby" along the treadling side of a draft, this indicates that there must be a plain weave base cloth woven at the same time as the pattern that is shown on the drawdown draft. It also tells you that the treadling shows only the pattern weft picks. Two shuttles are needed: one to weave the base cloth, and one to weave the pattern. "Use tabby" tells the weaver that between each pattern pick shown on the pattern, you need to weave a pick of plain weave (tabby) alternating the plain weave picks. The plain weave base cloth creates a stable foundation for the floats of weft that create the overall design of a fabric. The "use tabby" notation is commonly used with Overshot and Summer and Winter thread-by-thread drafts.

For block weaves, the area(s) of the fabric where you see the plain weave base cloth is called "background." Where the supplemental weft is on the surface, this is called "pattern."

With profile drafts, you will *not* see "use tabby" as a notation by the treadling because the profile draft can be used for many weave structures, and not all of the weave structures require a plain weave base cloth. Thus, profile drafts require that you have some initial understanding about how different weave structures work.

THREAD-BY-THREAD DRAFTS VS. PROFILE DRAFTS

Refer to the thread-by-thread draft in figure 1:

1 • Everything starts from the tie-up area on a draft, which is at the upper right-hand corner of this draft. I call the tie-up "home plate" because everything starts at home plate, just like in baseball.

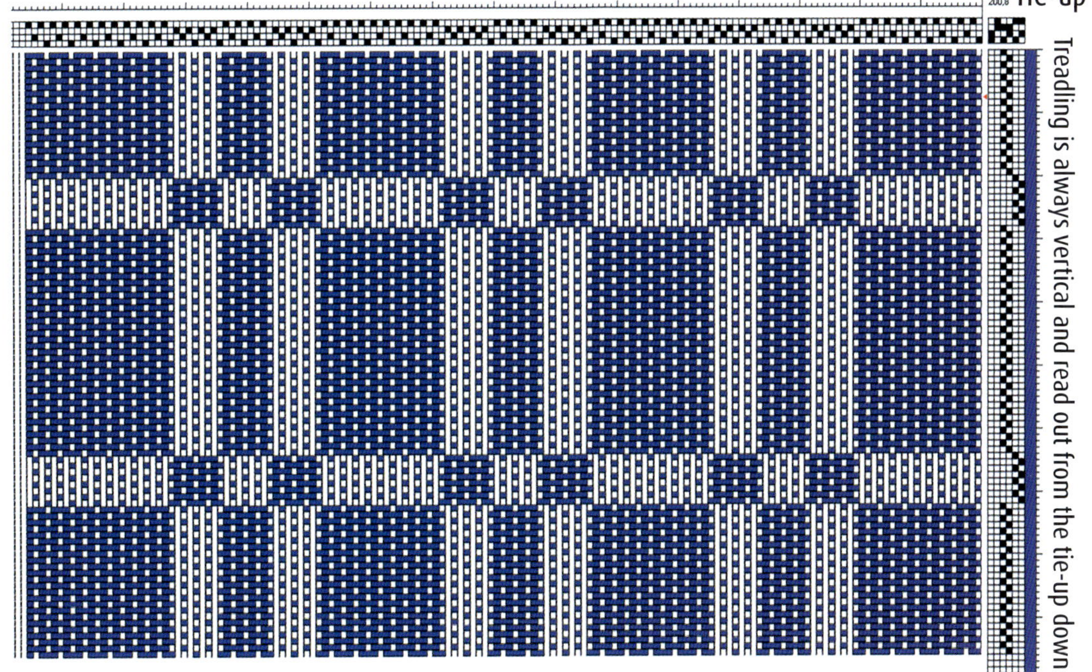

Figure 1: Two-block Summer and Winter thread-by-thread draft

2 • The horizontal grid section on the outside edge of a draft is always the threading. Each horizontal line of boxes represents a shaft on the loom. The row of squares closest to the drawdown area is always Shaft 1, the next row up is Shaft 2, the next row up is Shaft 3, etc. You always read the threading starting from the tie-up.

3 • The vertical grid section on the outside edge of a draft is always the treadling. You read the treadling starting from the tie-up. The vertical row of squares closest to the drawdown area is Treadle 1, the next vertical row is Treadle 2, etc.

4 • Threading and treadling are always read from the tie-up (home plate) out to the end of the draft, regardless of where the tie-up is located on the draft.

5 • Most weaving drafts have the tie-up at the upper right-hand corner. You may see some drafts in older books where the tie-up is at the lower left corner or upper left corner or lower right-hand corner. Regardless of where the tie-up is placed on a draft, the "reading the draft" rule still applies—the vertical is the treadling, the horizontal is the threading, and you read from the tie-up out.

6 • Weaving software uses the standard of locating the tie-up in the upper right-hand corner of the draft. I will be using this standard in the book.

Now let's look at a two-block profile draft (see figure 2) and how it differs from the thread-by-thread draft:

1 • The horizontal grid above the drawdown area is still the threading, but instead of each colored-in square representing an individual thread on a shaft, each square of the profile draft threading represents groups of threads that are called threading units. The rows of squares in the horizontal grid represent blocks of pattern threaded. Starting from the grid row of squares closest to the drawdown area, the threading blocks progress Block A threading, Block B threading, Block C threading, Block D threading.

2 • The vertical grid on the right-hand side of the draft is still the treadling, but each colored-in square represents a treadling group / unit of treadling repeats. The position of the square in the grid represents either pattern weft (blue) or background (white), where the base cloth shows on the fabric surface in specific blocks of threading for that block of pattern. The drawdown shows the pattern weft traveling from the top side of the fabric to the bottom side of the fabric. The vertical line of squares closest to the drawdown area is the treadle pattern in Block A; next is the treadle pattern in Block B. The remaining vertical rows of squares represent Block C and Block D.

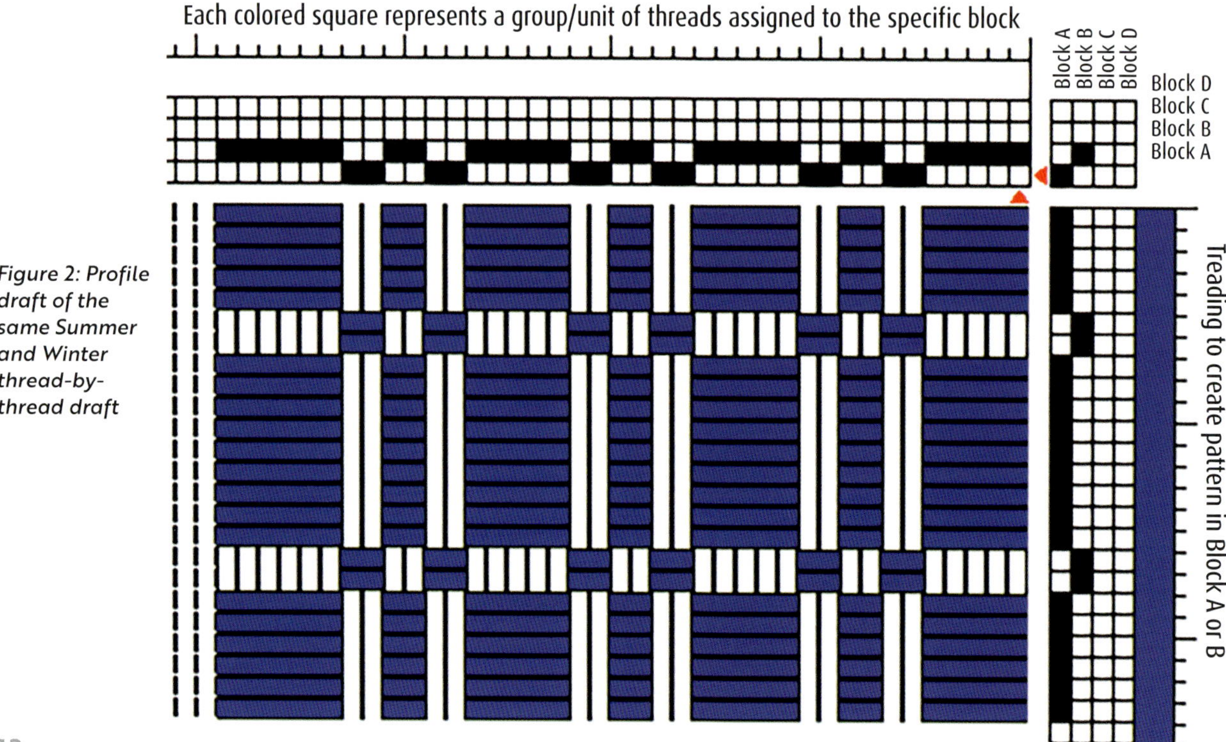

Figure 2: Profile draft of the same Summer and Winter thread-by-thread draft

You may be saying, "But wait! The treadling says to treadle for Block A! Why is the pattern weft showing in Block B threading?" Hold that thought: I will address why that happens on this draft in chapter 2. It has to do with rising shed vs. sinking shed looms. For now, let's just get a handle on reading the profile draft.

Look at the thread-by-thread draft in Figure 1: Note that the pattern weft floats in Block B are on the top and you get background (plain weave) in Block A, but remember the supplemental pattern weft floats in Block A sections are on the backside of the fabric, so the treadling is still weaving pattern weft floats in Block A. The weft floats are just not on the top surface of the fabric as you are weaving. This is an important concept to wrap your head around.

3 • The tie-up shows which block of pattern is being woven using the treadles/threading assigned to that block of pattern. Starting with the far left / bottom square in the tie-up, this is Block A. The next line of squares is Block B, the next line is Block C, and the last line is Block D.

4 • The threading reads horizontally out from the tie-up. The treadling reads vertically down from the tie-up. If squares are colored in in the Block A column, then the pattern is woven in Block A regardless of whether the pattern weft shows on the top layer or bottom layer of the fabric. If squares are colored in the Block B column, then the pattern is woven in Block B. This is a two-block profile draft pattern, but I labeled Blocks C and D as well. Since no squares are colored in for Blocks C and D, those blocks aren't used in the pattern.

5 • By knowing the threading units, treadling units, and how the tie-up raises or lowers warp threads for a weave structure, you can weave the fabric design without creating a thread-by-thread draft! You simply substitute the threading units for each colored-in square for the block of threading noted on the draft. The same thing goes for the treadling units. Hang with me; more details to come.

HOW WEAVE STRUCTURES WORK

Understanding how different weave structures work is the trickiest part of profile drafting, and that's one of the main reasons I wrote this book! Each project in the book has a threading key that shows the shafts involved for the project weave structure and the order to thread each unit. Each weave structure chapter/project has the threading, treadling, and tie-up for the weave structure. At the end of chapter 2, there's a Block Weaves Threading Chart for all of the weave structure in the book for a quick reference guide.

Profile drafts are designed to work with block weaves. Block weaves are weave structures where the warp and weft interlace in one way for pattern in the block vs. a different interlacement for background in the block. The mixture of pattern vs. background in the different blocks creates the overall design for a piece of fabric.

Log Cabin Blocks

Because we are so familiar with thread-by-thread drafts, I'm going to explore interlacement starting from a thread-by-thread draft and then to a profile draft, so you can see how the interlacement analysis works by using a couple of familiar weave structures, starting with Log Cabin.

Log Cabin is a simple 2-shaft block weave that is totally dependent on how the warp and weft threads interlace to achieve the pattern. (Log Cabin designs are created by alternating dark- and light-colored warp threads and weaving with alternating dark/

Fabric woven in two blocks of Log Cabin pattern created by alternating dark and light warp and weft threads. To change the block, 2 light warp threads are placed next to each other.

light weft threads to make vertical and horizontal lines in blocks of pattern across the fabric. To change the direction that the color lines travel in a block, you change the sequence of dark/light to light/dark by weaving or threading two light threads or two dark threads next to each other. The interlacement of the warp and weft creates the vertical vs. horizontal lines within the blocks.

Now refer to the thread-by-thread draft (see figure 3). The tie-up shows that Shafts 1 and 2 are used. There is a line above the threading grid that shows the colors of yarn to be used to thread the warp. The threading starts from the tie-up with a dark yarn (blue) vs. light yarn (white). Starting from the tie-up, you can see a wider band of pattern on the outside edges of the draft, where the lines of dark and light threads go horizontally from left to right. We are going to call that Block A. As you look across the draft, every section where you see the lines go from left to right is also Block A.

The other pattern sections have the dark/light lines going vertically. That is Block B. You make the transition from Block A horizontal lines to Block B vertical lines by threading either two dark threads or two light threads together where the blocks change. Every section where the lines are vertical is also Block B. Looking at this closely, when changing threading from Block A to Block B, two light threads are together. When changing from Block B to Block A, two dark threads are together.

Now look at the treadling (vertical grid). You can see that you alternate lifting Shaft 1 and Shaft 2 but also alternate the two colors of weft; thus, you know you need two shuttles, one for each color of weft. When you want to change the line directions in the blocks, you weave two dark threads together after weaving eight total picks alternating dark/light yarns.

Important! You weave alternating a dark yarn with a light yarn for 8 picks. Then you weave two dark yarns next to each other, and the vertical/horizontal lines change direction in the individual blocks to make the Log Cabin pattern. This change of direction does not change the designations of the warp threading blocks. The warp threading blocks remain A and B, but the interlacement of the yarns changes to make the pattern within the blocks to change from vertical stripes to horizontal stripes. Stick a pin in this, because when we move on to other weave structures, the interlacement of the warp and weft in the different blocks is what creates blocks of pattern for the overall design.

Now I'm going to convert the thread-by-thread Log Cabin draft to a profile draft (see figure 4). Log Cabin threading and treadling is in sets of two threads—one dark and one light. When we create profile drafts, each square on the threading and treadling grids represents a group of warp threads and weft threads. The squares in the tie-up represent which block weaves pattern.

Let's start by looking at the threading. For Log Cabin, the two colors of yarn are working as a unit, so one dark and one light thread equal one unit of threading. Remember, the blocks with the lines going

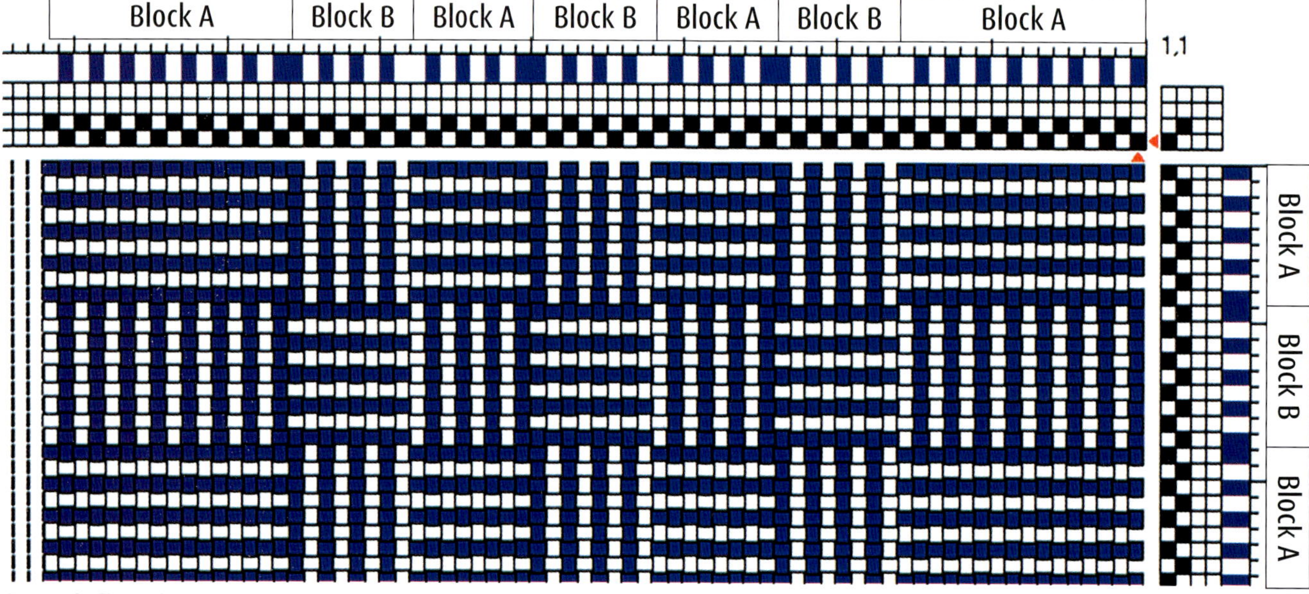

Figure 3: Thread-by-thread draft of two-block Log Cabin

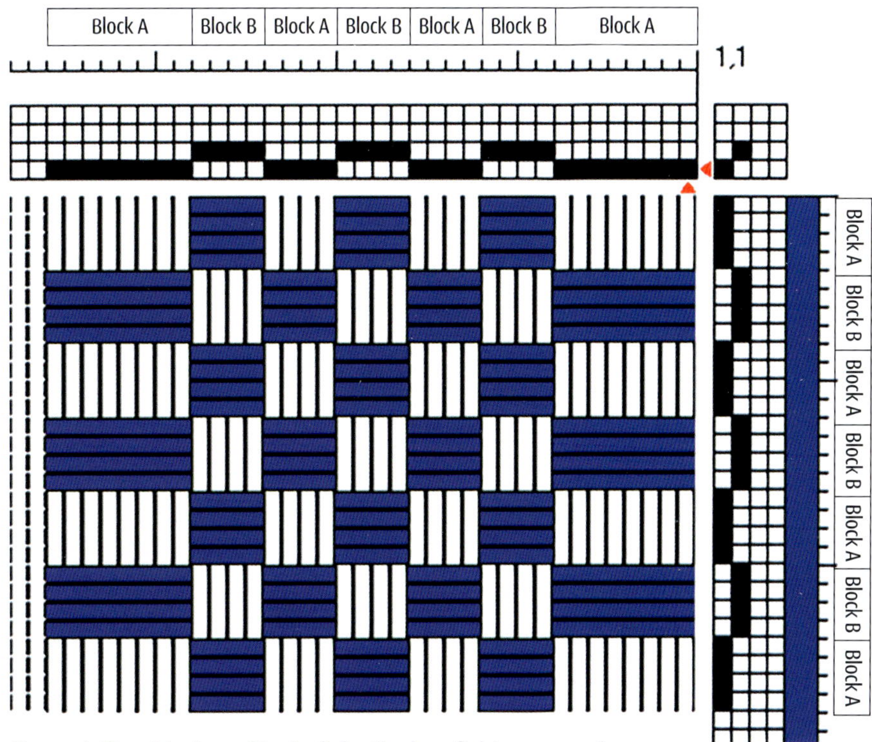

Figure 4: Two-block profile draft for the Log Cabin woven piece

from left to right are Block A. On the thread-by-thread draft, I have 16 threads total in the first Block A. Since a dark and light thread equal a unit of threading, I only need 8 squares on my profile draft because each threading square represents two threads.

Let's move on to the treadling. Log Cabin is plain weave, so I need only two shafts. Each pattern section of treadling is 8 picks, and each square in the profile draft still represents two threads (dark and light). Therefore, I only need to color in 4 squares for treadling, but I also have to remember that to change the blocks, I need to weave two dark threads together. The easiest way is to simply weave 8 picks dark/light and then, when you get to the end of a section, weave 2 picks of dark that you can count as either the first two picks of the next set of 8 threads, or they can be stand alone. You simply have to remember to be consistent.

Now let's look at the **tie-up**. Because this is a 2-shaft weave, the tie-up in the profile draft looks exactly like the tie-up for the thread-by-thread draft. This will not be the case when we get to more shafts/blocks.

With profile drafts, think of the tie-up area as "What do I need the threads to do?" For thread-by-thread drafts, each vertical column of squares of the tie-up represents a treadle on the loom, and the horizontal lines of squares represent the shafts on the loom. For our Log Cabin, we have Treadle number 1 tied up to Shaft 1 and treadle number 2 tied up to Shaft 2. This gives us plain weave.

	2		Shaft 2
1			Shaft 1

Thread-by-thread tie-up for two treadles

In profile drafts, the tie-up area looks the same, but instead of indicating which shafts are tied to which treadle, the profile draft tells us which block of pattern is being woven. In the tie-up area, blocks are noted from left to right and bottom to top. When a square in the tie-up is colored in, this instructs us to create pattern in a specific block of threading. Figure 6 shows a two-block profile tie-up.

A	B	C	D	
				D Block
				C Block
				B Block
				A Block

Blocks of pattern in the tie-up

For our Log Cabin, remember that Block A has horizontal lines of pattern. The threading on Block A is dark on shaft 1 and light on shaft 2. In Block B, we change the threading to light/dark. So when we press treadle 1, tied up to shaft 1, in Block A the dark threads are raised and in Block B the light threads are raised. When we press treadle 2, tied up to shaft 2, the light threads are raised in Block A and the dark threads are raised in Block B. Study the interlacements of the threads in the full drawdown/thread-by-thread draft. Note that depending on which color thread is raised in each block woven with the alternating colors gives you different interlacements in the two blocks, so you get different visual patterns in each block of pattern.

One key thing to note here: You may say, "But both blocks have a pattern," which is true. The key is that the pattern is different in the two blocks due to the interlacement of the warp and weft threads. Keep this in mind as we move to a different weave structure—Overshot.

Overshot

When using profile drafts, we must understand how a weave structure works to make a stable, patterned fabric. Each project in this book is here to help you understand different weave structures.

Overshot is a twill derivative weave structure that creates pattern on either the top or bottom of the fabric with floats of supplemental pattern weft. When you see an Overshot thread-by-thread draft, only the pattern weft picks are shown on the treadling and colored in on the drawdown. Next to the treadling grid is the notation "use tabby." This tells us that, between each pick of pattern weft, we have to weave a pick of plain weave to create a stable plain weave base cloth that the supplemental pattern picks interlace with the base cloth by traveling from the top of the fabric (pattern on top in that block) and then moving to the backside of the fabric in the other blocks of pattern.

Refer back to our 2-block profile draft (see figure 4) created for the Log Cabin. All the block notations and placement remain the same for the Overshot. What changes is the number of shafts needed, the threading, the tie up, and the treadling.

Figure 5 shows what the 2-block draft looks like when converted to a thread-by-thread draft for Overshot.

Well, that looks exactly like the profile draft in the drawdown! But here's what's different. The white areas where the lines go vertically are actually plain weave background. The blue areas where the threads go horizontally are showing pattern weft floats on top of the plain weave. (The background is on the other side of the fabric under the blue floats.) Note that where you see white for background, the pattern weft floats will be on the underside of the fabric.

Also note the tie-up. It likely doesn't look like any twill or Overshot tie-up you've seen. That's

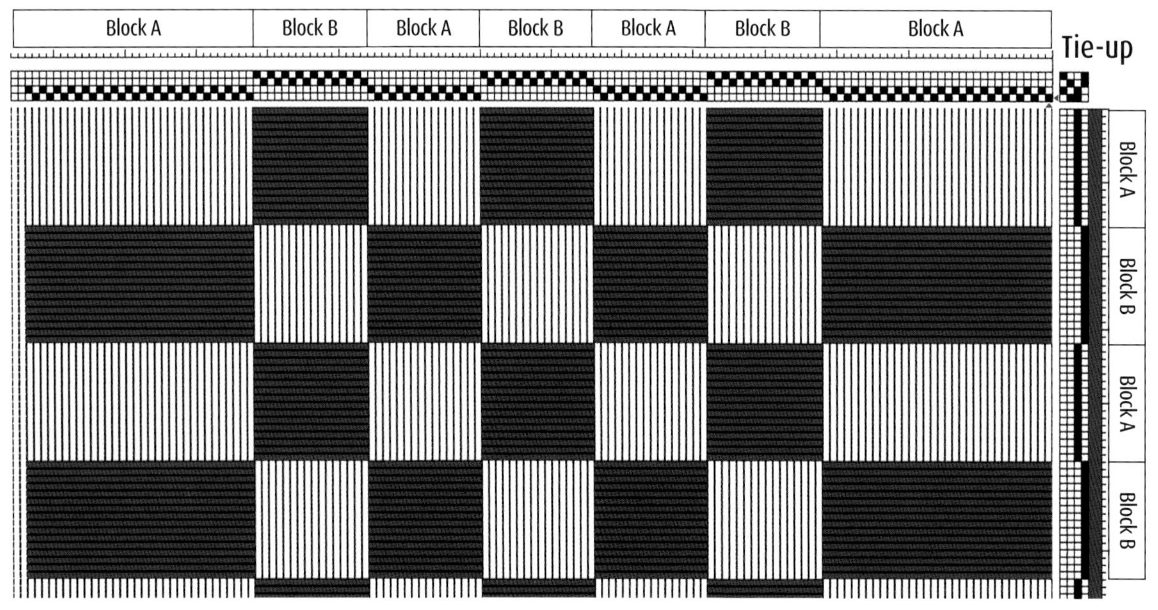

Figure 5: Thread-by-thread draft for Overshot, using the Log Cabin 2-block profile draft in Figure 4

because this particular draft has only two blocks of pattern, and Overshot is normally a 4-block weave structure on 4 shafts, with the threading assigned as follows:

Block A: Shafts 1–2
Block B: Shafts 2–3
Block C: Shafts 3–4
Block D: Shafts 1–4

Those shaft combinations for the blocks should look familiar, because those are also the tie-ups for weaving straight twill. Because there are only 2 blocks in this draft, you combine blocks of threading and treadling with our tie-up to create your two blocks and plain weave. First tabby treadle, then lift every other thread in Block A (Shafts 1 and 2) and Block B (shafts 3 and 4) so you tie up Treadle 1 to Shafts 1 and 3 (first set of tabby) and Shafts 2 and 4 (second set of tabby) to get clean plain weave in all the background (tabby only showing) areas of the pattern. I will talk much more about weaving/designing Overshot in the Overshot project. And yes, we will be working with four blocks in that chapter.

Figure 6 shows what the draft looks like with the tabby picks inserted in the first section of treadling. You can see that the white background sections now show plain weave. The blue pattern sections are a little odd, because my Fiberworks weaving software is showing the tabby intersections between the picks of blue plain weave base cloth. Now, let's move on to designing with profile drafts!

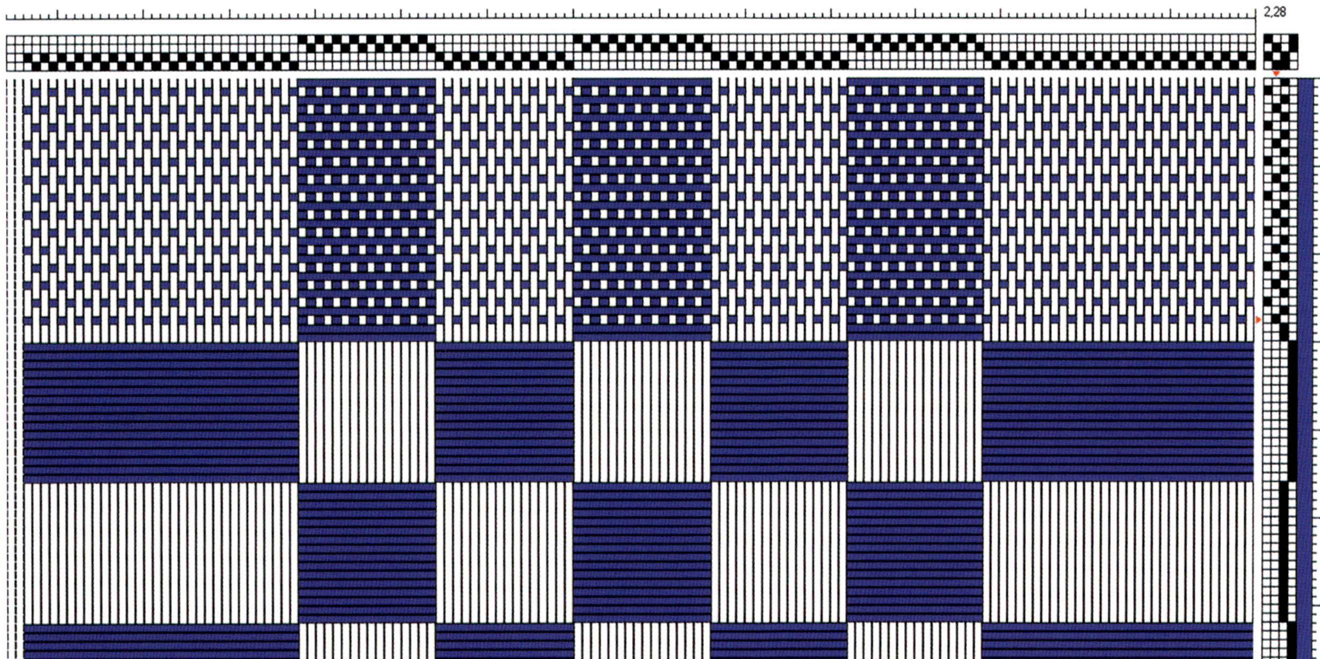

Figure 6: Thread-by-thread draft for Overshot in figure 5 with insertion of tabby picks in first Block A treadling

chapter 2

DESIGNING WITH PROFILE DRAFTS

Designing fabrics using profile drafts is fun, fast, and really quite easy. You can use graph paper, a weaving program, or even a spreadsheet program to quickly see the overall pattern design of a fabric. Profile drafts can also be used to "reverse engineer" a pattern in an existing fabric—as long as the existing fabric is a block weave structure. If you haven't read chapter 1, now is the time to do that before you plunge into this chapter on design.

USING A PROFILE DRAFT TO CREATE THE DRAWDOWN

The drawdown portion of your draft is the large area between the threading and treadling grids. This area shows the overall design of your fabric based on where the blocks of pattern are showing on one side of the fabric.

Rising vs. Sinking Shed Looms and Creating Drawdowns

There are two schools of thought for creating profile draft drawdowns, and they have to do with rising shed vs. sinking shed looms. First, a little background is necessary. Jack looms were invented by E.E. Gilmore in the 1930s in the United States and are a majority of the looms sold in the United States. Jack looms are rising shed looms. When you press a treadle, warp threads that are tied up to the treadle are raised, and the warp threads that are not tied up to that treadle stay in a neutral (down) position. Most of the drafts that are published in the United States are written for jack/rising shed looms.

Countermarche looms have been around for centuries and are sinking shed looms, even though technically the warp threads are both raised and lowered when you press on a treadle. Countermarche looms dominate drafts from Europe and older weaving drafts created prior to the 1930s in the United States.

The pattern shows on both the top side and the bottom side of the fabric. The threading for a block and what shafts are raised and lowered by treadling determines whether the pattern shows on the top side of the fabric in a block or the backside of the fabric.

Whether you are using a rising shed (jack) loom or a sinking shed (countermarche) loom will determine which side of the fabric the pattern will show on as you are weaving.

- **What do rising vs. sinking sheds have to do with profile drafts?** When I first learned about profile drafts, the instructions said that, if I was treadling in Block A, I would color in the squares for all the other blocks. This comes from the use of sinking shed countermarche looms and the conventional tie-up taught for those looms, where the pattern threads in a block are pulled down for all blocks except the block I am weaving for pattern.

  Now this isn't too difficult to remember when I have only two blocks in the pattern, but when using four blocks of pattern, it became quite confusing to keep track of which squares to color in and resulted in a lot of erasing.

  It occurred to me that, if I were to color in the drawdown squares that match the block threading/treadling, I would get the same drawdown for the overall design of the fabric. It technically would be the reverse image of the original drawdown technique. But it's still the same pattern!

  It's much easier to look across the drawdown, and if the threading is in Block A and my treadling is for Block A, then I color in the squares where Block A occurs across the drawdown. For all traditionalists who just gasped at this idea, traditions are sometimes meant to be broken.

◆ **Why does this matter?** I mention this because my Fiberworks weaving program still uses the "color in everything that is not Block A" method. So, when you look at profile draft drawdowns in this book created in my weaving program, it seems to be opposite of what you expect the fabric pattern to be.

◆ **Yes, there's pattern in all the blocks.** When I first started using profile drafts, I kept thinking, "But there's pattern in all the blocks!" This is true. The key is where the weave structure's pattern shows on the surface you are designating as the top / right side of the fabric!

It's all about the interlacement of the threads in a block.

Let's use the Overshot draft at the end of chapter 1 in figure 5. This draft is from my Fiberworks program (sinking shed). Note that the sections designated for Block A threading and treadling have white threads going vertically. That's the base cloth showing on the top side of the fabric, and the pattern wefts are weaving on the backside of the fabric.

In the same line of treadling, the blue pattern wefts are on top in the drawdown for Block B. That's because the threads for Block B pattern are not being engaged, and the pattern weft is now on top in Block B because of how the warp threads are being raised and lowered across the fabric. That interlacement of the warp and weft is different in Block A vs. Block B!

Using Jack Loom Draft with a Countermarche Loom

I learned to weave in 1993 on a jack loom and happily wove for several years on that jack loom. In the late 1990s, I took a class from Joann Hall, who owned Glimakra USA at the time, and a Glimakra loom followed me home. (What can I say—structure weavers collect looms!) The first project on my new loom was for an Overshot pattern, and I tied it up according to the instructions that came with the loom. When I started to weave, I discovered that the pattern dominant side of the fabric was facing down, and I was looking at the "back" (base cloth dominant) side of the fabric. This was different from my jack loom, and I wanted to see the side of the fabric that matched the jack loom drawdown draft that I had. What could I do?

Countermarche looms have two sets of lamms located above the treadles and below the shafts. The lamms are tied to the shafts and the treadles. When you press on a treadle, shafts tied to the upper lamms go down, lowering the warp threads for the sinking shed (I remember this by "What is up must come down"), and the shafts tied to the lower lamms go up, raising the warp threads tied to the lower lamms. Tie-up instructions with countermarch looms have you tie up the colored-in squares of the tie-up to the upper lamms (which pull the warps down), and the blank squares of the tie-up are tied to the lower lamms (which raise the threads). This is the opposite of what a jack loom does. Jack loom drafts mark only the warp threads that are raised (colored-in squares on the tie-up). Thus, this meant I was looking at the back of the fabric as I wove, using the jack loom draft.

Then I had a thought—what if I tied up the lower lamms (what is down must go up) to the colored-in tie-up squares so the warp threads would be lifted just like they are lifted by a jack loom and tie-up the upper lamms for all the other shafts (the blank squares in the tie-up) that aren't already tied to a lower lamm? Tah-dah! My fabric looks just like the jack loom drawdown when I am weaving.

CREATING A PROFILE DRAFT

Laying Out Your Fabric Design on Graph Paper

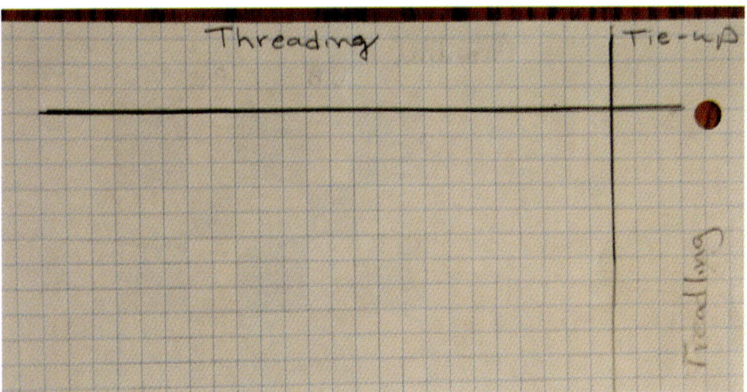

Your starting point for creating a draft—draw a horizontal line to mark the threading. Draw a vertical line to mark the treadling. The intersection of the two lines is the tie-up area.

Let's start by using graph paper and create a 2-block design. First, I create the drawdown area by drawing a horizontal line and a vertical line that intersect on the right-hand side of the sheet to create the standard form of a weaving draft. As discussed in chapter 1, the horizontal lines of squares are always threading. The vertical lines of squares are always treadling. The intersection of the two in the upper right-hand corner is the tie-up.

For now, I'm going to ignore the threading, treadling, and tie-up areas and create a 2-block fabric

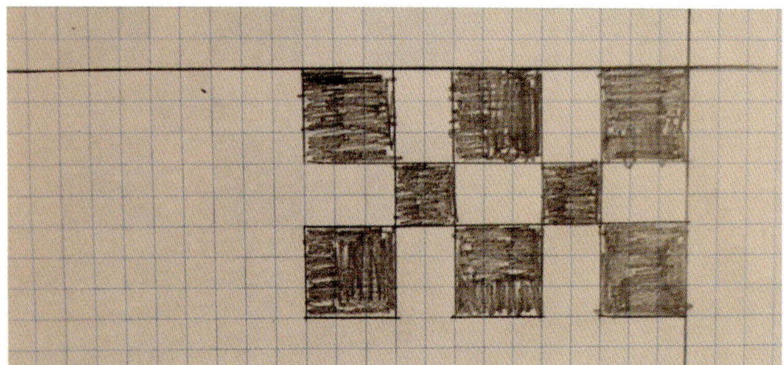

Create a two-block fabric design by coloring in the drawdown squares to create an overall pattern for the fabric.

design in the drawdown area by coloring in groups of squares. In other words, I'm creating the fabric design first and assigning the blocks based on the fabric design.

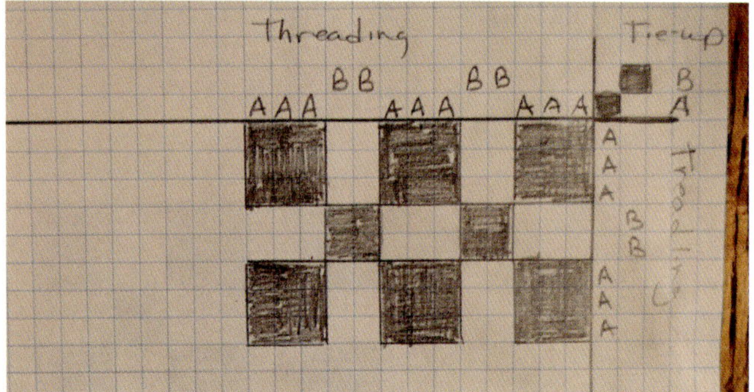

Label the threading for Block A on the lowest line of the threading grid, above where you have colored in squares in the first line across the drawdown. Wherever there are uncolored squares on the first line of the design, write B in the next line up of the threading grid.

Threading: After I've colored in the squares in the drawdown area, it's time to assign the block designations to the colored-in squares. I like to start with the threading. As mentioned in chapter 1, blocks of design are assigned the letters of the alphabet (A, B, C, D, etc.). I have assigned the letter A to the block of design closest to the intersection of the threading/treadling grids on the draft. Now, looking across the drawdown from tie-down out (right to left), every time I see a colored-in square in the drawdown, that drawdown square is labeled Block A in the threading grid. That tells me that the threading in these squares will be my Block A threading.

Now I look at the uncolored drawdown squares between the Block A colored-in squares. Those squares will have a different threading for Block B. In the threading area of my draft, I put a "B" in each square that lines up with blank squares in my first sequence of blocks across the drawdown.

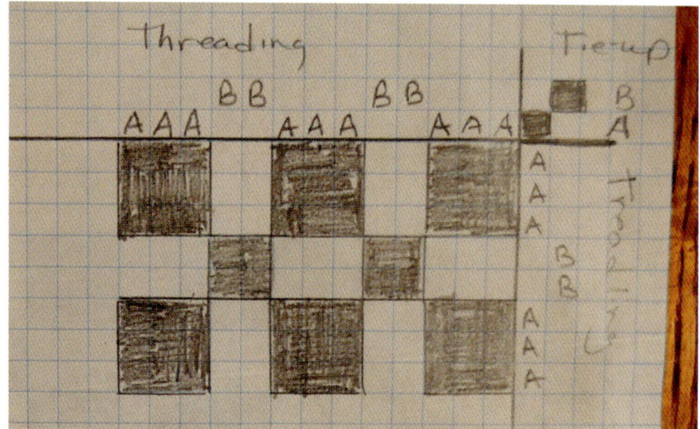

Color in the tie-up squares—Block A closest to the grid line intersection and B one step up and over. Refer to chapter 1 for positioning of the tie-up squares.

Tie-up and treadling: Referring back to chapter 1, I have two blocks of pattern, so I color in my tie-up squares for Block A and Block B. Then I say to myself, "I want pattern on top in a colored-in block," so I put an "A" in the treadling Block A column, where I have squares colored in for the pattern in Block A in the drawdown, and then shift over to the Block B column and write B in the squares that match where pattern is woven in Block B on the drawdown.

Once you've recognized the concept of threading in A and treadling in A vs. threading in B and treadling in B, the real fun can begin! You can repeat the same-sized blocks down the treadling. With this 2-block drawdown, I have created two different designs by adding or changing the sizes of the blocks.

You can change the number of threading squares colored in for a block to change the width of a block. You can change the number of treadling squares colored in to change the length of the block. (The combination of the two changes the overall design of the fabric.) This is the fun part (warning:

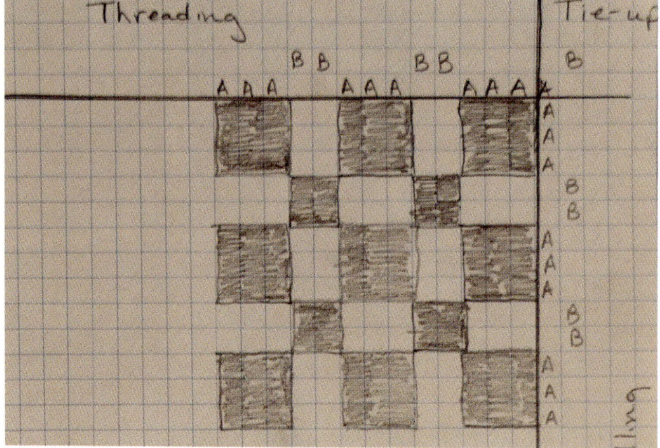

Repeating the blocks to expand the design

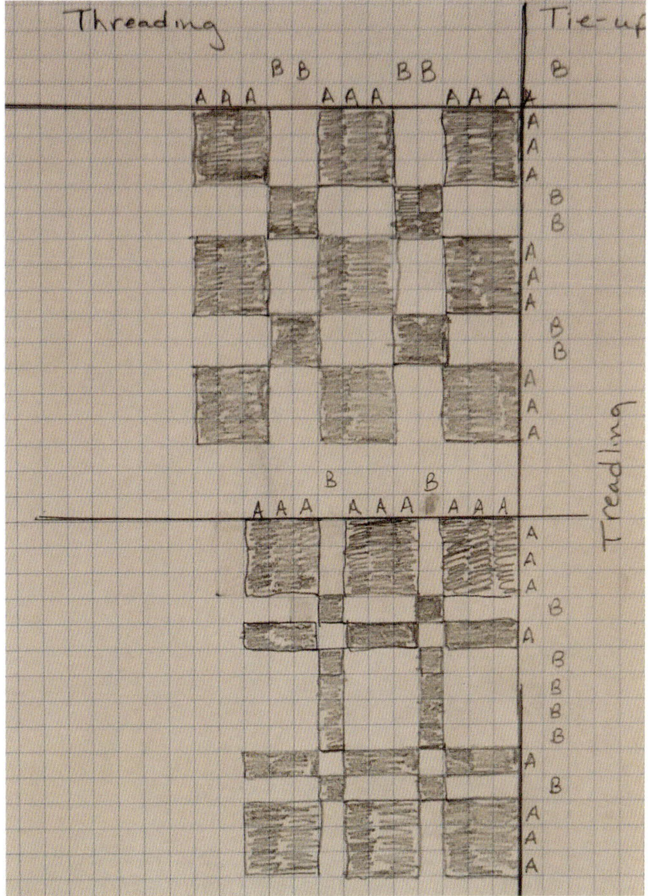

Creating a new fabric design by changing the size of the threading B blocks and the B block treadling blocks by adding or subtracting the number of squares representing the B block

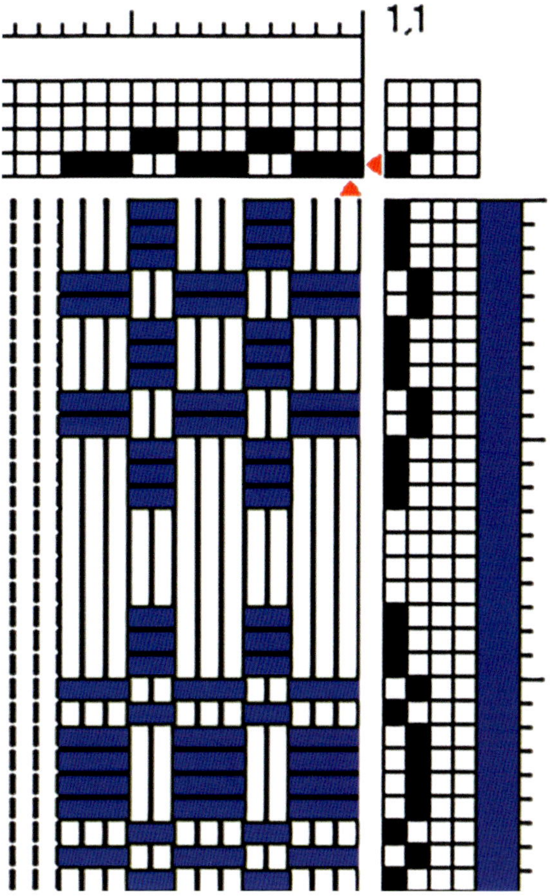

The same drawdown / profile drafts in Fiberworks weaving software. Note the colored-in vs. not-colored-in areas in the drawdown, due to Fiberworks creating a drawdown for a sinking shed loom. Refer to the beginning of chapter 2 about rising vs. sinking shed looms.

potential rabbit hole) of profile drafting. There are so many ways to combine block sizes/placement to create the overall fabric design. It is so much fun!

The second profile draft shows changing the size of only the Block B threading, and looking at the treadling, you can see I've changed the number of squares for the repeats of both Block A and Block B. And I got a very different, yet similar, fabric design.

And yes, you can set up the tie-up so that both Block A and Block B are engaged at the same time and you get pattern in both blocks all the way across the fabric.

Now let's look at how this same draft looks in my Fiberworks weaving program. Keep in mind what I was saying earlier about rising vs. sinking shed looms. You'll note that the opposite is happening in the blocks than what I colored in when drafting on the graph paper. Due to the Fiberworks program using the sinking shed blocks "rule," if I treadle in Block A, then the background (white) shows in A, so the pattern is on the backside in A and the pattern wefts are on the top/background on the back in Block B. But remember, the opposite side of the fabric will look like what I colored in on the graph paper. If you use a rising shed loom, treadling for Block A will mean the pattern floats on the top surface in the A blocks.

Using a Spreadsheet Program

Now let's play with a spreadsheet to create a drawdown/draft. This design started with my desire to weave a curved design down the length of a scarf. I have drawn out a curve on the right-hand side of the graph paper. I have numbered the columns of squares 1-2-3-4. These columns will represent specific blocks of pattern, so above the 1-2-3-4 labels, I have put A, B, C, and D for the necessary four blocks of pattern. To the left, I have replicated the curve by coloring in the squares that the curved drawn line crosses (or comes closest to). As you can see by

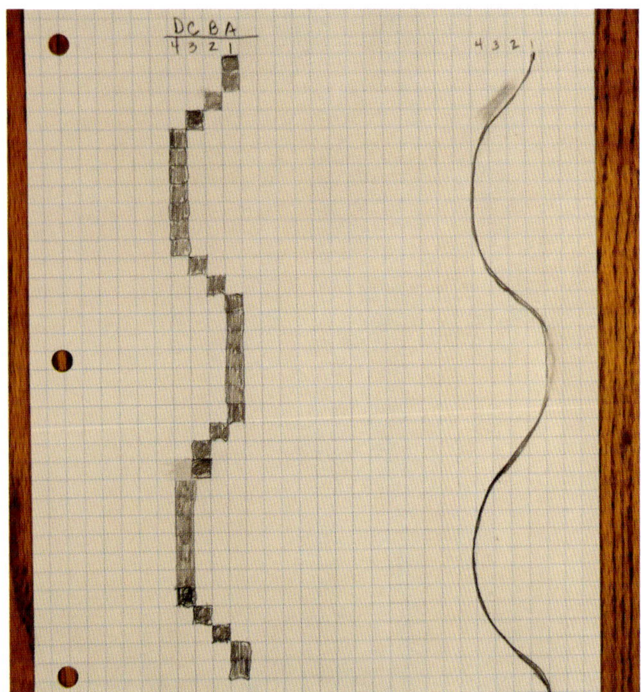

Mapping out the curves on graph paper

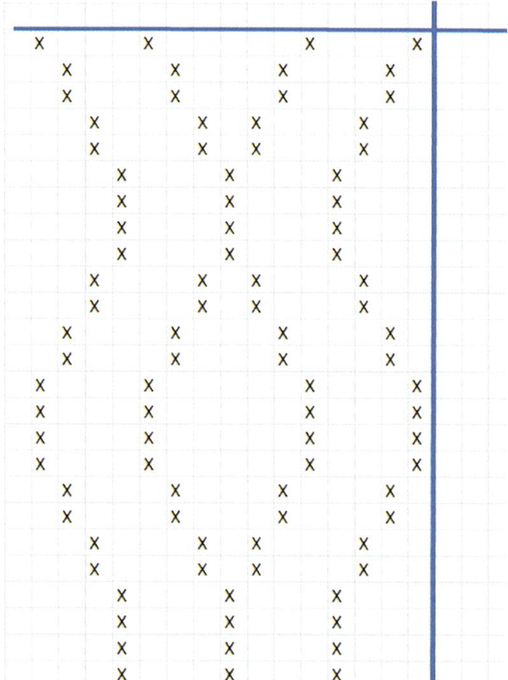
Creating the drawdown of the curves in a spreadsheet program

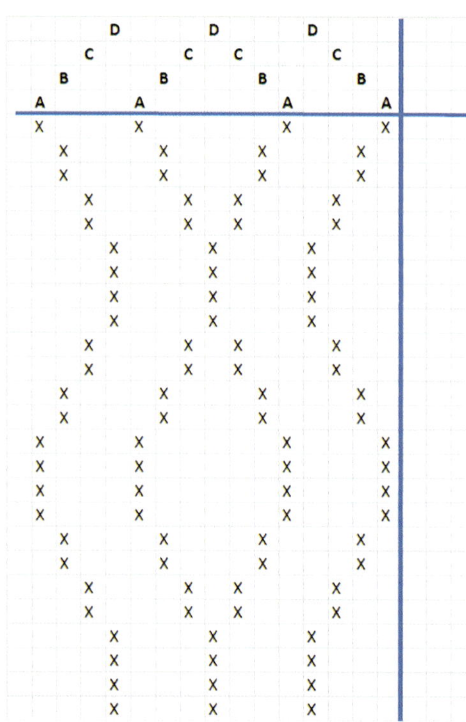

Inserting the threading block designations above the spreadsheet drawdown

the smudges on the paper, I changed the location of some of the colored-in squares to more closely mimic the original curve. A good eraser is important when using graph paper!

Now let's use a spreadsheet program to create the drawdown. My graph paper curve indicates that I need to stairstep the squares to mimic the curve. First, I want to make the cells in the spreadsheet smaller so I can see the whole design on my screen. To do this, I first highlight the top row of cells across columns A–Z. Then on the home tool bar, I select "Format," then "Column Width" in the pull-down menu. A box pops up, and I change the column width to 2. All 26 highlighted columns are now small squares.

Then I want the spreadsheet to mimic a weaving draft, so I click on the square in the fifth row down and fifth row from the right-hand edge. Then I change to the "View" tab and click on "Freeze Panes." You will get slightly darker lines that intersect (I have added a heavier line so it shows better) so the spreadsheet mimics a blank weaving draft.

Now I type an X in the squares where I want the pattern. I can easily move the position of the X's in the squares until I'm happy with the design—no eraser necessary and no smudges. If you want the squares to be a solid color, you can do this by using the little paint can on the "Home" taskbar to fill the square with a color. However, you must do this for every square, so it's kind of slow. Typing in an X in the cells/squares is faster.

Now it's time to assign block threading designations to the blocks in your design. I usually select the first/top line of colored-in squares as Block A. The next vertical line of colored squares in the design is Block B, the next vertical line is Block C, and the last vertical line is Block D.

I fill in the tie-up with Block A at the lower left-hand corner and Blocks B, C, and D going in a diagonal. See chapter 1 for the reason for this layout.

Now it's time to fill in the block treadling. The treadling is the vertical grid on the right-hand side. As I look across the drawdown design, my first section of treadling is Block A, so I color (or put an X) in that square. You can also use the block letter designation; in this case, type A in the treadling column. I continue filling in the treadling column based on what drawdown block has an "X" or is colored in on the drawdown.

Deciding on the Weave Structure

What weave structures can you use to create the fabric? Well, it depends on a couple of factors.

I have 4 blocks of pattern in this design, which tells me what weave structures I can use based on the number of shafts on my loom and the number of shafts used for threading each of the blocks. Refer to the "Block Weaves Threading" chart at the end of this chapter for the threading keys for the weave structures in this book. If I have a 4-shaft loom, I can weave 4 blocks of Overshot and Crackle, but that's about it! If I have an 8-shaft loom, I can weave four blocks of Overshot, Summer and Winter, Crackle, Bronson Lace, Spot Bronson, and Huck Lace.

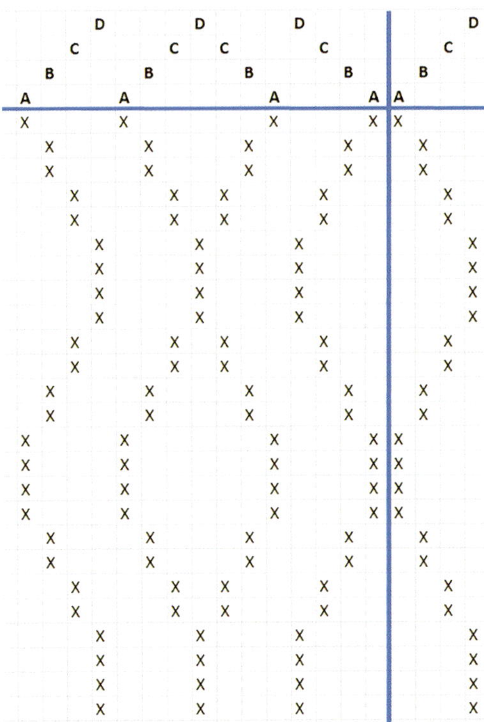

Adding the tie-up and treadling to the spreadsheet drawdown

Now before you despair that your options appear so limited, look closely at the threading key. Yes, you have more block number options with more shafts, but you can still weave many of the weave structures on a 4-shaft loom—you just need to design with fewer blocks of pattern. Will the curves work with fewer blocks? Not really, but you still have a ton of design options playing with the size, positioning, and color in blocks. Or it could be your excuse to buy a loom with more shafts!

Replicating a Fabric Design

For my curved design, I started by laying out the pattern in the drawdown. The same can be done with an existing fabric—simply consider the fabric as your drawdown.

Look at the photo below This is a sample for one of my kit designs called "Weaver's Choice" in Summer and Winter. For now, we are going to ignore the weave structure. We are going to identify the blocks first.

Lay a ruler across the picture at the bottom of one of the large squares. Remember that, when identifying blocks, the pattern shows on one side of the fabric in a block and the other side of the fabric for all the other blocks. Reading across the fabric, starting at the right-hand selvedge, we see the pattern weft on top, then the background for a rectangle, then the pattern on top again.

Lay a ruler across this photo to determine which blocks are the same for threading. Designate the different threading blocks. Then designate the treadling for each section of pattern.

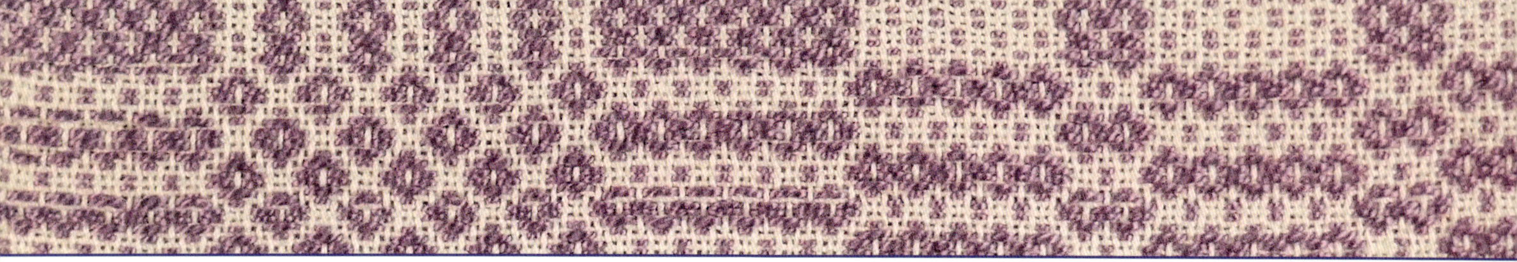

WOVEN SAMPLES ARE YOUR FRIEND!

WEAVING SAMPLES really is vital for profile drafting. A short, narrow warp will give you so much valuable information: making sure your threading/ treadling/tie-up is correct, whether the yarn sizes/ colors work well together, if the sett is appropriate for the weave structure and yarn you are using, and whether the feel/weight of the fabric is appropriate for the final product.

When I first started weaving, I thought sampling was a waste of time, money, and yarn. However, after a few unanticipated or unhappy results, I joined the "add a bit of warp length to your project" to check sett, threading, colors, etc. However, after a twill scarf project that needed to be re-sleyed to a much closer sett that made the piece too narrow for a scarf, I decided that weaving small samples was a smarter, more economic idea. These samples have become my Weaving Reference Library.

I use sampling to test sett, yarn color combinations (which is important to see how the colors I selected play together when woven), threading/ treadling, and overall design. Like many weavers, I tend to have favorite yarns that I use and know how they behave when woven. However, I also use "new to me" yarns and have found, for example, that an 8/2 Tencel from one manufacturer may not be the same as an 8/2 Tencel from another manufacturer. Tencel #1 may have less ply twist in the yarn than Tencel #2, which can change the drape / hand / light reflection of the fabric.

Yarn sett can change how a fabric feels. If you plan a cotton scarf, you want it to have a nice drape, so perhaps a more open sett should be used. However, you can use the same yarn for dish towels, using a closer sett for a firmer fabric that will hold up well to frequent use and many launderings.

Changing the weave structure may mean changing the sett for a yarn. A plain weave sett has fewer ends per inch sett than a twill weave sett, where the weft/warp has floats, and you need a closer sett to get a good fabric. The best way to find out what works best is to sample that yarn at different setts and different weave structures.

Save your samples for future reference in your version of your "Woven Samples Reference Library." People tend to fall into two camps when it comes to saving information: "Filers" and "Pilers."

Filers have a designated place for everything, and everything is labeled. Filers use file folders stored in file cabinets. The only papers on their desks are the papers they are working on.

Pilers have stacks of papers on their desk. Pilers know what's in each pile and approximately where that paper is in the pile.

I am a Piler with periodic fits of Filer tendencies. I keep woven samples in my "reference box" of samples, labeled with the yarn fiber content, yarn size, manufacturer, where the yarn was purchased, and the color names/numbers from the suppler. Sometimes that label is a scrap of paper pinned to the sample. Sometimes it's a paper price tag with a string attached, which allows me to put one of the tags at the selvedges so each woven section of the sample is labeled with what I did in that section.

Either way, whether you're a Filer or Piler, keeping some sort of record of a project is important. You'll find a "Record Sheet" in the appendix of this book that I use when I'm working on projects. I have the record sheet in my computer and print out copies. I fill in the information, and on the back of the sheet I make notes while weaving. You may find a three-ring binder with tabs for different types of projects such as "Scarves," "Runners," "Towels," and so on very helpful. Simply punch holes in the record sheet and place it in the appropriate section. Attaching your woven samples to those record sheets will keep track of everything in one place for future reference.

Not only does sampling give me good practice in warping my loom (I've gotten much faster and devised many tricks to make warping easier), weaving, and learning how different weave structures work, but it prevents a "dog on the loom" from haunting me. And that means I'm ahead of the game!

That tells me that the first block of pattern is the threading from the selvedge to the first section of background. We will designate that section Block A because it's the first section of pattern.

When we get to the rectangle at the bottom of the larger square shape, your first instinct is to say, "Well, that's Block B," because when you weave the pattern in Block A, you'd get background in Block B. It's pretty straightforward, until you move up to the next section up of pattern, and you have a block of pattern surrounded by background. Hmmm—that must be a different threading block, because if you have the same threading all the way across that large square, you can't get a square of pattern in the middle. That means each side of the large square is another block of threading. We will designate those blocks of background next to the center block of pattern Block C.

Now, go up to the alternating small squares between the boxed square. Here is your confirmation! You have a single small square of background, and if you move up another section, you have 2 small blocks of background on each side of the square of pattern. This tells you that there are actually 2 blocks of threading making up the longer block of background in the first section of pattern. Sometimes those blocks are treadled individually (small squares), and sometimes they are treadled together (in a long rectangle). So, we are going to designate those smaller squares Block B and Block C.

Now we have decided that we have 3 blocks of threading: Block A (selvedge to the design), Block B (the single pattern square), and Block C (with the two background squares on either side of the single small square). The longer rectangle and the larger square are actually Block B and Block C treadled at the same time! You can set up a set of treadles so that Block B and C are lifted at the same time with another set of treadles for Block A and another set of treadles for Block B.

The profile tie-up would look like this:

		C	Block C
	B	B	Block B
A			Block A

Figure 1: Profile tie-up combining blocks

Now, a question: Is Block A ever treadled on its own in the sample, or does it simply have the role of weaving pattern between treadling Block B and Block C? In the sample, Block A always has pattern on top, which happens whenever we treadle Blocks B and/or C. Therefore, we don't ever treadle for Block A alone, so we don't need to tie-up treadles for Block A.

Now, the number of shafts you need will depend on the weave structure you select. Refer to the threading units/block for each project in this book. For three blocks of Summer and Winter, you need 5 shafts. Therefore, you need an 8-shaft loom. If you decided to weave the pattern in Crackle or Spot Bronson, you would only need 4 shafts. The overall fabric design with the block relationships would be the same, but the pattern within the blocks would be different. See the Summer and Winter project on page 155 to learn about setting up threading, treadling, and tie-up.

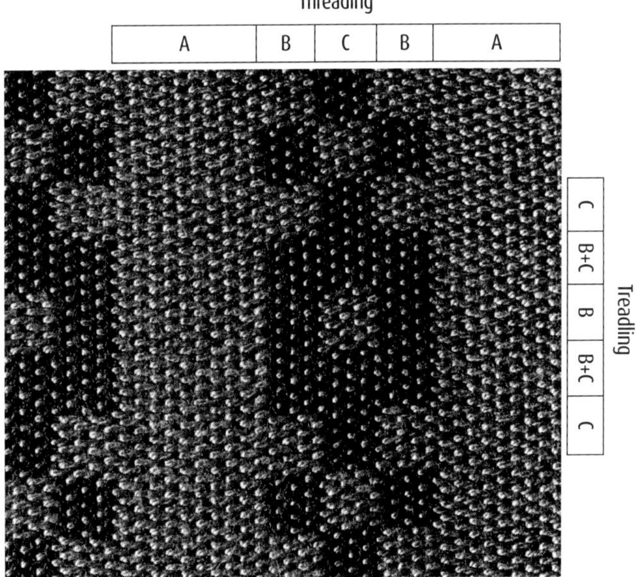

TIPS

TIP #1: You don't need to "translate" a profile draft into a thread-by-thread draft to weave! The profile draft gives you blocks of threading, treadling, and the drawdown. You can plug in the threading, treadling, and tie-up based on the squares that are colored in on the draft! All you need to know are the threading units and treadling groups for a weave structure (provided with each project). Each project walks you through how to figure out the tie-up for that weave structure. Refer to the Block Weave Threading Chart on page 26 for all the threading keys for the weave structures in this book.

BLOCK WEAVE THREADING CHART FOR PROJECTS IN THIS BOOK

	Block A	Block B	Block C	Block D
M's and O's	1-2-1-2-3-4-3-4	1-3-1-3-2-4-2-4		
Bronson Lace	1-3-1-3-1-2	1-4-1-4-1-2	1-5-1-5-1-2	1-6-1-6-1-2
Spot Bronson	1-2-1-2	1-3-1-3	1-4-1-4	1-5-1-5
Huck Lace	(2-3-2-3-2	1-4-1-4-1)	(2-5-2-5-2	1-6-1-6-1)
Turned Twill	1-2-3-4	5-6-7-8	9-10-11-12	13-14-15-16
Rep Weave	1-3 (Color A)	2-4 (Color B)	5-7 (Color C)	6-8 (Color D)
or alternate threading colors (example: Color A and Color B alternate in the same Block)				
Double Weave 4 shaft	1-2-3-4			
Double Weave Layers	1-2-3-4 (ABAB)	5-6-7-8 (ABAB)	9-10-11-12 (ABAB)	13-14-15-16 (ABAB)
(Note: 2 colors are used—Color A to weave the top layer and Color B to weave the bottom layer)				
Crackle	1-2-3-2	2-3-4-3	3-4-1-4	4-1-2-1
Satin	1-2-3-4-5	6-7-8-9-10	11-12-13-14-15	16-17-18-19-20
The following threading for Damask and Half Satin do not have a specific project but are included to expand your explorations for fabric designs.				
Damask	1-2-3-4-5	6-7-8-9-10	11-12-13-14-15	16-17-18-19-20
Half Satin threading	1-4-2-4-3-4	1-5-2-5-3-5	1-6-2-6-3-6	1-7-2-7-3-7
Overshot	1-2	2-3	3-4	1-4
Summer and Winter 4 shaft and 8 shaft)	1-3-2-3	1-4-2-4	1-5-2-5	1-6-2-6
Taqueté	1-3-2-3	1-4-2-4	1-5-2-5	1-6-2-6
Biederwand	(1-3-4-3-4	2-5-6-5-6)	(1-7-8-7-8	2-9-10-9-10)

TIP #2: When you calculate the number of warp ends needed for a project, count the number of colored squares for the blocks of threading. Multiply the total number of squares across the profile threading by the number of threads in each threading unit /group for the weave structure you are using. For example, Summer and Winter uses threading units/groups of 4 threads per square in the threading. If you have 30 total squares across the threading grid (regardless of different blocks), multiply 4 x 30 = 120 warp threads. Then add your floating selvedges (where necessary) for a total of 122 warp threads. Divide the total number of warp threads by the e.p.i. of the yarn you are using, and that equals the width of the project for that yarn.

Thread your heddles in batches of 4 threads each. Tie each 4-thread bundle with a slipknot.

TIP #3: When threading, bundle the threaded warp threads in bundles of threads that match the number of threads in a threading unit, and secure them with a slipknot. Simply count the number of threaded bundles until the number of bundles matches the number of threading squares in a block.

Using Summer and Winter again, the threads are in units of 4 threads for each threading profile square. Here's how I thread quickly. I am right-handed and thread from right side of the warp to the left. I place the number of total heddles I need over to the left side on the shafts. First, I move 4 heddles on the appropriate shafts over from the stash on the left. I reach back to the lease sticks, so my hand is to the left of the heddles I just moved.

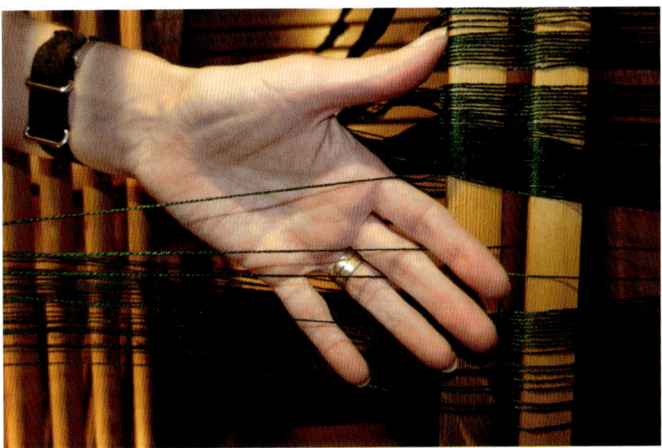

When threading, hold 4 warp threads in your non-dominant hand and separate the threads between your fingers. Now you can grab the threads for threading the heddles.

I separate 4 threads on the lease sticks. Then I place the threads between the fingers on my left hand. The farthest left thread is placed between my pointer finger and thumb, the next thread is between my pointer finger and middle finger, the next thread between my middle and ring fingers, and the last thread between my ring finger and pinky. Then I curl my fingers enough to catch the threads and pull my hand toward me, letting the threads slide between my fingers. Now I thread, starting with the thread between my ring finger and pinky. I thread the first heddle in the group, push that heddle to the right, pull the next thread (ring and middle fingers) from my fingers, and thread in the next heddle in the group. I continue until I have the 4 heddles I pulled over all threaded. I double-

When you complete the threading for a block, bundle the threaded warp threads together and secure with a piece of thrum. Now you can see at a glance where you are in the draft by simply counting the bundles or looking at the color of thrum. Green thrum is Block A threading, orange is Block B threading, etc.

check that the heddles are threaded correctly and no threads are twisted around another heddle, then I tie a slipknot in the bundle of 4 threads. Now I just have to count the number of bundles until they match the number of squares that I need to thread.

TIP #4: Once you have a block of threading done, bundle the four thread bundles together, and using a piece of thrum, tie the bundles together with a bow knot. Then thread the next block of threading and bundle those warp threads with another piece of thrum in a different color so you know that it's a new block. This helps immensely when threading gets interrupted (doesn't it always?), and you can simply count the number of threaded bundles to know exactly where you are in the profile draft.

Label your treadles with the letters of the block the treadle engages and whether it's the first or second treadle in a pair that work together (depending on the weave structure).

TIP #5: Label your treadles with the block letter and the treadle number for treadling that block. No, this isn't cheating. This is a great idea that I learned years ago from Madelyn van der Hooght. I will sometimes add a rubber band to the first treadle in each pair, so my foot can find the treadle easily. I use painter's tape to label the treadles and place the labels so my feet don't cover the labels when I treadle, and I can see the labels easily if I glance down to double-check which treadle I'm pressing.

TIP #6: Remember to keep good records, using the project sheet in the appendix. Keep the records organized in a three-ring binder with dividers for different types of projects, like towels, runners, placemats, etc. You, and future weavers, will greatly appreciate having those records easy to find. Also in the appendix are calculations for determining the amount of warp and weft you need for a project.

the WEAVE STRUCTURES and PROJECTS

There are 16 projects in this book, and each project has a profile draft and an explanation of the weave structure, tie-up, threading, and weaving for each weave structure.

THE PROJECTS HAVE ONLY THE PROFILE DRAFT. If you haven't read chapter 2 on how to use a profile draft, do this now or you will be lost without the information contained there. (This is for everyone who, like me, skipped right to the projects.)

Each project has a different profile draft. You can use the project profile drafts interchangeably between projects, depending on how many shafts on your loom and the number of shafts required per threading unit/blocks of the weave structure.

All the projects can be woven on a 4- or 8-shaft loom. If you have a loom of more than 8 shafts, I have included the threading units for additional blocks of threading for the different weave structures.

As a final note, your fabric isn't finished until it is wet-finished. With all these projects, I recommend a soak or gentle agitation in warm water. Lay the fabric flat to dry, smoothing the fabric into the shape of the project to block it. Yes, wool yarns should be washed in warm water. The warm water will help the yarns bloom up beautifully and removes remnants of spinning oil in the yarn from the manufacturing process. A little liquid dishwashing detergent added to the water can be useful to help remove the spinning oils. The exception to the warm-water "rule" is silk yarn, since you will get better luster from silk yarns using cold water. Gently squeeze the water out of your project, then roll it in a bath towel and press down on the rolled towel/fabric to help remove the excess water.

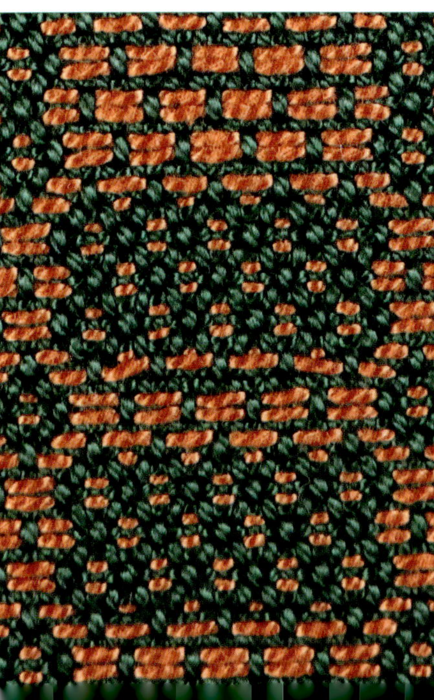

chapter 3

PLAYING WITH BLOCKS

M's and O's is a good introduction to block weaves where you can easily (a) see the blocks formation, (b) wrap your head around the concept of "what happens in Block A is different than what happens in Block B," and (c) figure out the tie-up and treadling for the weave structure. Plus, it's a fun, fast structure to weave!

WEAVE STRUCTURE

M's and O's

There is no definitive information about where M's and O's originated as a weave structure. It is speculated that the weave structure was first used in Finland and came over the ocean with immigrants to the United States. In Sweden, M's and O's is called Sålldräll, and we really don't know if Finnish weavers shared it with Swedish weavers or vice versa. At one point in weaving history the structure was called "Buckens and Owls" in New England, and the reasoning behind that name has been lost to time.

The M's and O's pattern. The two threading blocks work together to create the pattern in the fabric.

The name "M's and O's" appears to have been coined by Pennsylvania Dutch weavers because someone could see an "M" in the weft float areas and "O" in the plain weave areas once the fabric is washed. On the loom, the fabric frankly looks rather blah. The magic transformation happens when you wet-finish the cloth. When the yarns get wet, the floats move closer together, drawing the plain weave blocks into an "O" shape. This "O" shape can be more oval (side to side or top to bottom) or rounder, depending on the number of picks that you weave in each section of pattern.

M's and O's is a unit weave structure. The threading key shows that each threading unit is 8 threads. Because of the way we thread the shafts and tie up the shafts for treadling, each block weaves either plain weave or rib weave. Plain weave has threads going over/under each warp thread, while rib weave lifts 4 warp threads next to each other and leaves the next 4 threads down to create weft floats. When you change which warp threads are lifted for plain weave, you also change which 4 warp threads are lifted for the rib weave. The rib floats intertwine in the center of the block. You change which block weaves plain weave vs. rib weave with the tie-up and treadling.

Interpreting the Profile Draft

Let's examine how this works. A 2-block profile draft alternates Block A with Block B and repeats across the fabric.

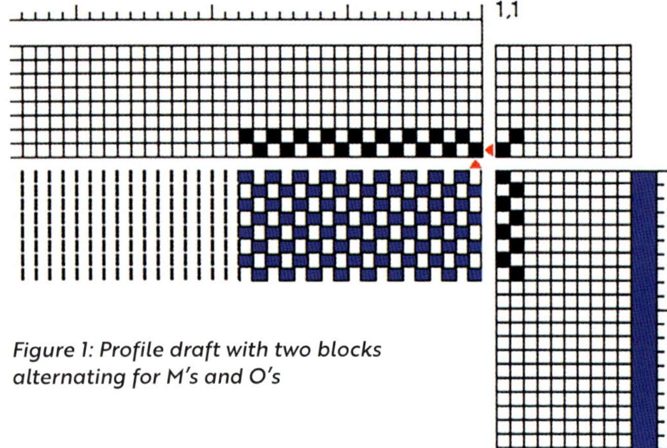

Figure 1: Profile draft with two blocks alternating for M's and O's

The threading units per block:
Block A: 1-2-1-2-3-4-3-4
Block B: 1-3-1-3-2-4-2-4

Note that in Block A, the threading is 1-2-1-2 followed by 3-4-3-4, as opposed to Block B, where the threading is 1-3-1-3 followed by 2-4-2-4. So the same shafts are being used for each block, but with a slightly different threading sequence in each block of pattern. Tuck this away for when we discuss the tie-up/treadling shortly.

DETERMINING THE SETT

Each unit of threading is 8 warp threads. Because there are sections of plain weave across the warp, the sett for an M's and O's fabric is based on the plain weave sett for the yarn chosen. For the M's and O's project, I chose a yarn that has a sett of 16 e.p.i. I will use that sett for this example as well.

USING THE PROFILE DRAFT TO DETERMINE WIDTH

The threading units tell me that each block of threading (colored-in square) on my profile draft represents 8 warp threads. With a sett of 16 e.p.i., each block on the profile draft will be ½ inch wide (8 threads) at a sett of 16 e.p.i.

Remember, the two blocks work together to create a section of pattern—the plain weave and the rib weave sections. When you combine those two blocks, you have 8 threads in Block A and 8 threads in Block B. These two blocks combine to make a section of pattern across your fabric.

Counting the squares across the profile draft threading, we have a total of 18 threading squares colored in, alternating between Block A and Block B. This means we would have 144 warp ends when converting to thread by thread (18 blocks multiplied by 8 warp ends/block). At my sett of 16 e.p.i., this gives me a scarf 9 inches wide (144 warp threads divided by 16 ends per inch = 9 inches).

The other option is to have each colored-in square of a block represent two threading repeats of each block. However, remember that when Block A is weaving plain weave, then Block B is weaving ribs, with floats over 4 threads. That means, if you repeat the threading for a block, then in the rib weave sections there would be 4 columns of ribs. It also means your Block A plain weave would be 1 inch across. Thus, the M's and O's pattern would be much larger. This may make you very happy! The best way to find out is to weave a short sample.

Repeating threading units in a block could be necessary if you are using finer yarns. For example, if you use a yarn that requires a plain weave sett of 24 ends per inch, then each threading unit/block of one repeat of the 8 threads would be only ⅓ inch wide (24 divided by 8 = 3). If you do two repeats of each threading unit, then each block would be 16 ends per block for 0.67 inches (16 divided by 24), or just over ½ inch wide. Again, repeating threading units would mean that the ribs would still go over/under 4 warp threads, but there would be 4 columns of ribs.

Another option is to use a larger grist (size) of yarn. I've woven M's and O's with DK weight knitting yarns sett at 8 e.p.i. This sett/yarn size makes fabulous fabric, and the pattern blocks really show up well. Plus, the elasticity of the knitting yarn pulls the blocks of M's and O's into high relief after wet-finishing.

FIGURING OUT THE TIE-UP/TREADLING

The threading is straightforward, but how to tie-up the shafts/treadles? First ask yourself, "What do I want the threads to do in each block?"

If Block A is plain weave, then Block B is rib floats.

Let's start with Block A plain weave. Plain weave means that the weft alternates going over/under the individual threads. The threading unit for Block A is 1-2-1-2-3-4-3-4.

To create plain weave with the Block A threading, we need to raise every other thread for the first pick. Every other thread in Block A is 1 and 3. Thus, we tie up to raise Shafts 1 and 3, because these threads are every other thread in the Block A threading unit (Shafts 2 and 4 will stay down).

For the second pick of plain weave, we need to again raise every other thread, which are on Shafts 2 and 4 (Shafts 1 and 3 will stay down). This gives us the 2 picks needed to complete the plain weave.

So our first 2 treadles will be tied up to get plain weave in Block A:

Treadle 1: tied up to Shafts 1 and 3
Treadle 2: tied up to Shafts 2 and 4

Block B rib floats happen at the same time. This tells us that Block B is threaded differently than Block A.

Block B threading is 1-3-1-3-2-4-2-4. That means, when you press Treadle 1 which is tied up to Shafts 1 and 3, it will raise the first 4 warp threads in Block B, because Shafts 1 and 3 are threaded next to each other and leave the next four warp threads on Shafts 2 and 4 down. This is your first pick of rib in Block B, and it happens at the same time you weave plain weave in Block A. When you press Treadle 2, threads on Shafts 2 and 4 are raised. This means you will have the four threads on Shafts 1 and 3 left down, and the four threads on Shaft 2 and 4 are up. This gives you rib weave in Block B. Sweet!

CHANGING THE PATTERN SO BLOCK B IS PLAIN WEAVE AND BLOCK A IS RIB FLOATS

Block B is threaded 1-3-1-3-2-4-2-4.

Raising every other thread in the Block B threading unit for plain weave means Shafts 1 and 2 work together and Shafts 3 and 4 work together. Thus, we need Shafts 1 and 2 tied up together on a treadle and Shafts 3 and 4 tied up together on another treadle. Rib floats will happen in Block A because Shafts 1 and 2 are threaded next to each other and Shafts 3 and 4 are next to each other.

So our second set of two treadles are tied up:

Treadle 3: tied up to Shaft 1 and Shaft 2
Treadle 4: tied up to Shaft 3 and Shaft 4

Figure 2 (below) shows what the thread-by-thread draft looks like. Take note of what the weft threads are doing in each block, depending on the tie-up and treadling.

As you continue with the other weave structures, you will be asking the same question: "What do I want the threads to do in each block of pattern?" This is the key to figuring out all tie-ups.

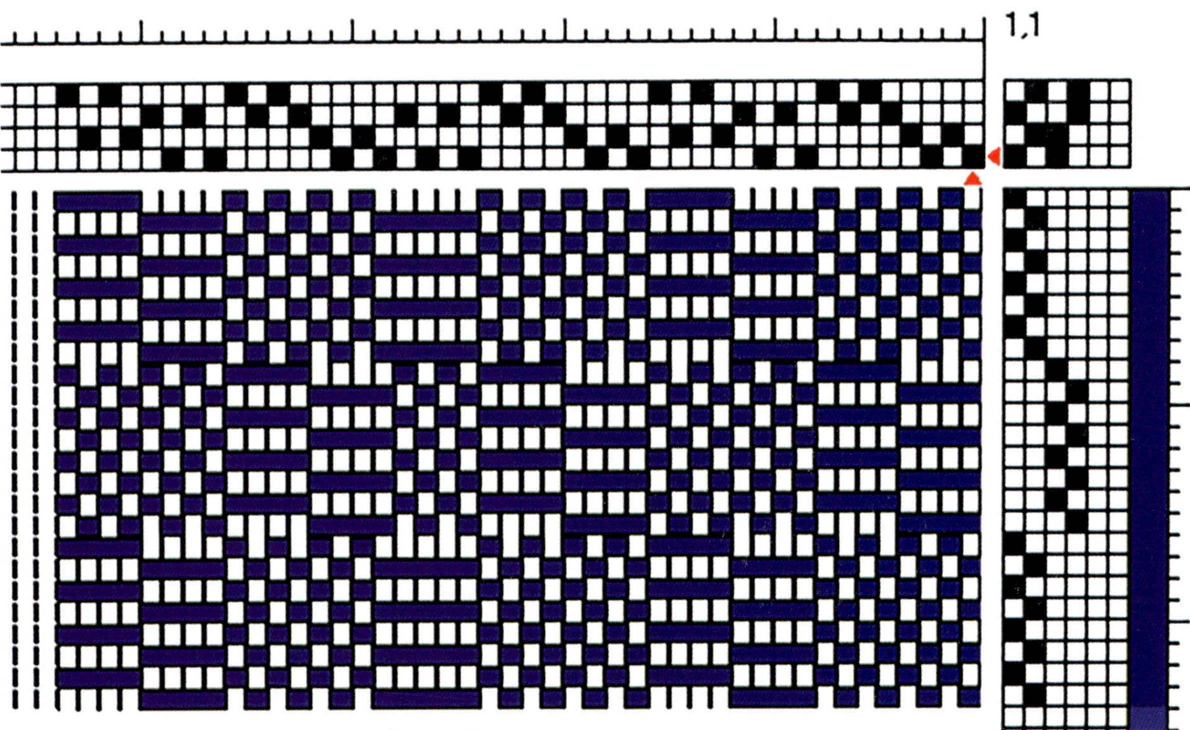

Figure 2: Thread-by-thread draft for M's and O's

◆ PROJECT ◆

M's and O's SCARF

4 SHAFTS

M's and O's is a fast weave. Each block is woven alternating between 2 treadles. The treadles work together in pairs so that you get plain weave in one block and the ribs in the other block. It's easy to be weaving along and lose count of the number of picks, but simply stop and count the number of rib floats!

The sett is based on the plain weave sett for the yarn you select. For this sample, I used Lunatic Fringe Yarns Hemp Bold. Cotton and wool yarns also work well in M's and O's. Hemp bold wraps out to a sett of 16 e.p.i. (see page 10 for calculating sett). This sett also just happens to work perfectly for the threading units of 8 ends per block. Remember, the threading units must be the full 8 threads/unit, or your pattern won't weave correctly.

You can change the number of weft picks in a block. Make sure you complete both treadles in the treadling pair for a block. For example, there are 8 threads in each threading unit, so you can treadle 8 total picks (pressing each treadle in the treadling pair four times). Perhaps you've decided that you want a taller block, so you could alternate the treadles for 12 picks of weft (pressing each treadle 6 times). This is "legal."

Please note: Beat M's and O's on a closed shed and press the wefts into place. The sett may seem a bit open (with correct beat, you should have a tiny square at the intersections of warp and weft), but once you wash the piece, the spaces between the warp/weft will close up, helping to pull those rib floats together, accentuating the overall fabric pattern. For this hemp yarn, I washed the scarf in hot water with a vigorous agitation and laid the scarf flat to dry. The ribs / plain weave were really well defined. I then spritzed the scarf with water and pressed it firmly, looking to produce a shine to the fabric. I achieved the shine, but hard pressing caused the ribs to flatten and move apart just a bit. But the pattern is still there. If you want the ribs closer together, I suggest weaving a sample and cutting the sample apart to try various wet-finishing techniques (including machine wash / dry) to test your yarn in the woven form.

I decided not to wet-finish further because I got a fabulous iridescence in the scarf fabric. The fabric is very stiff after washing and drying but softens up nicely with handling.

EQUIPMENT NEEDED

4-shaft loom
1 shuttle
8-dent reed (sleyed 2 ends per dent)

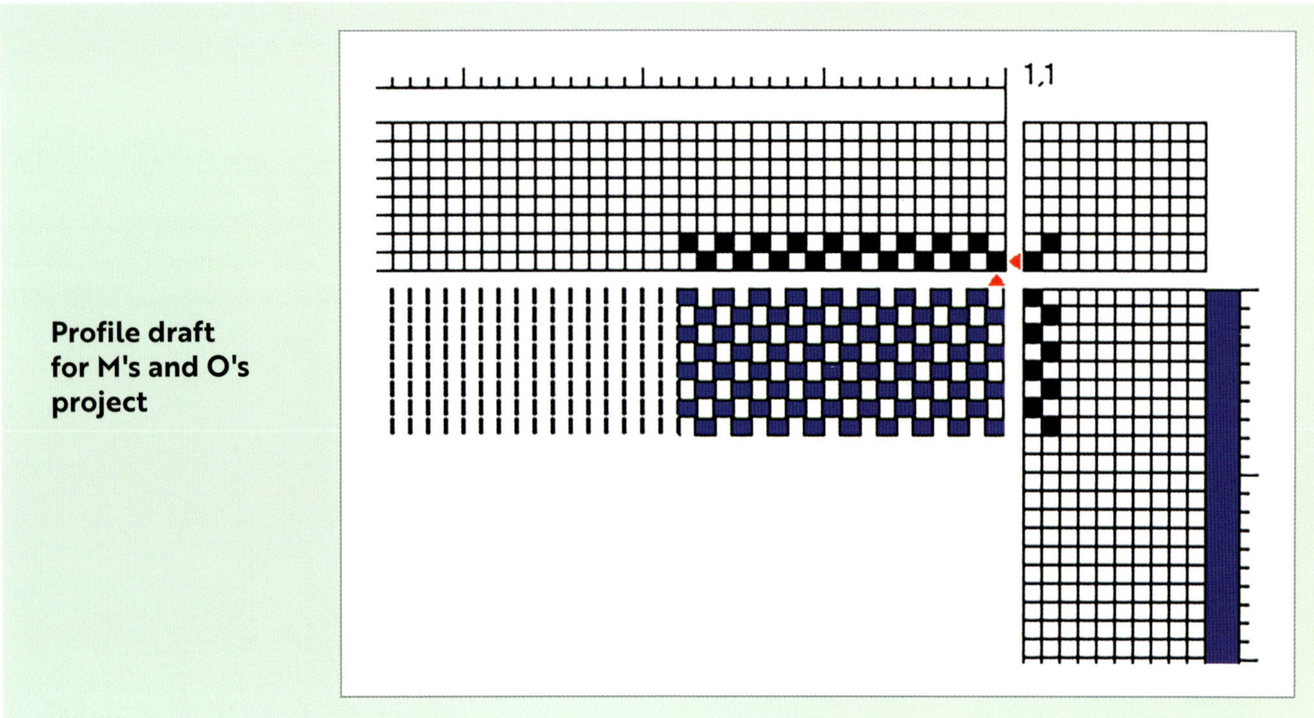

Profile draft for M's and O's project

Threading units:

Block A: 1-2-1-2-3-4-3-4
Block B: 1-3-1-3-2-4-2-4

Calculate the number of warp ends:
Each threading block is 8 warp ends. Thus, each colored-in square on the profile draft represents 8 warp ends. There are 18 squares in the threading;
18 squares × 8 threads/square = 144 warp ends.
A total of 144 warp ends at 16 e.p.i. gives you a scarf 9 inches wide. Do not add floating selvedges. Floating selvedges are unnecessary and also mess up the interlacement of the rib weave floats at the selvedges.

Calculate the number of heddles/shaft:
Use the profile draft to calculate heddles needed on each shaft.

Each square colored in on the threading grid of profile draft represents threads on all 4 shafts.

Both threading blocks (regardless of the Block A threading order or the Block B threading order) use:

Two threads on Shaft 1
Two threads on Shaft 2
Two threads on Shaft 3
Two threads on Shaft 4

Therefore, 18 blocks multiplied by 2 threads per Shaft = 36 heddles needed on each shaft.
Check your work: 36 heddles × 4 shafts = 144 warp threads total.

Yarns
Warp Yarn: Lunatic Fringe Yarns Hemp Bold in Peacock
Weft Yarn: Lunatic Fringe Yarns Hemp Bold in Amethyst

Sett: 16 e.p.i.

Warp Length: 96 inches
This warp length allows 68 inches of woven length on loom (allows for 6 inches take-up shrinkage), 6 inches fringe/tie-on for beginning of scarf, and 20 inches loom/thrum waste (fringe will come out of the thrum waste).

Width in Reed: 9 inches

Hems: Start and end scarf weaving the pattern. Do not weave plain weave hems.

Finished size after washing: 64 inches long by 8 inches wide

Shrinkage:
Woven length on loom: 68 inches
Length after washing: 64 inches
Shrinkage: 9%
Width in reed: 9 inches
Width after washing: 8 inches
Shrinkage: 9%

Tie-Up
As explained in the M's and O's weave structure overview.

Block A: Treadle 1 tied up to Shafts 1 and 3
Treadle 2 tied up to Shafts 2 and 4
Block B: Treadle 3 tied up to Shafts 1 and 2
Treadle 4 tied up to Shafts 3 and 4

Treadling:
10 picks of weft per block of treadling

Block A: Alternate treadles 1 and 2 for a total of 10 weft picks
Block B: Alternate treadles 3 and 4 for a total of 10 weft picks
Repeat

Finishing:
Knot fringe in knots of 4 ends each. For twisted fringe, use 8 warp ends (two 4 end knots). Wash in hot water with vigorous agitation. Lay flat to dry. Press if desired.

chapter 4

LACE WEAVES

There are several lace weave structures that can be used with profile drafts. For this book, I have selected Bronson Lace, Spot Bronson, and Huck Lace. These three lace weaves are related, but the pattern within the blocks depends on the threading, treadling, and tie-ups. Bronson Lace and Huck Lace are unit weave structures.

Bronson Lace has threading units that work independently from each other to create the overall pattern, but the interlacement of warp and weft is the same within the blocks.

Huck Lace uses two blocks of threading that work together to create a pattern unit (see the definitions in chapter 1). The interlacement of warp and weft within the pattern blocks can be changed via the tie-up and treadling to give different designs within a block.

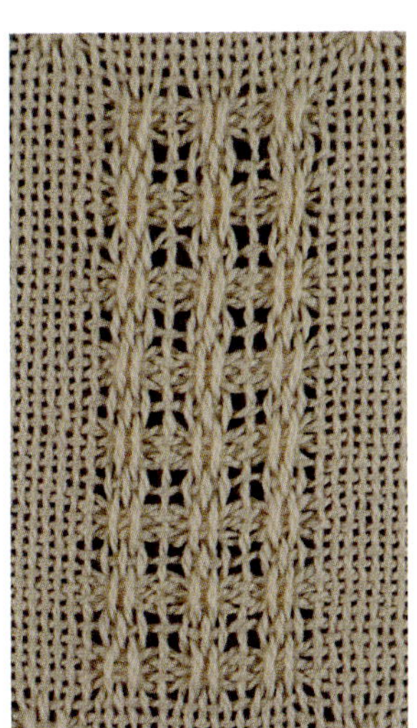

Bronson Lace—note the little "window" panes in the blocks.

Spot Bronson is a non-unit weave structure, which means the pattern created by warp and weft floats can be woven independently from the other blocks of pattern threading. One side of the fabric features warp floats; the other side features the weft floats in the blocks.

Huck Spots creates spots of warp and weft interlacements with plain weave between the spots. Huck Spots can be woven on the same warp as Huck Lace; you just need to change the treadling.

When using profile drafts with lace structures, I have a slightly different way of approaching the overall fabric design, depending on the lace structure I'm using. Those approaches are in the individual lace chapters.

Another option using profile drafts with lace weaves is to create stripes or boxes of pattern that are proportionally based on the size of the blocks in the profile draft. Tuck that away, because you can also create color stripes or plaids by using profile drafts.

Huck Lace—note the open windows between interlaced floats.

Spot Bronson—each "spot" is a block of pattern.

Huck Spots—note the interlaced warp/weft in the lace spots that pull the plain weave blocks into ovals.

WEAVE STRUCTURE
Bronson Lace

Bronson Lace is a lovely weave structure that is easy to design, thread, and treadle. The fabric pattern is created by weaving weft floats on one side of the fabric and warp floats on the reverse side of the fabric, interspersed by plain weave. Like M's and O's, the patterns look rather "blah" on the loom, but magic happens when you wet-finish the fabric. Wet-finishing causes the floats to slide together and create little windowpanes (at least to my eye) in the center of the blocks on the fabric surface. Stacking up these blocks of lace creates the overall designs in the fabric.

You may have heard the term "Atwater-Bronson Lace" rather than just Bronson Lace. The "Atwater" refers to Mary Meigs Atwater, whose research into the weave structure in her 1923 book *The Shuttle-Craft Book of American Hand-Weaving* led her to an "ancient" book published in England, called *The Domestic Manufacturer's Assistant*. The earlier book was written by the Bronsons and described the weave structure but didn't give the structure a name. *The Domestic Manufacturer's Assistant* doesn't sound like a weaving book, until we remember that prior to the

invention of powered mechanized looms in 1784, all weaving was done by hired weavers working in their homes. Now the book title makes sense and gives us a hint at how old the book Mary found really was!

In her book, Mary Atwater stated that she found the weave structure to be very useful and decided to include it in her book. Lacking an official name for the weave structure, she decided to call it "Bronson" weave for the authors of *The Domestic Manufacturer's Assistant.* At some point, the word "Atwater" got attached to the weave structure as Atwater-Bronson Lace, but now it's just referred to as Bronson Lace. Bronson Lace is a wonderful structure for shawls, scarves, and household linens such as towels, curtains, and blankets.

THREADING UNITS

There are 6 threads per threading unit. Shafts 1 and 2 are used for plain weave, and the other shafts in the threading units create the warp/weft floats that create the lacy patterns within the blocks.

The rule for the number of blocks you can weave is that the number of shafts on your loom minus 2 (for the two shafts weaving plain weave) equals the number of blocks of Bronson lace you can weave.

This means that you can weave two blocks of pattern on 4 shafts and up to 6 blocks of pattern on an 8-shaft loom. If you have more shafts on your loom, you can use the "number of shafts minus 2" rule to keep building more pattern blocks.

Note the threading sequences in the threading units. Shafts 1 and 2 are used in every threading unit, but the other shafts are assigned one at a time to the threading units.

The amount of pattern designs you can coax out of two blocks without changing the threading and just simply changing the treadling repeats is amazing. This weave structure is worthy of a sample where you play with different threading block combinations and treadling repeats.

Note that each block of threading ends on Shafts 1 and 2 to create picks of plain weave between the blocks, and each block starts on Shaft 1. This 1-2-1 threading sequence stabilizes the fabric around the pattern float areas by creating three picks of plain weave between the pattern float areas. The warp and weft floats travel over 5 threads.

Yes, you can repeat the threading units in a block to make larger blocks of pattern.

Threading Units:
Block A: 1-3-1-3-1-2
Block B: 1-4-1-4-1-2
Block C: 1-5-1-5-1-2
Block D: 1-6-1-6-1-2
Block E: 1-7-1-7-1-2
Block F: 1-8-1-8-1-2
Block G: 1-9-1-9-1-2
Block H: 1-10-1-10-1-2

CHOOSING THE YARNS

You can use any fiber content yarn that you wish, but slippery yarns such as silk or Tencel can be a challenge to make behave in the block floats. Yarns with body such as cotton, linen, and wool work well with the weave structure.

Some teachers and books suggest a slightly more open sett for lace weaves. However, I have found that Bronson Lace works well using the plain weave sett of your chosen yarn (see "Calculating Sett" on page 10 in chapter 1). One caution: Beat on a closed shed with this more open sett. If you beat on an open shed, it's very easy to overbeat the fabric; it becomes weft-face-emphasis fabric, and the block patterning can get lost. A little sampling, especially with new yarns, goes a long way in helping determine the sett that you like best. And remember to wet-finish that sample before making your final decision.

When selecting your yarns and sett, keep in mind that Bronson Lace warp and weft floats always travel over 5 threads. Finer yarns will make the pattern blocks smaller and more delicate. Larger grist yarns with a lower sett will create longer floats because the weft and warp floats travel a farther distance due to the yarn size. For example, with a yarn sett at 20 e.p.i., the float distance over the 5 threads is about ¼ inch. However, with a yarn sett at 10 e.p.i., those warp/weft floats will be ½ inch long. Now, that heavier yarn sett creating the longer float length could be really lovely in a shawl or scarf but may not work in a blanket where fingers could easily catch the floats. Keep this in mind when planning what the fabric will be used for.

To increase the size of the individual blocks, you simply increase the number of threading repeats within the blocks. Repeating threading units places the float sections next to each other, but the floats are tied down by Shafts 1 and 2 between the threading repeats at the end/beginning of the threading units. Very convenient!

Bronson Lace designs show up best when you're using the same color of yarn in the warp and weft. You can use a different color of weft, but it can make the pattern look very different. It's a design option worthy of some play.

TREADLING

When you treadle for pattern floats in a block, the other blocks will weave plain weave due to the threading units in the blocks. Shaft 1 is the constant being raised between all the pattern threads for a block, and Shaft 2 stays down until you transition at the end of the block. Shaft 2 threads then tie down the ends of the floats. This transition thread on Shaft 2 also weaves plain weave between the rows of weft. You can do as many treadle repeats as you wish for a block, creating fun "designing at the loom" adventures.

TIE-UP

Keeping in mind that Shaft 1 is the constant in every block of pattern, let's figure out a plain weave pick across the width of the fabric as the first step of our tie-up.

First pick of plain weave across the fabric: All blocks of threading alternate a thread on Shaft 1 with a thread on another shaft. This means Treadle 1 is tied up only to Shaft 1 to raise every other thread across the warp.

Second pick of plain weave across the fabric: In every threading unit, all the threads alternate threading with Shaft 1, so now we want to raise all the threads that are not Shaft 1 for the second pick of plain weave. In a design with two blocks (A and B), those threads would be on Shafts 2 (second half of plain weave), 3 (Block A pattern floats), and 4 (Block B pattern floats). Therefore, Treadle 2 is tied up to Shafts 2, 3, and 4. Again, every other thread is raised across the warp, because Shaft 1 threads stay down between each of these threads.

Now to create the warp and weft floats in the blocks for pattern. The warp and weft floats will travel over a threading unit using Shaft 2 as the tie-down on each end of the float for both warp (one side of fabric / float) and weft (the other side of the fabric). Thus, for treadling the pattern floats in a block, we need another set of treadles. Shaft 1 is always lifted for the plain weave between threading blocks, and then you alternate with another treadle for lifting the float shafts.

The two block tie-up is:
Treadle 1: Tied up to Shaft 1 (plain weave pick 1)
Treadle 2: Shafts 2, 3, and 4 (plain weave pick 2)
Treadle 3: Tied up to Shaft 1 plus Shaft 3 to create floats in Block A
Treadle 4: Tied up to Shaft 1 plus Shaft 4 to create floats in Block B

Here's the tie-up grid (figure 1). Remember that Treadle 1 vs. Treadle 2 weaves plain weave in all blocks.

When treadling, you need to alternate the plain weave treadles (Treadles 1 and 2) with the block pattern treadles, depending on which block you want float pattern in:

Figure 1

	4		4	
	3	3		
	2			
1		1	1	
P1	P2	A	B	Blocks with float pattern

Now it's time to figure out the treadling order.

Plain weave across the fabric: Note in the tie-up, Shaft 1 is engaged in all picks/treadles except Treadle 2, which is tied up to all the pattern float shafts plus the other half of the plain weave between blocks. Thus, to weave plain weave all the way across the warp, you alternate between Treadle 1 and Treadle 2. Use these two treadles for plain weave hems, and if you decide you'd like to have sections of plain weave between lace block repeats. Yet another fabric design option!

Pattern in the blocks: If you want pattern floats in Block A, you press Treadle 3, which raises Shafts 1 and 3. But wait—you also need to weave a pick with Shaft 2 to get the plain weave sequence in blocks that are not weaving pattern. Thus, you need to alternate a treadle weaving pattern in a block with the plain weave treadles.

So here's the treadling sequence for Block A pattern floats using the tie-up in figure 1.
Treadle 2 (raises first half of plain weave plus all pattern shafts)
Treadle 3 (raises float threads in Block A only / second half of plain weave on Shaft 1)
You want to balance the warp float length with the weft float length (5 threads) so you repeat treadling.
Treadle 2
Treadle 3
The weft floats go over 5 threads so we need to tie down the warp length floats at 5 threads.
Treadle 2
Treadle 1 (creates a line of plain weave between float sections)

However, there is an easier way! Figure 2 is the classic tie-up for Bronson Lace. Below each treadle tie-up, I have noted plain weave (P) vs. block (A or B) floats. Note that the plain weave treadles have changed places from the first tie-up grid.

Figure 2

4			4	Floats in Block B
3		3		Floats in Block A
2				Plain weave #2
	1	1	1	Plain weave #1
P1	P2	A	B	Blocks with float pattern

With this tie-up, we can treadle the following sequence alternating a plain weave pick (on Treadles 1 and 2) with a pattern block pick (Treadle 3 for Block A pattern and Treadle 4 for Block B pattern):

Block A: Treadle 1-Treadle 3-Treadle 1-Treadle 3-Treadle 1-Treadle 2 (1-3-1-3-1-2)
Block B: Treadle 1-Treadle 4-Treadle 1-Treadle 4-Treadle 1-Treadle 2 (1-4-1-4-1-2)

Wait! That treadling sequence is now the same as the threading sequence for each block! Isn't that delightful! And it's so much easier to remember!

TIP: When I tie up my treadles, I like to put Treadles 1 and 2 on the left, then leave a treadle down (not tied up), then tie up treadles 3 and 4. Then I can press treadles 1 and 2 with my left foot and treadles 3 and 4 with my right foot. Leaving the empty space between the sets of treadles helps me avoid pressing the wrong treadle.

MORE THAN TWO BLOCKS OF PATTERN

So what happens if you have 3 blocks of pattern? You will need 5 shafts; thus an 8-shaft loom. Figure 3 has the tie-up for more than 2 blocks of pattern:

6					6	Floats in Block D
5				5		Floats in Block C
4			4			Floats in Block B
3		3				Floats in Block A
2						Second half of plain weave
	1	1	1	1		First half of plain weave
P1	P2	A	B	C	D	Blocks with float pattern

Figure 3

Your treadling sequences:
Block A pattern: 1-3-1-3-1-2
Block B pattern: 1-4-1-4-1-2
Block C pattern: 1-5-1-5-1-2
Block D pattern: 1-6-1-6-1-2

Notice the pattern here? Bet you can figure out more blocks!

◆ PROJECT ◆

BRONSON LACE NAPKINS

4 SHAFTS

This Bronson Lace project has only 2 blocks in the profile draft, but you can play with the length of the blocks by changing how many repeats of the treadling for a block that you do. The treadling is easy to remember, and you can just fly with the weaving. Be sure to use a generous weaver's angle to avoid draw-in at the selvedges. The sections that are plain weave across the fabric will need a slightly deeper weaver's angle for the weft picks than the sections that include the blocks of pattern. You will have to experiment a bit to find the sweet spots for each.

The design has plain weave borders around the napkins. You can leave those off if you like. The plain weave borders are *not* shown on the profile draft! The profile draft has only the central section of the napkin with the Bronson Lace design.

Plain weave borders are easy to add to Bronson Lace. Simply thread the borders on Shafts 1 and 2 until you have the width of border you want. Then proceed with the threading units for the blocks of pattern. Yes, you can do the same thing between pattern blocks if you want to isolate the Bronson Lace blocks!

The profile draft really doesn't look anything like the final fabric design unless you remember that pattern shows up only in the block you are treadling. The other block weaves plain weave. For example, when you are treadling three repeats of Block A and where the threading is also three repeats of Block A, you get the larger center "medallion" in the fabric design. Isn't that grand fun?

EQUIPMENT NEEDED

4-shaft loom
1 shuttle
8-dent reed (sley 2 ends/dent)

Two-block profile draft for napkins

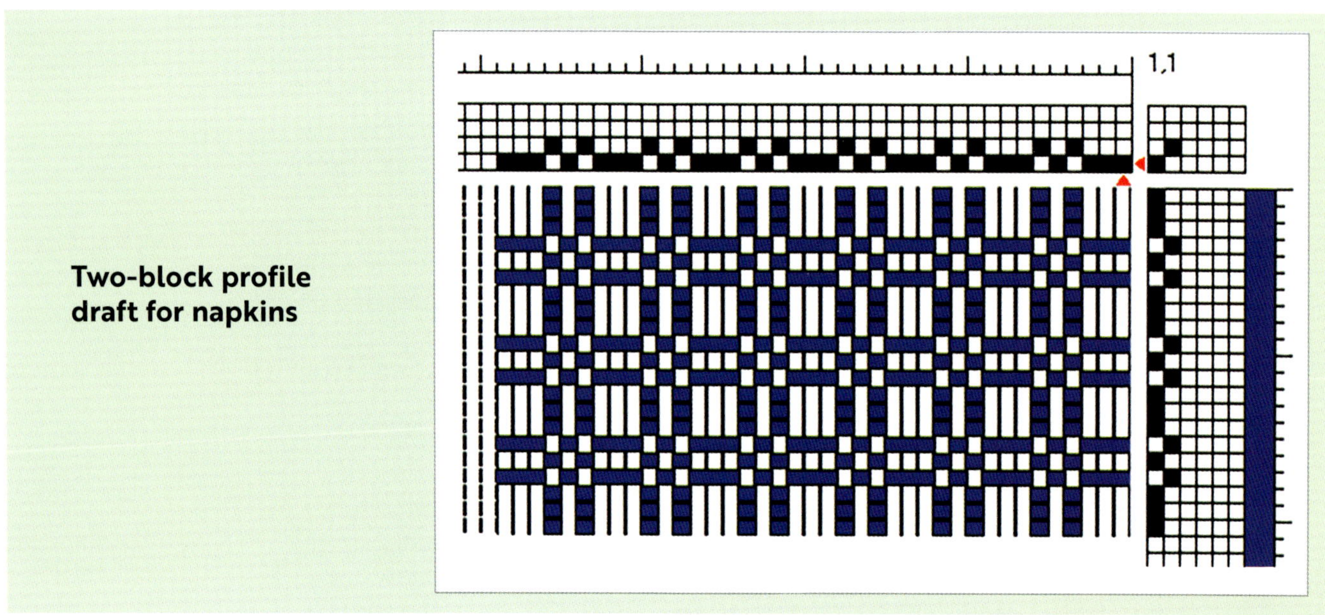

Threading Units:
Block A: 1-3-1-3-1-2
Block B: 1-4-1-4-1-2

Yarns:
8/2 Valley Yarns cotton for warp and weft
Cotton Candy (variegated yarn) Color #9951
Turquoise Blue (solid) Color # 2194

Sett: 16 e.p.i.

Calculate the number of warp ends: Count the number of colored-in squares on the threading grid and multiply the number of squares times 6. This only gives you the width of the center of the napkin. If you want borders, add the appropriate number of threads for the border width you desire.

For my sample: There are 39 squares in the threading × 6 threads per square = 234 ends for the center patterned area of the napkin.
I added 1.5 inches of plain weave border on each side. The threading in the two borders is 1-2, repeat. The sett of 16 e.p.i. × 1.5 inches = 24 ends for each side of border, for a total of 48 ends.

234 ends (patterned center) + 48 ends (borders on each side) = total of 282 warp ends

Calculate the number of heddles:
Shaft 1 is used 3 times for every colored-in square of the threading.

Multiply 3 × 39 squares = 117 heddles on Shaft 1 plus 12 for each border (24 total threaded on Shafts 1 and 2 for the 2 side borders)

Shaft 1: 117 + 24 (2 sections of border) = 141 heddles

Do the same calculation for the number of heddles on the other shafts, but this time you will need to pay attention to which block is being threaded in the profile draft.

Shaft 2: 39 squares x 1 Shaft 2 thread/threading unit = 39 heddles. Plus 24 total for the borders = 63 heddles.

Shaft 3: 27 squares for Block A × 2 threads/square on Shaft 3 = 54 heddles

Shaft 4: 12 squares for Block B × 2 threads/square on Shaft 4 = 24 heddles

Check your work: 141 (Shaft 1) + 63 (Shaft 2) + 54 (Shaft 3) + 24 (Shaft 4) = 282 heddles / warp ends

Tie-up:
Treadle 1: 2–3–4
Treadle 2: 1
Treadle 3: 1–3
Treadle 4: 1–4

Block treadling sequences:
Block A: 1-3-1-3-1-2
Block B: 1-4-1-4-1-2
Plain weave without pattern in blocks: Treadle 1–Treadle 2 (repeat to length desired)

Note! Watch your weaver's angle. You will need a deeper weaver's angle for the borders on each end than the center part of the napkin with the pattern floats. If you see the pattern weft floats bubbling up / not lying flat on the fabric surface, you need a shallower weaver's angle. If you see draw-in at the selvedges, you need a deeper weaver's angle.

Warp length: Allow 20 inches of warp length per napkin plus allowance for tie-on and loom/thrum waste. The 20 inches of warp length per napkin allows for shrinkage and hems.

Width in reed: 17.67 inches

Woven length on loom (measured off-tension): Start and end each napkin weaving 2.75 inches of plain weave with Cotton Candy (variegated yarn) to allow for 1.5 inches for the napkin border plus an additional 1.25 inches for hem/shrinkage. Weave the center section to a length of 13.5 inches with the Turquoise Blue (solid), followed by another 2.5 inches for the other border with the Cotton Candy.

When you get to the end of a napkin, weave 2 picks of plain weave, using thrums or yarn of a different color. This creates the cutting line between the napkins. When finishing, cut between these two picks for a straight cut. Remove the thrums after cutting the napkins apart.

Hem allowance: Included in the border. See "Woven Length on Loom" section above.

Finished size after washing: 14 inches long (hemmed) × 14 inches wide

Shrinkage: 9%

Finishing: Cut the napkins off the loom and machine zigzag stitch both raw ends and on each side of the thrum / cutting line yarn picks. Before you cut the napkins apart, soak the fabric in warm water, with some agitation. Lay flat to dry to block the napkins. This step helps keep shrinkage to a minimum with future machine laundering. To hem, lay a napkin flat and fold the raw edge toward the backside of the napkin until the border is the width you desire. Press fold. Now flip the napkin over and turn the raw edge under so it is between the napkin and the hem. Hand- or machine-stitch the hems.

Weave two picks of plain weave, using a contrasting color yarn between napkins. Cut the napkins apart between the two picks for a perfectly straight cut. After cutting, remove the contrasting yarn.

WEAVE STRUCTURE
Spot Bronson

Spot Bronson is similar to Bronson Lace, except Spot Bronson creates pattern using spots of warp/weft floats across the fabric to create the overall fabric pattern rather than larger blocks of pattern found in Bronson Lace. With the Spot Bronson pattern, spots of floats interact with each other across the surface of the fabric. It's a more delicate weave pattern, and like Bronson Lace, it is easy to thread and treadle.

Spot Bronson on 4 shafts can create 3 blocks of pattern, unlike Bronson Lace, where 4 shafts can weave only two blocks. However, to weave 3 blocks on 4 shafts, you sacrifice the ability to thread plain weave at the selvedges or between vertical sections of block pattern sections. If you do Spot Bronson on 4 shafts, you must use floating selvedges to catch the weft floats on each selvedge. However, you can weave plain weave at the beginning and end of a piece for hems by alternating Treadle 1 (tied up to Shafts 2, 3, 4) and Treadle 2 (tied up to Shaft 1).

The weft/warp floats to create the pattern go over 5 threads in each block. If you decide you'd like larger blocks of pattern due to using a fine thread, you can repeat the threading unit for a block. Each repeat of threading unit adds four more threads that the pattern weft floats cover. For example, one threading of Block A uses 4 threads and creates a weft float over 5 ends of warp. Adding another threading repeat uses 8 threads and creates a float over 9 threads. The size of yarn you are using will determine if those longer float lengths will work or not.

To weave 3 blocks of Spot Bronson with solid, lengthwise, plain weave borders on each edge of the fabric, you need to use 5 shafts; thus you need an 8-shaft loom.

Threading units for 3 blocks on 4 shafts (floating selvedges required):
Block A: 1-2-1-2
Block B: 1-3-1-3
Block C: 1-4-1-4

Threading units for 3 blocks on 5 shafts with plain weave sections that run lengthwise:
Block A: 1-3-1-3
Block B: 1-4-1-4
Block C: 1-5-1-5
Shafts 1 and 2 are used for threading the plain weave sections that run the length of the fabric.

Threading units for 4 blocks on 5 shafts without plain weave lengthwise—need floating selvedges:
Block A: 1-2-1-2
Block B: 1-3-1-3
Block C: 1-4-1-4
Block D: 1-5-1-5

Threading units for 4 blocks with plain weave borders:
Block A: 1-3-1-3
Block B: 1-4-1-4
Block C: 1-5-1-5
Block D: 1-6-1-6
Shafts 1 and 2 are used for threading the plain weave borders lengthwise.

Tie-up:

Let's look at the threading first. Note that no matter how many blocks, Shaft 1 is used in every block and is every other thread, regardless of what block you are threading. To get the plain weave pick that ties down the warp and weft floats and weaves plain weave in all the other blocks, you have to engage Shaft 1 vs. all the other shafts being used. This is the same as Bronson Lace in the previous chapter.

All the other shafts except Shaft 1 will be raised between every pattern pick for the block. To create pattern floats within a block, Shaft 1 will rise with the pattern shaft for the block.

Thus, your tie-up for 3 blocks on 4 shafts is:

4				4	Shaft 4, Block C pattern
3			3		Shaft 3, Block B pattern
2		2			Shaft 2, Block A pattern
	1	1	1	1	Shaft 1 is plain weave
P1	P2	A	B	C	

Figure 1

To weave plain weave for hems at the start and finish of a piece, you alternate treadling P1 and P2.

When weaving pattern in a block, you alternate Treadle P1 with the treadle tied up for the block you want pattern floats in. You do not need to Treadle P2 in the pattern blocks, because each of the pattern blocks engages Shaft 1 with the tie-up.

The tie-up and treadling create pattern floats in the block weaving pattern and plain weave in all the other blocks of pattern.

To weave plain weave across the fabric for hems or pattern separation, alternate Treadle 1 with Treadle 2.

Tie-up for 3 blocks on 5 shafts with lengthwise plain weave edges/borders:

				5	Shaft 5, Block C pattern
4			4		Shaft 4, Block B pattern
3		3			Shaft 3, Block A pattern
2					Shaft 2, plain weave lengthwise
	1	1	1	1	Shaft 1, plain weave lengthwise
P1	P2	A	B	C	

Figure 2

To weave plain weave lengthwise as a border or stripe, you need to thread the warp sections where you want to weave only plain weave bands the length of the fabric (no pattern floats for either block) on Shafts 1 and 2 only.

The profile draft for the project does not reflect lengthwise bands of plain weave. Only the pattern blocks are noted on a profile draft. You can illustrate lengthwise bands of plain weave on your profile by coloring in the threading squares on a different block line that is not part of the pattern threading. For example, in the 3-block draft on 5 shafts, you could color in each square for plain weave threading on the Shaft 6 line, since Shaft 6 is not used in the pattern blocks. Your weaving notes with the profile draft should include the information that blocks on Shaft 6 are plain weave running the length of the piece. Your future self will thank you for that reminder.

LEARNING OPPORTUNITIES

PRIOR TO WEAVING the project sample for this book, I hadn't played much with Spot Bronson. The structure just didn't call to me. Boy, did I learn a lot—including that I love this simple weave structure!

Lesson #1: Less is more for pattern! The first profile draft I created had interlocking diamonds using 6/2 white cotton, since I was thinking that the spots would show better with the larger yarn. The fabric design looked really interesting on the draft, pretty good on the loom, and really awful in the fabric off the loom. The overall design is far too busy, and my eye couldn't easily discern the individual designs. Keep the interactions of the blocks simple for the fabric design.

Lesson #2: Use finer yarns. I've used 6/2 cotton in Bronson Lace and love the definition of the blocks with the heavier yarn. However, Spot Bronson doesn't play as well with larger yarns. The float distances have to travel a longer distance due to the yarn sett, and the overall pattern is not as crisp. I was much more pleased with a second sample, woven with 10/2 cotton.

Lesson 3: Use a yarn with a bit of shine like mercerized cotton, Tencel, silk, linen, bamboo, etc. The light reflection provided by the shinier yarns helps the warp/weft pattern spots show up much better.

Lesson 4: Shrinkage on all Spot Bronson samples is about 9%–10% in both take-up (length) and draw-in (width). Plan for that amount of shrinkage, but if using a new yarn, be sure to sample first to confirm the shrinkage with the yarn.

Lesson 5: As with other lace weaves, the magic really happens in the wet-finishing. Use warm water (no detergent) and a bit of agitation and let the pieces soak for about 5–10 minutes. Squeeze out the water and roll the piece in a towel, pressing down on the rolled towel to remove excess water. Lay the piece flat to dry. Once it's dry, give the piece a good steam ironing, but don't press hard with the iron. The spots will really shine!

Lesson 6: Set up your treadles so the plain weave (Treadles 1 and 2) are on the left, then drop a treadle and tie up the pattern Treadles 3, 4, and 5 (treadle 5 is used only in the five-shaft design). The separation between the sets of treadles helps easily alternate between Treadle 1 and whichever treadle is assigned to the particular block. Treadle 2 is used only for weaving plain weave on each end for optional hems.

Lesson 7: Use a deeper weaver's angle for the plain weave picks (Treadle 1: Shafts 2, 3, 4) than for the pattern weft picks. The pattern sections will be crisper if you use a shallower weaver's angle for the pattern weft picks.

Lesson 8: Weave with firm tension on the warp. If the warp tension is soft, it's easy to catch the warp float threads with your shuttle.

Treadling:

On the profile draft, you color in the threading and treadling squares where you want pattern (the warp / weft floats). If the treadling square for Block A is colored in, then you treadle for Block A pattern.

There are 4 warp threads per block of threading; therefore, there are 4 picks of weft per colored-in square in the treadling. These weft picks alternate between Treadle 1 (tied up to Shafts 2, 3, 4, etc.) and the pattern treadle assigned to that block of pattern.

For example: If you are treadling for Block A with 3 blocks on 4 shafts, the treadle sequence using our tie-up on page 49 is:

P1 (Treadle 1) then Block A Treadle (Treadle 2)
P1 (Treadle 1) then Block A Treadle again
or Treadle 1-2-1-2
Note that pattern for Block A is threaded on Shafts 1-2-1-2.

Block B:

P1 then Block B (Treadle 3)
P1 then Block B
Treadling for Block B using the tie-up above: 1-3-1-3

Aha! The treadling sequence for each block is the same as the threading sequence for the block!

For 3 blocks on 5 shafts, treadling for each block is using the 5-shaft tie-up above:
Block A: Treadle 1-3-1-3
Block B: Treadle 1-4-1-4
Block C: Treadle 1-5-1-5

Both scenarios work so that the treadling is the same sequence as the threading, because we have Shafts 2, 3, 4, etc. tied up to Treadle 1. This makes your treadling order easy to remember!

◆ PROJECT ◆

SPOT BRONSON INFINITY SCARF

As pictured, this 3-block project requires an 8 -shaft loom due to the lengthwise plain weave band on each selvedge edge. However, you can weave this as 3 blocks on 4 shafts by eliminating the plain weave bands on each side. The plain weave along each edge is *not* shown on the profile draft. Only the pattern section is shown on the profile draft.

With a 4-shaft loom, you must add floating selvedges on each side since you will not be able to have plain weave bands running lengthwise. I wove the sample for this project on 4 shafts, and the floating selvedges worked very well.

If you have an 8-shaft loom, decide how wide you would like the plain weave bands on each selvedge edge. Add the appropriate number of warp threads based on your yarn's ends per inch, and add to the warp ends calculation.

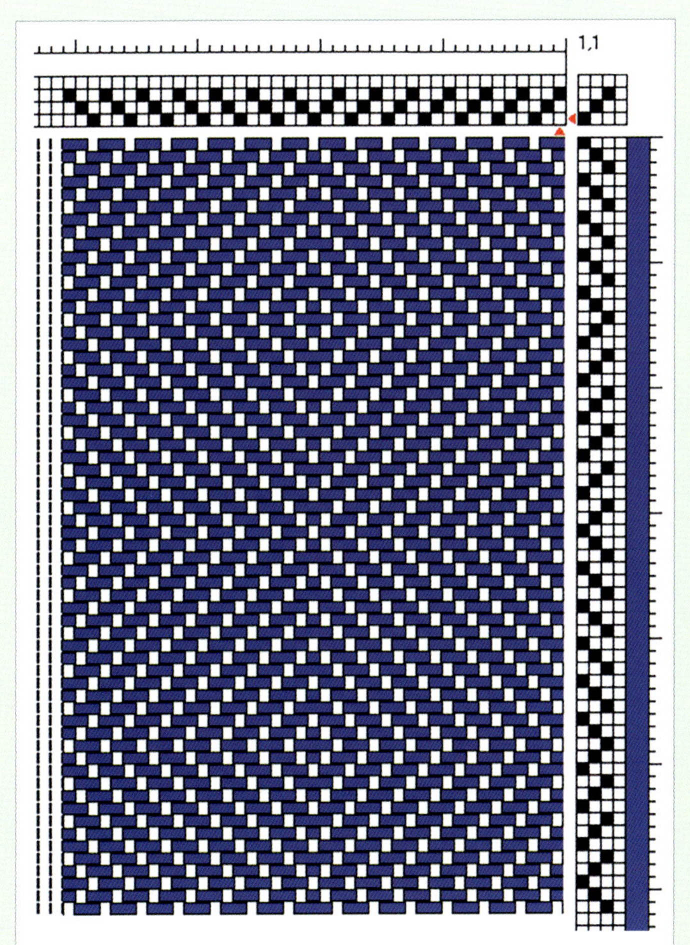

Profile draft for 3-block project

EQUIPMENT NEEDED

4- or 8-shaft loom
1 shuttle
10-dent reed (sleyed 2 ends per dent)

Threading units:

4-shaft loom:
Block A: 1-2-1-2
Block B: 1-3-1-3
Block C: 1-4-1-4

8-shaft loom:
Block A: 1-3-1-3
Block B: 1-4-1-4
Block C: 1-5-1-5

Plain weave sections lengthwise on the scarf: Thread 1-2 (repeat for the number of threads you want in the lengthwise band of plain weave).

Yarns: 10/2 Lunatic Fringe Tubular Spectrum mercerized cotton in #5 Blue

Warp and Weft: 10/2 mercerized cotton in Tubular Specturm #5 Blue

Sett: 20 e.p.i.

Calculate the number of warp ends:
Each colored-in square of the threading represents 4 threads, and there are 41 squares.
41 squares × 4 threads/square = 164 warp ends for the pattern section only.

If you are using a 4-shaft loom, you don't have enough shafts to do the plain weave bands, so add 2 more threads for floating selvedges for a total of 166 warp threads. This will give you a width in the reed of 8.2 inches.

This is designed for an 8-shaft loom, so you can weave the plain weave bands along each selvedge. These bands of plain weave are *not* noted on the profile draft.

I added 1-inch-wide plain weave bands on each selvedge, for a total of 40 ends (20 ends on each selvedge).

164 pattern warp ends (pattern) + 40 warp ends (2 borders) = total of 204 warp ends. This gives you a width in the reed of 10 inches.

Calculate the number of heddles—8-shaft version:
Shaft 1 is used in every threading unit alternating with the pattern warp threads, so each threading square represent 2 threads on Shaft 1 × the number of pattern squares.
41 pattern square × 2 = 82 heddles for pattern plus 10 ends in each plain weave band, for a total of 20 ends.

Shaft 1 total: 82 ends for pattern squares + 20 borders = 102 heddles

Shaft 2 is only used for the plain weave selvedge bands that are each 1-inch-wide sett at 20 e.p.i × 2 inches; this is a total of 40 ends needed for the selvedge bands. Only half of those threads will be on Shaft 2.

Shaft 2 total: 40 total threads divided by 2 = 20 heddles

Shaft 3 = Block A sections: There are 13 squares for Block A, which is threaded on Shafts 1 and 3. There are two threads in each Block A section on Shaft 3.

Shaft 3 total: 13 squares × 2 threads per square = 26 heddles

Shaft 4 = Block B: 14 squares, and these are on Shafts 1 and 4, with two threads on Shaft 4 per square.

Shaft 4 total: 14 squares × 2 threads / square= 28 heddles

Shaft 5 = Block C: 14 squares and two Shaft 5 threads per square

Shaft 5 total: 14 squares × 2 threads/square = 28 heddles

Check your work:
Shaft 1 = 102 heddles
Shaft 2 = 20 heddles
Shaft 3 = 26 heddles
Shaft 4 = 28 heddles
Shaft 5 = 28 heddles

The total of 204 heddles matches the 204 warp ends calculated.

Calculating heddles—4-shaft version
With 4 shafts, you do not have enough shafts to weave the plain weave borders. But you can weave the pattern using floating selvedges on each side.

Shaft 1: Both blocks use Shaft 1 on every treadle. There are 41 squares of pattern, and each square requires two threads on Shaft 1 for the threading units.
41 squares × 2 = 82 heddles

Shaft 2: This shaft makes pattern for Block A. There are 13 squares for Block A threading and 2 threads per threading unit.
13 squares × 2 threads/unit = 26 heddles

Shaft 3: This shaft makes pattern for Block B. 14 squares for Block B and 2 threads on Shaft 3 per threading unit.
14 squares × 2 threads/unit = 28 heddles

Shaft 4: Pattern in Block C. 14 squares for Block C and 2 threads on Shaft 4 per threading unit.
14 squares × 2 threads/unit = 28 heddles.

Check your work:
Shaft 1: 82 heddles
Shaft 2: 26 heddles
Shaft 3: 28 heddles
Shaft 4: 28 heddles

Total of 164 warp ends plus 2 floating selvedges = 166 warp ends for 4 shaft version

TIP: If you have an 8-shaft loom, don't have enough heddles on Shaft 1, and hate to move heddles as much as I do, you can use another shaft that is not being used to complete the threading. Since Shaft 6 isn't being used, thread on Shaft 1 until you run out of heddles, then substitute Shaft 6 for Shaft 1 to finish threading. Remember to tie up the plain weave Treadle 2 to Shafts 1 and 6, plus every pattern treadle needs to include both Shaft 1 and Shaft 6.

Unfortunately, with three blocks of pattern, 4-shaft looms do not have an empty shaft to use, so you may have to move heddles. Count heddles before you start to thread! (We've all been there, haven't we?)

Tie-up:
4-shaft loom:
Treadle 1: Shafts 2, 3, 4
Treadle 2: Shaft 1
Treadle 3: Shafts 1 and 2
Treadle 4: Shafts 1 and 3
Treadle 5: Shafts 1 and 4

8-shaft loom tie-up for plain weave bands lengthwise:
Treadle 1: Shafts 2–3–4
Treadle 2: Shaft 1
Treadle 3: Shafts 1–3
Treadle 4: Shafts 1–4
Treadle 5: Shafts 1–5

Treadle 1 and Treadle 2 alternating will weave plain weave widthwise across the fabric for both 4-shaft and 8-shaft looms.

Treadling:
Regardless of whether you are using a 4-shaft or 8-shaft loom, Treadle 1 is engaged between every block pattern pick. Thus, if you are treadling a Bronson Spot in Block A, you will press Treadle 1, throw a weft pick, and then, for the pattern treadle for the block you are treadling pattern in, throw a weft pick. Repeat for a total of 4 picks of weft.

Note that the profile draft starts on Block A treadling.

Treadling—4 shafts:
Block A spots: 1-2-1-2
Block B spots: 1-3-1-3
Block C spots: 1-4-1-4

Treadling—8 shafts:
Block A spots: 1-3-1-3 for 4 picks
Block B spots: 1-4-1-4 for 4 picks
Block C spots: 1-5-1-5 for 4 picks

See the pattern here? The treadling is exactly the same as the threading for each block!

Warp length: 84 inches

Width in reed: 10.2 inches (center pattern area is 8 inches wide, and the plain weave bands on each side are 1 inch)

Weft: Lunatic Fringe Tubular Spectrum 10/2 mercerized cotton in #5 Blue

Woven length on loom (measured off-tension): 55 inches

Hem allowance: 1.5 inches plain weave on each end

Finished size after washing: 8.5 inches wide × 50 inches long hemmed

Shrinkage: 10%

Weaving: Weave 1.5 inches of plain weave for hems. Repeat the pattern blocks a total of 6 times, then weave the turn (point). End with 1.5 inches of plain weave for the hem.

Finishing: Soak in warm water, then lay flat to dry. Iron with steam. Turn the hem under on one end, so you have 1 inch of plain weave showing. Fold this end back on the scarf. Take the other end of the fabric and turn it so the bottom is now the top (this gives you the infinity twist). Turn the end under so you have 1 inch of plain weave. Place the turned-back hem edges on top of each other and tuck the raw ends between the folded-over edges and the main fabric. Pin and hand-hemstitch the ends.

WEAVE STRUCTURE
Huck Lace

If you've already played with Bronson Lace, you may be tempted to skip over Huck. Resist the temptation! The possibilities in weaving Huck are more than you may ever imagine! Once you set up the blocks, you could literally weave the designs you can make by simply changing treadling sequences and tie-up for months and still have things to explore! I think Madeline van der Hoogt said it best in her introduction to *The Best of Weaver's: Huck Lace*, page 4 (see "Resources," page 190):

"If I were shipwrecked on a desert island and had to choose only one weave to have with me, it would be huck lace. Huck has everything a weaver could wish for. This lovely, lacy structure:

- provides maximum pattern on a minimum number of shafts
- produces fabrics with a beautiful hand in all types of fibers
- can be used for a wide range of fabric types, from light and lacy to thick, warm, and insulating
- looks very complicated but is really very simple (so much better than the other way around)
- defies the vertical and horizontal grid (always a weaver's goal)
- is especially suitable for creating original designs
- allows, but does not require, the interplay of color
- is quick and easy to weave with only one shuttle

What more could you ask for?" (Madeline van der Hoogt, teacher and former editor of *Prairie Wool Companion, Weaver's,* and *Handwoven* magazines)

I totally agree with everything Madeline wrote. Playing with Huck can occupy your creative itch for a long, long time. It's grand fun to

create dramatically new designs with a simple treadling sequence change or a quick tie-up adjustment and then toss in color and weave effects—oh, my!

Consider this section and project an introduction to Huck to set you on the exploration path. In older weaving publications, such as *A Handweaver's Pattern Book* by Marguerite Porter Davison, this weave structure was called "Huck-a-back." Over the years, this name has been shortened to "Huck." The Huck weave structure is closely related to Swedish Lace, a weave structure that is also very similar to Bronson Lace.

HOW HUCK DIFFERS FROM BRONSON LACE

Huck differs from Bronson Lace by using **two blocks of threading that work together as a unit**. Within the threading units, you can have 5 thread repeats (most common), 7 thread repeats (best for fine threads, so the floats don't get too long), and 3 thread repeats within the block. By alternating the threading for each block, the two blocks work together as a unit to make the design. The threading units for 5 thread repeats are:

Threading unit for Block A / B
Block A: 2-3-2-3-2
Block B: 1-4-1-4-1

Threading unit for Block C / D
Block C: 2-5-2-5-2
Block D: 1-6-1-6-1

Threading unit for Block E / F
Block E: 2-7-2-7-2
Block F: 1-8-1-8-1

If you want a 7-thread block, simply repeat the threading sequence in a block for 7 threads total. For example, Block A would be 2-3-2-3-2-3-2, and Block B would be 1-4-1-4-1-4-1. For a 3-thread, Block A would be 2-3-2, and Block B would be 1-4-1.

Threading for Blocks A and B works as a team (unit), and only 4 shafts are needed. Blocks C and D work as a team and create another design area on the fabric that can be connected to Blocks A and B or stand alone within the fabric design.

When you treadle the designs, one threading block in a unit will weave warp floats, and the other threading block in the unit will weave weft floats. The

Interlacement of warp and weft threads in classic Huck Lace

combination of the two blocks can give you classic "framed open window" interlacement for Huck Lace.

By playing with the tie-up, you can get floats in one block and plain weave in the other block(s) for weaving Huck spots, ovals, boxes, and more! If you have enough treadles on your loom (or the willingness to retie treadles as you weave), you can mix different Huck textures in one piece. For example, you can have classic Huck Lace windows in one part of your fabric combined with other blocks weaving Huck spots. The Huck Lace runner project explores these options within the piece.

HOW HUCK WORKS

Shafts 1 and 2 are your plain weave/tie-down shafts for the blocks. When threading, you can alternate threading for different blocks, or you can thread the same block over and over as long as you have the opposite tie-down shaft between each group of threading on the same block.

Each full block of Huck Lace is actually two blocks of threading units. Note that earlier, I refer to these blocks as A/B, C/D, and E/F for the threading units that combine to make up a threading block.

For a traditional Huck Lace threading, you alternate threading one Block A sequence followed by one Block B sequence where you want the Huck Lace to appear in your fabric. To achieve lengthwise plain weave areas (stripes) between the unit blocks of pattern, you thread only on Shafts 1 and 2. Here's what the threading looks like for 2 blocks / one unit

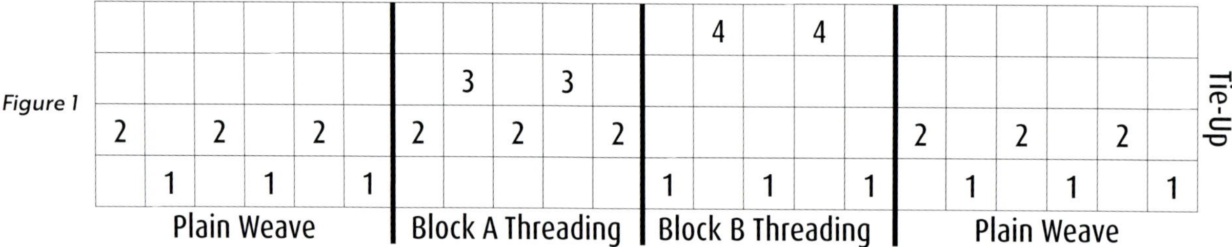

Figure 1

in classic Huck Lace (see figure 1) separated by sections of plain weave:

Refer to the example labeled figure 1. When you transition threading from the plain weave sections to the pattern section, you need to maintain the alternation between Shafts 1 and 2. I've placed a box "Tie up" to the right of the threading where the tie-up located on standardized weaving drafts. The threading starts with six threads of plain weave on Shafts 1 and 2. The next thread on Shaft 1 is part of the threading for Block B. Yes, you can start threading in either Block A or Block B. For this example, I have chosen to start threading on Block B. Take note that the alternating of plain weave tie-downs on Shafts 1 and 2 continues between the blocks of threading.

Here's another option for threading blocks with plain weave borders.

In the second example, labeled figure 2, notice that I ended the threading of the first plain weave section on Shaft 1 so the transition to Block A threading (starts on Shaft 2 for Block A) maintains the plain weave threading of 1-2. If you end on Shaft 2 for the plain weave section (as in the example in figure 1) and start threading Block A threading of 2-3, there would be two threads next to each other on Shaft 2, which creates a doubled warp thread when you weave. We do not want doubled warp threads.

Tie-Up

The first thing to remember is that you need to alternate engaging those tie-downs on Shafts 1 and 2 with your treadles. Also, the threading of pattern on Shafts 3 and 4 must alternate between warp floats in one block and weft floats in the other block. This is controlled by how you tie up the treadles.

Let's take this a step at a time. If you want to start your project with plain weave all the way across the fabric for hems or a border, you want to raise every other warp thread with each pick of weft for plain weave. Refer to threading grid in figure 3.

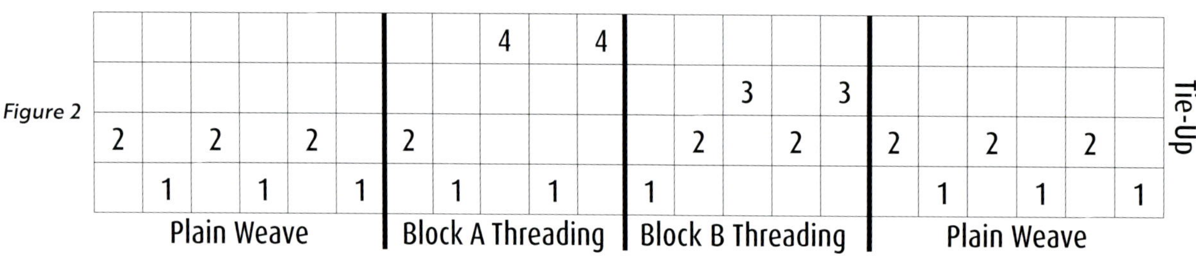

Figure 2

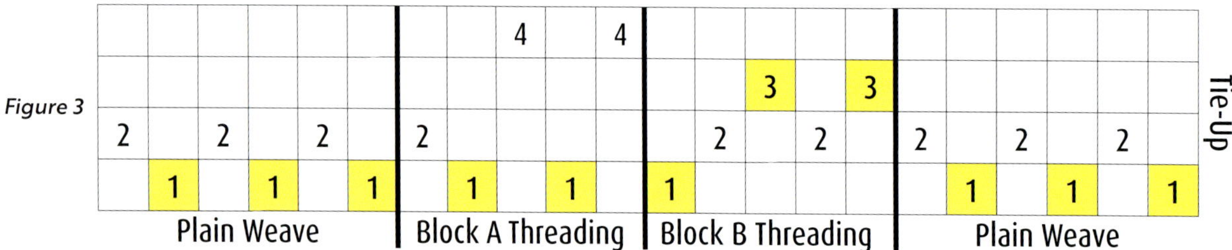

Figure 3

The first section of threading is on Shafts 1 and 2 for plain weave. You want to raise one of those shafts. I have highlighted Shaft 1 for the first pick.

If you want plain weave in Block A (threaded 2-3-2-3-2), you want to continue to raise every other thread in Block A, so you tie up a treadle to Shaft 3. You can't use Shaft 2, because then, two warp threads would be raised together on Shafts 1 (plain weave) and Shaft 2 (Block A threading).

In Block B (threaded 1-4-1-4-1), every other thread is on Shaft 1. I've colored in the squares, showing every other thread in yellow being raised for the first pick of plain weave. Note that since Block B ends on Shaft 1, I can continue raising Shaft 1 in the plain weave threading in the border.

This illustrates that, to weave plain weave across the entire width of the fabric, you need to tie up Treadle 1 to Shafts 1 and 3, which will raise every other thread across the piece regardless of plain weave threading or block threading.

The other squares which are not colored in are on Shafts 2 and 4. That means that for the second pick of plain weave across the piece, you tie up Treadle 2 to Shafts 2 and 4. Again, this will raise every other thread in the threading.

Stick a pin in this. More to come.

Now let's talk about the floats in each block that create pattern. The beauty of Huck is that the two blocks of threading in a unit interlace to create a stable fabric within the lace pattern blocks. This means you can make the combined blocks as big as you want by repeating the threading for the two blocks in a unit. When you weave, the fabric looks like stacks of floats. When you wet-finish the fabric, these loose interlacements will move together and create the Huck Lace panes in the areas threaded for the lace blocks.

Remember, when you have warp floats in Block B threading, you will have weft floats in Block A threading. If you treadle for warp floats in Block A, then you will have weft floats in Block B.

Please note: The following is for a rising shed (Jack loom) tie-up. If you have a countermarche loom, you can use this same tie-up by tying up the lower lamms to the marked (rising) shafts (see "Rising vs. Sinking Shed Looms," page 18). If you prefer to use a traditional countermarche tie-up, note that the warp/weft floats will be opposite.

So how do these all pull together in our tie-up for pattern in the blocks and plain weave on the edges? Keep in mind that Shafts 1 and 2 are also the tie-down shafts for the warp and weft floats created in the blocks of pattern. Thus, one of these tie-down shafts (1 and 2) has to be engaged with a treadle plus the float pattern shaft that is designated for that block.

I know—you just said "WHAT?!?!" Refer to figure 4, where the tie-up has been added to the threading grid we've been using.

Treadle 1 is tied up to Shafts 2 and 4, and Treadle 2 is tied up to Shafts 1 and 3. Alternating between these Treadles 1 and 2 creates plain weave across the fabric, because each treadle is lifting every other thread in both blocks.

To get warp floats in Block B, Treadle 3 is tied up to Shafts 1 and 4, the two shafts designated for Block B threading. Because Shafts 2 and 3 stay down, you get weft floats in Block A.

To get warp floats in Block A, Treadle 4 is tied up to Shafts 2 and 3 so both threads for Block A are raised to create warp floats in Block A. When there are warp floats in A, then there are weft floats in Block B, because Shafts 1 and 4 stay down in Block B.

Now let's put this all together. Because you are using threading units of 5 threads, to complete the treadling sequence for both blocks, you need to repeat the treadling sequence for 5 total picks for each block, starting and ending the treadling

Figure 4

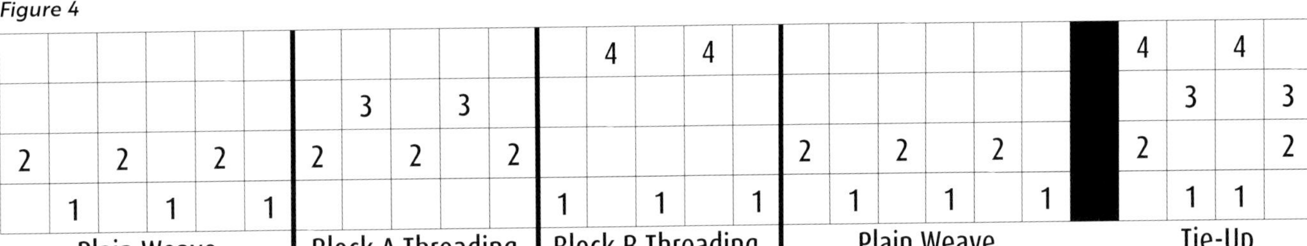

sequences with the plain weave shafts treadle assigned to the block. For this tie-up, Block B is Treadle 1 and Block A is Treadle 2.

Here are the treadling sequences starting with plain weave across the fabric:

Plain weave across fabric: Treadle 1 (raises Shafts 2 and 4) vs. Treadle 2 (raises Shafts 1 and 3) until you have the length of plain weave across the fabric that you desire.

Block A warp floats / weft floats in Block B: Treadle 2 (raises 1 and 3) vs. Treadle 4 (raises 2 and 3). So the treadle sequence for the tie-up in the figure 4 grid is 2-4-2-4-2.

Block B warp floats / weft floats in Block A: Treadle 1 vs. Treadle 3. So the treadle sequence is 1-3-1-3-1.

Hmm, it would be easier to treadle if the treadles tied to shafts that weave in a block are next to each other. So let's rearrange the tie-up to make it easier to treadle.

Tie-up change:
Treadle 1: 2-4 (Block B warp floats)
Treadle 2: 1-4 (Block B warp floats)
Treadle 3: 1-3 (Block A warp floats)
Treadle 4: 2-3 (Block A warp floats)

Block A warp floats / Block B weft floats: Treadle 3-4-3-4-3
Block B warp floats / Block A weft floats: Treadle 1-2-1-2-1
Plain weave all the way across: Treadle 1 (raises Shafts 2 and 4), then Treadle 3 (raises Shafts 1 and 3)

This means you can tie up the Block A treadles next to each other, drop a treadle, and then tie up the Block B treadles next to each other. Now you can treadle Block A with your left foot and Block B with your right foot and alternate between Treadle 1 (first treadle in the first pair) and Treadle 3 (first treadle in second pair) to weave plain weave across the fabric. That's much easier!

Feel free to try your own easy-to-treadle tie-ups!

OTHER HUCK DESIGNS

You can change up your Huck designs while weaving the same piece! In the *Weaver's Book of Huck Lace*, Lynn Tedder has a sample project that has nine (!) different Huck designs created just by changing the treadling, using a skeleton tie-up. Skeleton tie-ups can be quite wonderful but confusing to treadle if you have to press multiple treadles at the same time. For countermarche looms, you can't press multiple treadles at the same time, which eliminates the option of a skeleton tie-up.

Here are some 2-block tie-ups to try out without using a skeleton tie-up. The same shafts are tied up, but the treadles are tied up in a different order. You can weave all of these on the same warp, but depending how many treadles your loom has, changes in pattern may mean changing tie-ups within a project. I have noted which treadles to use in sequence to get plain weave across the fabric for each tie-up.

Huck Lace tie-up

4	4		
		3	3
2			2
	1	1	
B	B	A	A

Warp floats in B / weft floats in A: Treadles 1-2-1-2-1, repeat.
Weft floats in B / warp floats in A: Treadles 3-4-3-4-3, repeat.
Full sequence: Treadle 1-2-1-2-1 then Treadle 3-4-3-4-3
For plain weave between blocks of Huck Lace, use Treadle 1 vs. Treadle 3; repeat for the amount of plain weave you want between blocks.

You do not have to treadle plain weave between Huck Lace blocks. You can simply continue treadling for the Huck Lace, and the Huck blocks will continue for the entire length.

Huck Spots based on weft floats tie-up

		4	
3			
	2	2	
1			1

Treadle 1-2-1-2-1 followed by Treadles 3-4-3-4-3; repeat. Plain weave is Treadle 1 vs. Treadle 3.

Huck Spots based on warp floats tie-up (notice that the tie-up is different from the weft floats tie-up)

4	4		4
	3	3	3
2			2
	1	1	

Treadle 1-2-1-2-1, followed by 3-4-3-4-3; repeat. Plain weave is Treadle 1 vs. Treadle 3.

Lacy Huck squares

		4	4
3	3		3
	2	2	
1			1

Treadle 1-2-1-2-1, followed by 3-4-3-4-3. You will get long floats outlining plain weave in the middle. This design is much more effective with a really open sett for your fabric with a careful, gentle press in place beat. Plain weave across is Treadle 1 vs. Treadle 3.

Huck ovals

4	4		4
	3		
2			2
	1	1	

Treadle 1-2-1-2-1, followed by 3-4-3-4-3. This creates Huck spots around plain weave, and when the fabric is washed, the threads draw the plain weave section into an oval shape. Note: If you want to weave plain weave between design sections, you will have to add one more treadle for Shafts 1 and 3. Putting that treadle last would make easy treadling between Treadle 1 and Treadle 5. Yes, there are two treadles tied up the same—Treadles 1 and 4. Tying up these two treadles the same means easier treadling in pairs, but you could treadle 1-2-1-2-1, followed by 3-1-3-1-3.

This will just get you started. As you can see, almost anything goes. Try different treadling combinations and see what happens. Be sure to write down what you've done when experimenting.

As Madeline said, you could weave different designs with Huck for a lifetime!

◆ PROJECT ◆

HUCK LACE and HUCK SPOTS SCARF or RUNNER

This project was designed to play with changing treadling for two Huck patterns and to discover new patterns produced when using contrasting color weft. I consider it a sampling project that you can wear.

On the loom, the colored weft yarn sections looked like the yellow sections, but off the loom and wet-finished fun patterns emerged. From a distance, these sections look like little boxes within a larger box of Huck Lace, and it was achieved simply by changing weft color. I was inspired by Tom Knisley's *Huck Lace Weaving Patterns* (see "Resources," page 190), where he uses the same two-Block threading, changes up the tie-ups, and plays with color in warp and weft for a total of 574 variations. After years of being told that Huck "must" use the same yarn for the warp and weft, it's fun to break the "rules."

Huck is different from other weave structures when interpreting a 2-block profile draft. You are technically using two blocks/units of threading within one block of pattern. When I use a profile draft for Huck, I consider each colored-in threading square on the "A" Block line to be the combination of Block A / Block B threading repeats. The colored-in threading squares on the next line up are usually called Block B, but I consider those squares to be plain weave sections between the pattern blocks on the first line.

I designed this piece with 4-shaft looms in mind. If you have 8 shafts available, you can create two different blocks of pattern: unit A/B (Blocks A and B threading) and unit C/D (Block C/D threading). Refer to the threading units/blocks information at the beginning of the Huck Lace Weave Structure section.

EQUIPMENT NEEDED

4-shaft loom
1 shuttle
8-dent reed (sleyed 2 ends per dent)

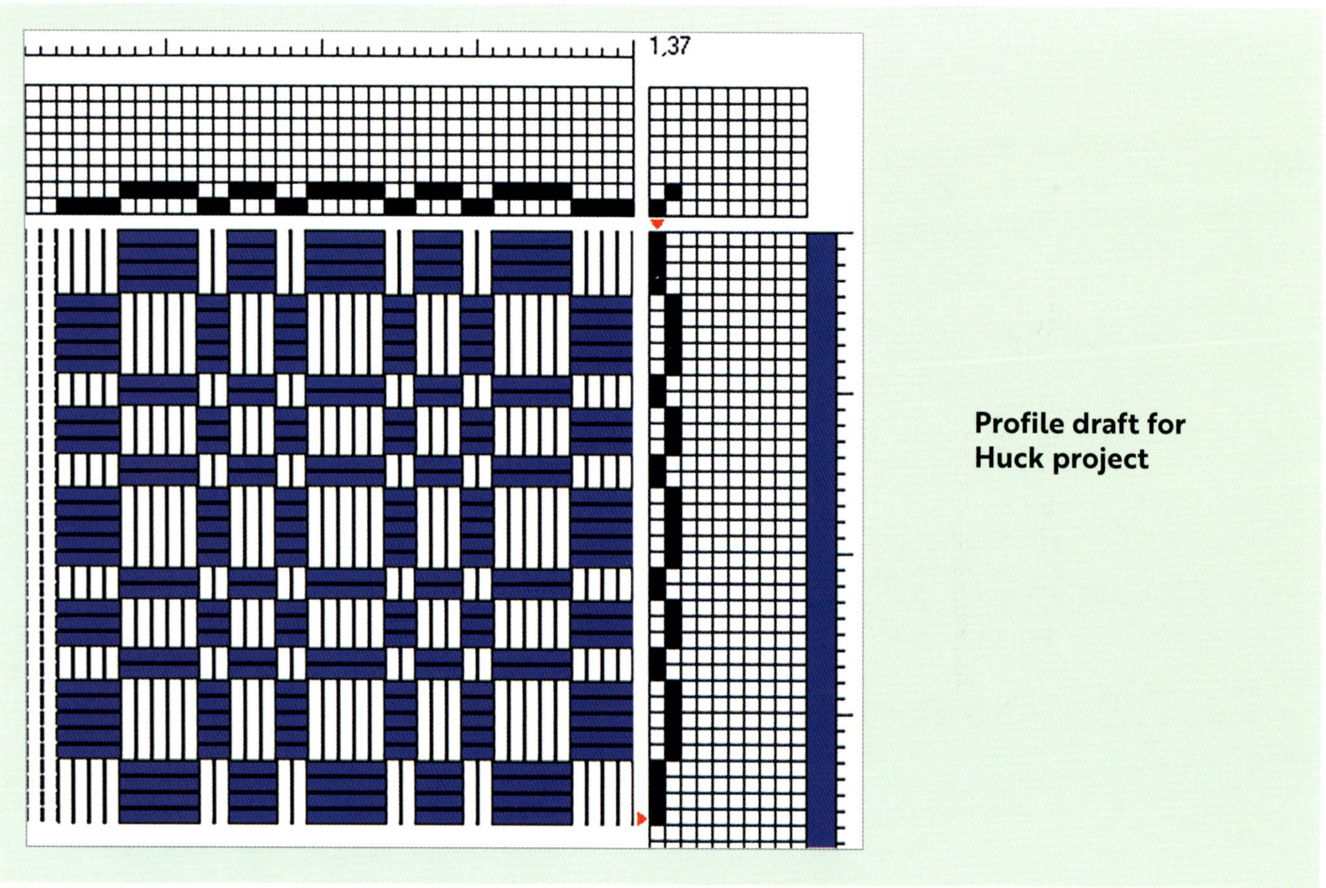

Profile draft for Huck project

Threading units: Remember that Block A threading and Block B threading work together as a unit to make a larger block of pattern.
Block A: 2-3-2-3-2
Block B: 1-4-1-4-1

Plain weave sections between blocks of pattern are threaded on Shafts 1–2; repeat. For the narrow plain weave separations between blocks of pattern, I used 10 threads. In these sections of the warp, I wound four threads in yellow, 2 threads in purple, then 4 threads in yellow. This centers the purple stripe between each section of pattern.

For the profile draft, I designated any colored-in squares on the Block A line to be block pattern for the A/B Huck units threading, starting and ending each pattern block with the Block B threading unit.

Each colored-in square on the Block A line of the profile draft represents one of the threading units—either Block A threading or Block B threading. Therefore, when the profile draft has 5 colored-in squares on the Block B line, I threaded this pattern: Block B threading / Block A / Block B / Block A / Block B.

I designated the colored-in squares on Block B line of the profile draft to be plain weave threading between the units of Huck pattern. Initially, I figured 5 threads of plain weave threading for each colored-in square on Block A and with 4 colored-in squares on each selvedge, equaling 20 threads. Then I decided to add purple threads on each selvedge to balance with the purple dividers. So I simply decided that the selvedge edge bands of plain weave would be 24 warp ends. Yes, you can do things like that!

I have 5 sections of pattern: Sections 1, 3, and 5 are five threading repeats alternating Block B with Block A, ending on Block B. So your threading is B, A, B, A, B in the wider sections.

Sections 2 and 4 are narrower, and only three sections of pattern threading: B, A, B.

Yarns: I wove the scarf using WEBS Valley Yarns Cotolin (50% cotton / 50% linen blend) from my stash. However, the Valley Yarns line no longer has cotolin. You can substitute another cotolin yarn or 8/2 cotton.

Colors:
Pale Yellow #1171
Dark Teal #2746
White #8001
Eggplant #6256
Madder Brown # 7327

Warp: 8/2 cotton or Cotolin

Sett: 16 e.p.i. If you want a very lacy fabric, use a more open sett.

Calculate the number of warp ends: Each square colored in on the threading represents either plain weave sections or Huck sections. You have to consider whether this is (1) Blocks A/B combined (which is 5 threads / repeat) or (2) plain weave. To keep things simpler, I consider each colored-in square on the B line of the profile draft to be the threading units equaling 5 threads per square.

For the sample, my outside borders are plain weave threading on Shafts 1 and 2 for 24 threads, ending on Shaft 2 because my pattern threading actually starts on Block B threading with Shaft 1. It also ends on Block B threading because I wanted both sides of the lace pattern sections to start and end on the same block threading. That means my plain weave divider sections must start on Shaft 2 to maintain the plain weave.

At this point, my brain threatened to have a major meltdown.

For these reasons, I decided to use my computer drafting program to do full a thread-by-thread draft so I could see the stripe proportions/placement clearly and make sure I was threading each transition correctly between pattern and plain weave.

Does that break the profile draft rules? No, it does not. The profile draft still gives you the proportions / overall design of the fabric. Tools are for making your life easier, so use the tools when you need them!

The sample is 193 warp ends for the design. The reason for the odd number of warp threads is there are an odd number of threads in the pattern sections.

Calculate the number of heddles: I'll be honest—if you have created a thread-by-thread draft in weaving software, the easiest way to determine heddle count is already in the software. In Fiberworks, this command is in the Print function. Just click the box "Heddle Count" in the menu that appears; the program counts the heddles for you and will print the information on your draft copy.

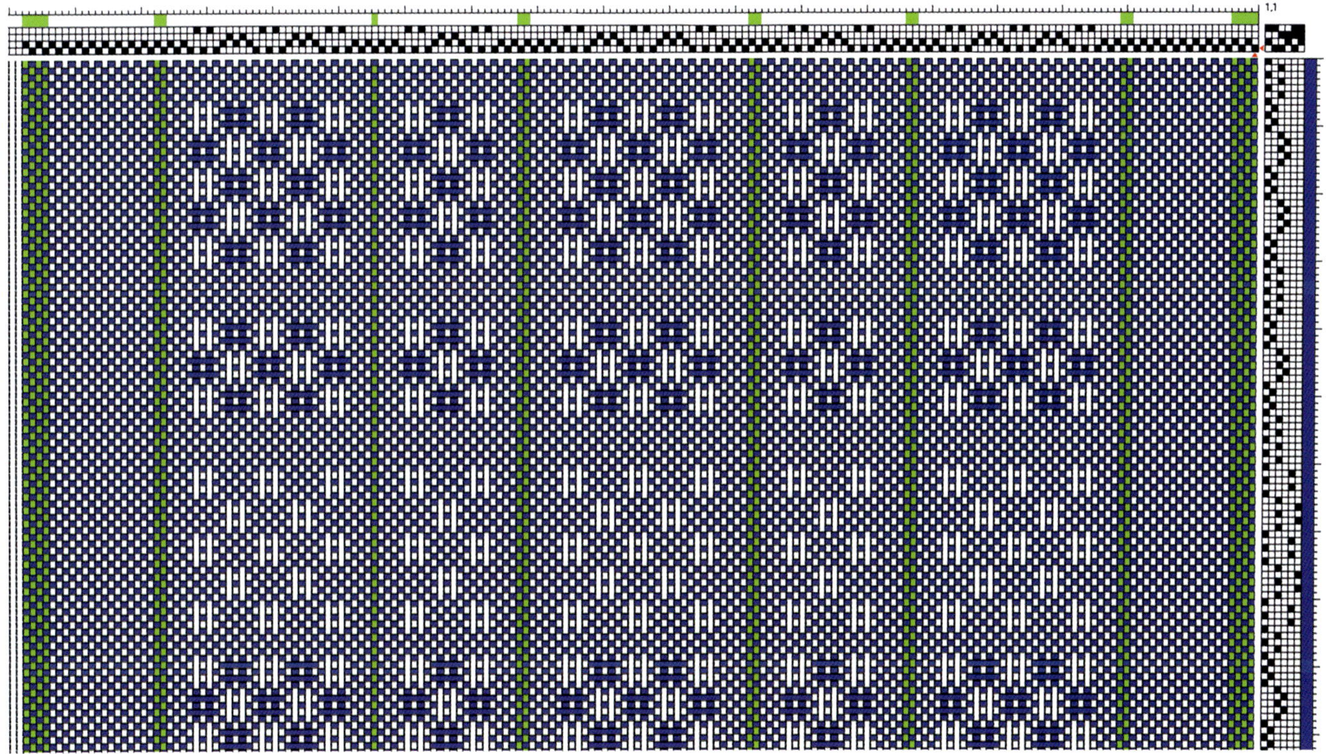

Thread-by-thread draft for Huck project

For calculations by hand (because yes, it can be done):

Shaft 1: Plain weave plus the tie-down for Block B threading. We need 9 heddles per large pattern section. 9 heddles × 3 sections = 27 heddles for the wider pattern sections.

For the narrower sections: 2 repeats of Block B, so 2 repeats × 3 Shaft 1 threads = 6 heddles per section × 2 sections = 12 heddles.

Shaft 1 pattern heddles: 27 + 12 = 39 heddles for pattern only.

The borders are 24 threads total, half on Shaft 1 and half on Shaft 2, and 10 plain weave threads between each section of pattern. There are 4 plain weave dividers, so Shaft 1: 12 + 12 (each border) + 20 (dividers are 4 sections × 10 threads divided by 2) = 44 heddles

Add these all together: 39 pattern + 44 plain weave = 83 heddles on Shaft 1.

Shaft 2: The same thing happens for Shaft 2, only using Block A threading.
8 repeats of Block A threading across the pattern × 3 threads / repeat = 24 on Shaft 2
Plus 44 heddles for plain weave dividers
24 pattern + 44 plain weave = 68 heddles on Shaft 2

Shaft 3: Now it gets easier: Wide sections have 2 repeats of the Block A threading, and each repeat has 2 threads on Shaft 3. Narrow sections have 1 repeat of Block A threading, so only 2 threads on Shaft 3 for the two narrow sections.

This makes a total of 8 repeats of Block A threading × 2 threads/repeat = 16 heddles on Shaft 3.

Shaft 4: Wide sections have 3 Block B repeats with two Shaft 4 threads each threading repeat = 6 Shaft 4 threads per wide section × 3 section repeats = 18 heddles.

There's only 1 Block B threading in each narrow section, so 2 Shaft 4 threads × 2 sections = 4 heddles total for the narrow sections.
Shaft 4 total: 18 heddles in wide sections + 4 heddles on narrow sections = 26 heddles

Check your work: 83 heddles on Shaft 1 + 68 on Shaft 2 + 16 on Shaft 3 + 26 on Shaft 4 = 193 heddles

Tie-up:
Treadle 1: 2–4 (Warp floats in B threading / weft floats in A threading)
Treadle 2: 1–4 (Warp floats in B threading / weft floats in A threading)
Treadle 3: 1–3 (Warp floats in A threading / weft floats in B threading)
Treadle 4: 2–3 (Warp floats in A threading / weft floats in B threading)
Treadle 5: 1–3–4 (Warp floats in B threading, plain weave in A threading)
Treadle 6: 2–3–4 (Warp floats in A threading, plain weave in B threading)

Treadling sequence:
Plain weave across the fabric: Treadles 1–3; repeat until you have desired length of plain weave

Huck Lace squares:
Treadle: 1-3-1-3-1 (B threading warp floats), followed by Treadle 3-4-3-4-3 (A threading warp floats)
Repeat these two treadles to the desire block size.

Huck Lace Squares are the first section of the thread-by-thread draft.

Huck Spots:
Spots in B threading / plain weave A threading: Treadle sequence 1-5-1-5-1
Spots in A threading / plain weave in B threading: Treadle sequence 3-6-3-6-3

Huck Spots treadling is the last section on the thread-by-thread draft.

I wove 8 picks in plain weave between each block of Huck Lace and Huck spots. I started the scarf with 1.5 inches of plain weave for hem allowance.

TIP: You will be alternating between plain weave sections with Huck sections. To minimize draw-in and help with tidy selvedges, use a slightly deeper weaver's angle on the plain weave across the fabric sections and use a slightly shallower weaver's angle for the weft in the areas with the pattern floats. If you see the weft bubbling up / not lying flat on the fabric surface, you need a shallower weaver's angle. If you see draw-in at the selvedges, you need a deeper weaver's angle.

Warp length: 94 inches

Width in reed: 11.75 inches

Weft: 8/2 Cotolin or 8/2 cotton, the same yarn as the warp. Colors listed in "Yarns."

Woven length on loom (measured off-tension): 74.5 inches. Each color section measures 5.5 inches on the loom. Add 1.5 inches to each end of the scarf for hems.

Hem allowance: 1.5 inches plain weave on each end

Finished size after washing: 10 inches wide × 63 inches long, including hem allowance.

Shrinkage: 15% in both length and width

Weaving sequence:
Weave 1.5 inches plain weave treadling for the hem.
Weave 5 repeats of pattern for large squares (Treadle B, A, B, A, B).
Weave 3 repeats of pattern for small squares (Treadle B, A, B).
Weave 8 picks of plain weave after each last pattern section, then change to new weft color. Weave 8 picks of new color, then repeat the pattern section.
Weave 3 pattern sections per color section: 1 large, 1 small, 1 large.
End by weaving 1.5 inches plain weave for the hem.

Weft color sequence:
5.5 inches per color / 13 large sections total
Yellow
Madder Brown
Yellow
Dark Teal
Yellow
Eggplant
Center section: White for 1 large pattern
Yellow for 1 large pattern
White for 1 large pattern
Eggplant
Yellow
Dark Teal
Yellow
Madder Brown
Yellow

Treadling sequence:
Plain weave hems and dividers:
1-3-1-3 repeat until desired length of plain weave section

Large Huck Lace pattern blocks:
1-2-1-2-1
3-4-3-4-3
1-2-1-2-1
3-4-3-4-3
1-2-1-2-1

Small Huck Lace pattern block:
1-2-1-2-1
3-4-3-4-3
1-2-1-2-1

Huck Spots: Repeat for however long you want spots. I wove some segments as continuous stripes of spots and some segments with blocks of spots. Notice how different the sections woven with yellow weft look from the sections using a contrasting weft. Fun!
1-5-1-5-1
3-6-3-6-3

Finishing: For runner: Zigzag raw ends. Hand wash in warm water; lay flat to dry. Trim warp ends next to zigzag stitching and hem so you have the same distance from the start of the first color block from the hem edge to pattern as you do between pattern and color changes. Hand- or machine-hem. For scarf: You can follow the hemming directions or tie overhand knots for fringe.

chapter 5
TWILL-BASED WEAVES

Twill threading has to be the most versatile threading available to weavers. Until I wrote this book, I didn't have a full appreciation of the wide variety of weave structures that use twill threading. It's apparent that weavers have been playing "what if" with this threading forever.

I am featuring five different block weaves that all use twill threading as the basis for the designs. All the weave structures look very different, and yet, the familiar threading of 1-2-3-4 is there.

Because twill threading units require four shafts, some of these weave structures will require more than four shafts—but there's something in this section for everyone. I've designed the projects for 4- and 8-shaft looms, but for those who have more than 8 shafts on your loom, the world is your oyster for expanding the number of blocks of pattern you can use. Have fun!

WEAVE STRUCTURE
Turned Twill

Ahh, Turned Twill—how do I love thee? I can create textiles in yarns ranging from 3/2 to 20/2 (and smaller), and the pattern always dances. I can use the same warp and simply change the weft color to create dramatically different pieces or create multiple designs within the same piece—great fun when weaving towels or napkins or placemats or anything else. I can change my overall fabric pattern design simply by adding or subtracting treadling repeats. Turned Twill plays well with any yarn fiber content. I could go on and on.

There's only one catch: You must have at least an 8-shaft loom to do two blocks of turned twill. Sadly, you can't do Turned Twill on 4 shafts, since each block of threading requires 4 shafts. Three blocks of Turned Twill require 12 shafts, and four blocks require 16 shafts. But don't despair—you will be amazed at the design possibilities with only two blocks, especially when you start playing with color.

Turned Twill is simply blocks of 3/1 vs. 1/3 twill, using a straight twill threading. To achieve the patterns, the rising shed tie-up is done so each treadle engages threads in both blocks of threading. If you are treadling for Block A, the tie-up will raise 3 warp threads (weft goes under these warp threads) in Block A threading and leave one warp thread down (weft goes over this warp thread), making Block A warp-dominant. The reverse happens in Block B because of the tie-up. Hang with me; there are more details in the tie-up section.

Combining the warp vs. weft dominance in the blocks changes the overall fabric design.

The size of the threading blocks can be any size as long as the blocks are threaded in sets of 4 threads.

The treadling can create blocks of different heights using treadling repeats in sets of 4 weft picks.

Oh, the places we can go! The designs we can create! Let's dig into the details.

THREADING

The threading in each block of pattern is straight twill threading of 1-2-3-4 for Block A and 5-6-7-8 for Block B. The width of the blocks is determined by the number of threading unit repeats in the block.

Threading units:
Block A: 1-2-3-4 (repeat to make wider blocks)
Block B: 5-6-7-8 (repeat to make wider blocks)

Tie-up:
The profile tie-up is where the fabric design takes shape. To create the tie-up, think of it as drawing the

fabric design in the tie-up. Keep in mind: What happens in Block A is the opposite of what happens in Block B.

Let's start with the first half of the 3/1 twill vs. 1/3 twill tie-up.

Shafts 1 through 4 are for Block A threading. Shafts 5 through 8 are for Block B threading.

Treadle 1: 1-2-3-5 (Shafts 1, 2, and 3 are raised in Block A, and Shaft 5 is raised in Block B)
Treadle 2: 1-2-4-6 (Shaft 1, 2, and 4 are raised in Block A, and Shaft 6 is raised in Block B)
Treadle 3: 1-3-4-7 (Shafts 1, 3, 4 are raised in Block A and Shaft 7 is raised in Block B)
Treadle 4: 2-3-4-8 (Shafts 2, 3, 4 are raised in Block A and Shaft 8 is raised in Block B)

Here's what this sequence looks like in a tie-up grid for a rising shed loom. The blue squares are warp threads that are lifted, and the white squares are warp threads left down.

			8	
		7		Block A
	6			
5				
	4	4	4	
3		3	3	Block B
2	2		2	
1	1	1		

Look at this closely. Shafts 1–4 are assigned to Block A for the threading and in the tie-up. When you press Treadle 1, Shafts 1, 2, 3 are lifted (blue warp floats created over 3 threads) in Block A threading, and at the same time, only Shaft 5 is lifted for Block B and Shafts 6, 7, 8 stay down, creating a white weft float in Block B over threads on Shafts 6, 7, 8. So we are creating blocks of pattern that are warp-dominant in Block A and weft-dominant in Block B.

Now we need to set up, so when we treadle for Block B, the warp floats are dominant in Block B and the weft floats are dominant in Block A and, at the same time, have the twill lines head in the opposite directions in both blocks. Thus, the Turned Twill design is created.

Treadle 5: 1-5-6-7
Treadle 6: 2-5-6-8
Treadle 7: 3-5-7-8
Treadle 8: 4-6-7-8

Here's what the entire tie-up looks like:

	1	2	3	4	5	6	7	8
Block A				8		8	8	8
Block A			7		7		7	7
Block A		6			6	6		6
Block A	5				5	5	5	
Block B		4	4	4				4
Block B	3		3	3			3	
Block B	2	2		2		2		
Block B	1	1	1		1			
Treadles	Block A				Block B			

As you can see, whatever happens in one block, the opposite happens in the other block.

The first 4 treadles are for Block A treadling, and the last 4 treadles are for Block B treadling.

Remember the two simple rules for Turned Twill using a profile draft:

1) Each colored-in square in the threading represents the 4 warp threads in the threading unit for a block.
2) Each colored-in square in the treadling represents the treadling unit of 4 weft threads/picks treadled in the straight twill progression for that block of pattern.

Treadling
Each colored-in square of the profile draft represents one repeat of four picks of weft in a block.

1) If one square is colored in for Block A treadling, you treadle 1-2-3-4, using the tie-up shown earlier.
2) If one square is colored in for Block B treadling, you treadle 5-6-7-8.
3) If there is more than one square colored on the treadling grid for a block, you simply repeat the treadling in sets of 4 picks for that block. For example, if there are 3 squares colored in next to each other on Block B treadling, you treadle 5-6-7-8 for a total of 3 repeats of the treadling unit.

◆ PROJECT ◆

TURNED TWILL TOWELS

I like a dish towel that's big enough to hold a dinner plate with one corner of the towel and still have enough towel to dry the plate. It must also be absorbent, and after years of testing, I like to use a good unmercerized cotton yarn for my handwoven towels. Using a weave structure that features warp and weft floats means more yarn surface area, which also equals a more absorbent towel. One note: Don't use liquid fabric softener when washing towels. It can make your towels water-repellent!

I used a new-to-me yarn for these towels, and I love it. The yarn is "Ad Astra" 4/2 organic cotton, grown, spun, and dyed in the United States, available exclusively from The Yarn Barn of Kansas. The Yarn Barn has created 45 colors, and the yarn is so soft and absorbent! Note that the yarn comes on 8-ounce cones with 840 yards per cone, so plan and purchase accordingly.

I decided to play with color interactions in the design. Think of it as a color and design sample that is put to practical use! You don't need to follow my lead, but be aware that, if you use the same color of weft as warp, you will get texture in the towels, not the highly visible pattern from the Turned Twill weave structure. Contrasting colors for the warp and weft are very important for Turned Twill.

I also played with the sizes of the blocks in the threading and treadling to create an optical illusion of a rounded square of each pattern. Feel free to experiment!

EQUIPMENT NEEDED

8-shaft loom with minimum 24-inch weaving width
1 shuttle
8-dent reed (sleyed 1-2-2-2 ends / dent for 14 e.p.i.)

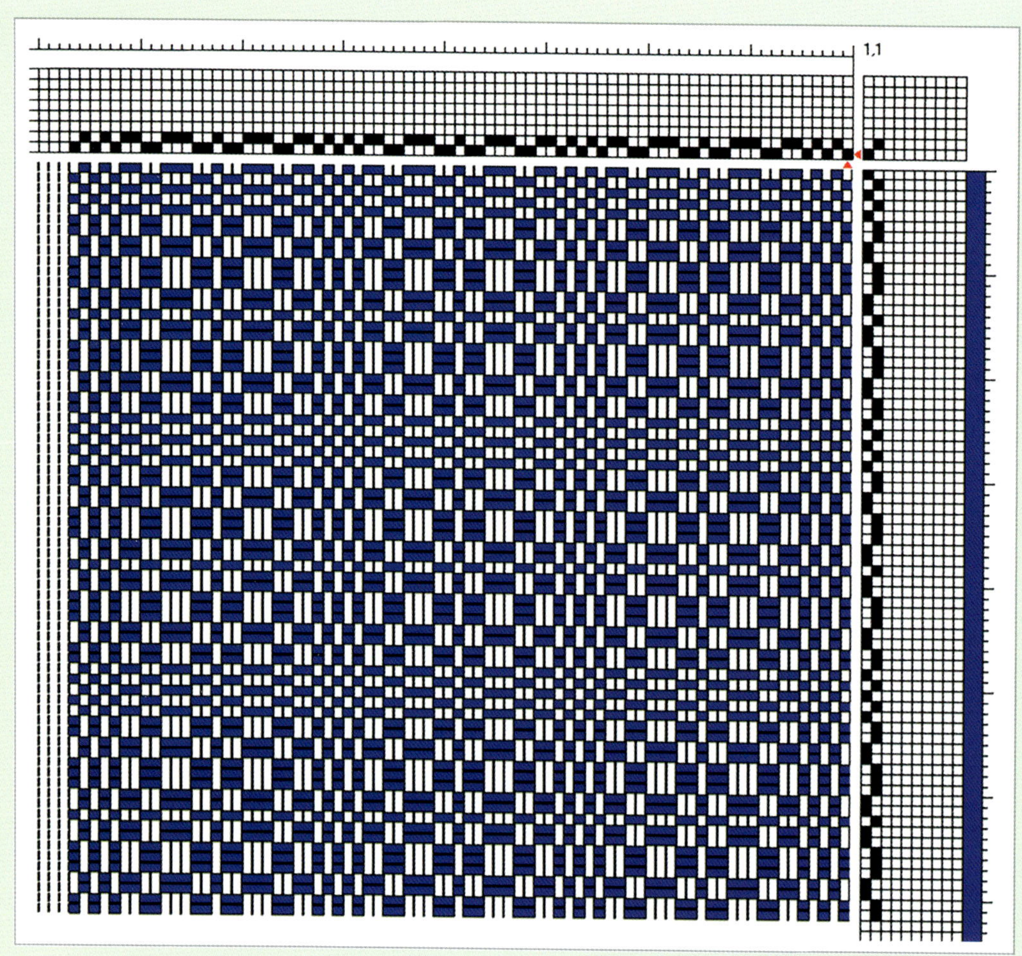

Profile draft for turned twill towels

Threading
Block A: 1-2-3-4
Block B: 5-6-7-8
Yarns:
Ad Astra 4/2 organic unmercerized cotton, available exclusively from The Yarn Barn of Kansas

Warp:
Bluebird (Color #42) on outside edges
Cosmos (Color #49) on middle section

Sett: 14 e.p.i. (This yarn wraps to 10 e.p.i. for plain weave. Increase the e.p.i. of whatever yarn you use by 4 ends per inch for twill sett.)

Calculate the number of warp ends: Each colored-in square in the threading represents 4 warp threads. There are a total of 77 squares in the threading.
77 squares × 4 threads/square = 308 warp threads plus 2 floating selvedges for a total of 310 warp ends.

Calculate the number of heddles:
Block A: There are 36 squares of threading for Block A. Each colored-in square represents 4 threads that are threaded 1-2-3-4. Because each of these shafts is used one time per square, you will need 36 heddles on each shaft used for Block A (Shafts 1, 2, 3, 4).

Block B: There are 41 squares of threading for Block B. Each square represents threading 5-6-7-8, and again, each of these shafts is used one time per colored-in square, so you need 41 heddles on each shaft used for Block B.

Tie-up: Use the tie-up in the Turned Twill weave structure chapter.

Treadling sequence: See treadling instruction in the Turned Twill weave structure section. Multiple colored-in squares for a block means a full repeat of the treadling for each square in the block.

Block A: Treadle 1-2-3-4 for each square in the treadling, using the tie-up in the chapter
Block B: Treadle 5-6-7-8 for each square in Block B treadling

Warp length: 94 inches

Width in reed: 22 inches

Wefts:
Multicolored towel
Apricot—Color #24 (light orange for section 1)
Garnet—Color #54 (deep red in center section 2)
Daffodil—Color #25 (pale yellow for section 3)
Striped towel
Second towel on the same warp; weft is White #10 only.

Woven length on loom (measured off-tension):
Multicolored towel: 3 full repeats of the pattern plus 3 extra repeats of the small blocks to start and end the towel for hems on each end (total of 8 repeats of the small blocks on each end)
Measured on the loom = 28 inches

Striped towel: 4 full repeats of the pattern plus 3 extra repeats of the narrow small blocks at beginning and end
Measured on the loom = 34 inches long

Hem allowance: For Turned Twill, I don't do a plain weave hem. Using plain weave for the hems can cause your hems to flare out wider than body of the towel woven in twill, due to the density of the yarns in the plain weave hems. I simply weave extra repeats of the first and last sections of pattern for the hem allowance.

For the towels, I wove 3 additional sections of narrow blocks to add a hem allowance, then followed the profile draft. Then I wove the body of the towel according to the profile draft.

When you hem the towels, turn under the raw ends 1 small pattern repeat and then turn under again 1 small pattern repeat. Hand- or machine-stitch the hems.

Finished size after washing and hemming:
Multicolored blocks towel: 24 inches long × 19 inches wide

Striped towel: 29 inches long × 19 inches wide

Shrinkage: 9% in width and length

Weaving:
Multi-colored towel:
Start with 2 extra repeats of Treadles 1 through 8 for hems for 7 total repeats of the narrow block. After hem, follow the profile draft for 1 full repeat of the pattern, ending with 4 bands of the narrow blocks.

Change to Color #2 and weave 4 bands of the narrow blocks, then one full repeat of the larger pattern with Color #2, ending with 4 bands of the narrow blocks.

Change to Color #1. Weave 4 bands of the narrow blocks and one full repeat of the larger pattern with Color #1. Add 2 extra repeats of the narrow blocks for the hem.

Striped towel (white weft): Start with the hems, weaving the narrow blocks for 7 narrow bands. Then treadle each repeat according to draft, for a total of 4 full repeats of the pattern. End with 7 narrow bands to balance the pattern and create the hem.

TIP: To get a perfect cutting line, weave 2 picks of thrum yarn in a contrasting color between the towels. When you are ready to cut the towels apart, cut between the 2 picks of thrum for a perfectly straight cut.

Finishing: Cut the towels off the loom and zigzag stitch the raw ends and on each side of the thrum picks separating the towels. Hand wash in warm water and lay flat to dry. This blocks the towels into shape, and you will be able to machine wash / dry later with minimal shrinkage.

Cut the towels apart between the two picks of thrum yarn and trim extra warp ends next to the zigzag stitching at each end. Turn under the towel ends, using the narrow sections of pattern for your fold line. Machine- or hand-stitch the hems.

TIP: If you machine hem, lighten up the presser foot pressure so the presser foot doesn't push the fabric ahead of it and create a triangle of extra fabric at the end of the hem.

WEAVE STRUCTURE
Rep Weave

Rep Weave is a warp-faced weave that plays well with profile drafts. However, we need to think of the profile blocks as blocks of color rather than blocks of structure.

Rep Weave uses a dense warp sett to cover two sizes of weft threads—weft #1 is larger in grist (size) and can be multiple strands of yarn woven as one. Weft #2 is smaller than weft #1 and is usually the same yarn as the warp, but it doesn't have to be. The concept behind Rep Weave is to cover the weft threads with the warp threads to create a warp-faced fabric.

Profile drafts are very handy for designing Rep Weave because you can easily create proportionately pleasing stripes or blocks of colors (or both). The number of weft picks per inch is dependent on the size of the large weft yarn. Stick a pin in that.

Rep Weave is based on plain weave but uses the straight twill threading to help accommodate all the warp threads necessary to weave the warp-faced fabric. The dense sett of the warp yarns covers the weft yarns to create the warp-faced fabric, using half of the warp yarns to weave the top layer and the other half of the warp yarns weave the bottom layer of the fabric.

If you use only one color of yarn in a block threading section, you will get solid stripes of color running the length of the fabric. By using two different-colored yarns in a block, you can have the yarn colors change positions from top layer to bottom layer simply by weaving two picks of the finer weft threads. This gives you the blocks of pattern like you see in a profile draft.

So if Rep is based on plain weave, why is this weave structure in the Twill threading group? It's about spreading out your densely sett warp threads over more shafts. You can weave Rep using only two shafts, but due to the dense sett of the warp threads, you need a lot of heddles on each of those two shafts. If you have the same aversion as I do to moving heddles between shafts, you can spread the warps out over 4 or more shafts, using a straight twill threading. More shafts equal fewer heddles needed per shaft, so a lesser chance of having to move heddles around! Rep Weave takes a long time to thread, due to the high number of warp yarns, but it weaves up really fast.

Let's take this step by step.

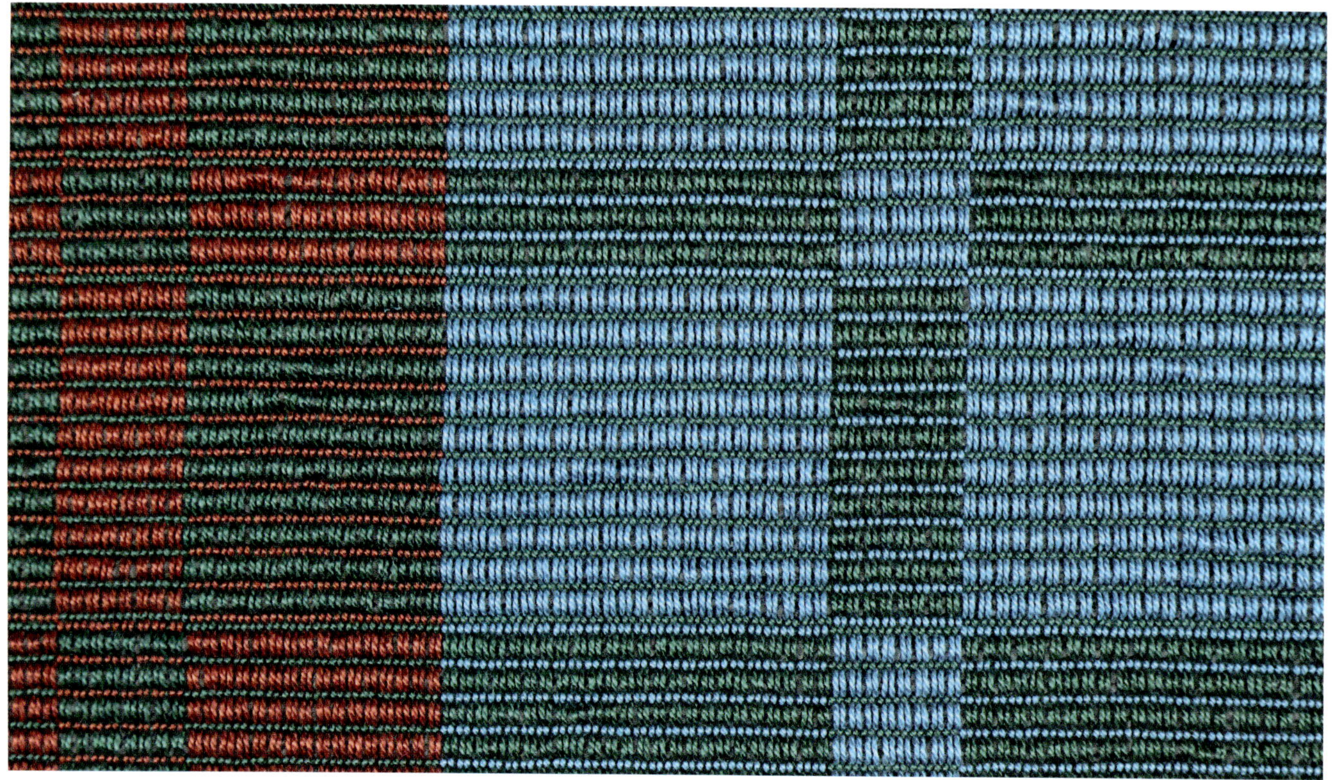

Step 1: Select your warp yarns and calculate the ends per inch.
In Rep Weave, we want a very dense sett for the warp so the warp yarns cover the weft yarns. For the smaller weft thread woven between picks of large weft, the general rule is that the smaller weft is the same yarn size as your warp yarn. However, you can play with this a bit. For example, I wove a set of placemats years ago using 10/2 cotton as the warp, piping cord for the large weft, and 10/2 cotton for the small weft. Then on the same warp, I wove a set of napkins by switching the large weft to 10/2 cotton and the small weft to sewing thread. Both created the same Rep Weave patterns, but the placemats were nice and firm to lie flat on the table, and the napkins were softer fabric due to the finer wefts, so they could be folded nicely—all thanks to changing the weft sizes.

When calculating the warp sett for Rep Weave, wrap your warp yarn around a sett gauge or ruler for 1 inch. Count the number of wraps. Normally, the number of wraps per inch is divided by 2 for a plain weave sett. For Rep Weave, the number of wraps in 1 inch tells us the sett for a warp-faced fabric. Half the total number of wraps / warp threads will be on the top side of the fabric, and the other half of the warp threads will be on the bottom side of the fabric.

For Rep Weave, the wraps per inch give us the minimum Rep Weave sett.

For example: In the Rep Weave project, I used 5/2 cotton for the warp that wraps to 28 wraps per inch, which for a plain weave sett would be divided by 2 for a sett of 14 e.p.i. However, for my warp-faced fabric, my minimum Rep Weave sett should be 28 ends per inch or the same as the number of wraps per inch. Half of the warp ends (14 ends) will weave the top layer of fabric, and half (14 ends) will weave the bottom layer of the fabric. Will this sett give me the coverage I want for the large warp ribs? That is dependent on the size of the large weft yarn you select.

Step 2: Select your weft yarns for the ribs.
You need two weft yarns. The first yarn is larger in grist to create the larger ribs that define the blocks of pattern. The second weft is a smaller grist yarn, generally the same yarn size used in the warp, and the smaller weft is woven between each pick of the large weft. The smaller weft creates small ribs that nestle between the picks of larger weft and holds the large ribs in place.

When you are selecting the weft yarns to use, keep in mind what the fabric is going to be used for. For a rug, you will likely prefer larger pattern ribs across the warp for a heavier, firmer fabric that will lie nicely on the floor. For placemats or a table runner, you may want to use a smaller grist yarn to make smaller pattern ribs that are proportionally pleasing in smaller pieces.

You can use strips of fabric, piping cord, large yarns, mop cotton, or multiple strands of yarn wound on the same shuttle for the large weft. The larger the yarn used for the large weft, the more pronounced the ribs will be across the fabric and the more warp ends per inch that you will need to have good coverage of the large weft yarn(s) by the warp.

The large weft yarns will show at the selvedges. I tend to select my large weft yarn color so it coordinates with, or matches, the warp yarn colors at the outer edges of the project. However, you can select a large weft yarn that contrasts with the warp yarns to create a noticeable edging as a design feature. Do what makes you happy!

Step 3: Calculate warp sett for good rib coverage.
Warp coverage of the wefts is affected by the size of the large weft that you are using. On a general basis, the bigger the large weft being used, the more warp threads in an inch will be needed for good coverage of the large weft. This can mean increasing the number of warp threads per inch for the project.

Here's a little test that can give you an idea of the coverage of the weft by the warp. First decide how pronounced you want the large pattern ribs to be and the number of strands of the large weft yarn you plan to use to achieve that size of rib.

For the Rep project in this chapter, I used a 1/2 cotton yarn from my stash for the large weft, and the warp is 5/2 cotton. Because I planned a rug, I decided to use two strands of the 1/2 yarn for every large weft pick so I would get well-defined ribs and stiffer fabric for the rug. To test my warp sett coverage of the large weft, I cut two small lengths of the 1/2 cotton yarn, twisted them together, and placed them on a ruler, taping the yarn ends to the ruler to keep them in place. Then I wrapped my 5/2 warp yarn around the ruler for 14 wraps (half of the 28 wraps per inch) that will be on one side of the rug at a time, spacing out the warp threads across an inch of weft. I decided that too much of the large weft showed between the warp yarns, so I increased the warp sett to 32 ends per inch (16 warps per inch on the top layer and 16 on the bottom layer when woven) to get better coverage of the large weft ribs.

Step 4: Wind the warp.
If you want stripes of solid colors running the length of the piece, each block of the profile draft represents one color of yarn. Each square of the threading will represent 1 inch of warp.

If you want blocks of color, you wind two warp threads in different colors at the same time in a section of warp based on your profile draft blocks. Each colored-in square of the profile draft will represent which color in the combination will show on each surface, depending on the treadling/threading in the blocks of pattern. We'll get back to this.

2 Shafts vs. 4 Shafts for threading
Rep Weave uses a lot of warp threads, so you need a lot of heddles. You can weave 2 blocks of Rep Weave on 2 shafts, but I like to spread the warp threads across 4 shafts so I don't have to move a bunch of heddles between shafts!

For example, imagine that a placemat design has 32 ends per inch for the Rep warp. Placemats are generally 12 inches deep, so that is our warp width on the loom. To calculate the number of warp ends, multiply 32 ends per inch × 12 inches for a total of 384 warp ends.

Now, using only 2 shafts, we divide 384 warp ends by 2 shafts, so we need 192 heddles on Shaft 1 and 192 heddles on Shaft 2. For most of us, needing this many heddles on each shaft likely means we have to move heddles from other shafts.

However, if I thread the same placemat on 4 shafts threading 1-2-3-4 straight twill threading, I can divide the 384 warp ends by 4 shafts and only need 96 heddles on each shaft. There's a pretty good chance you have that many heddles on each of your first 4 shafts, or if not, you at least won't have to move very many heddles.

Tie-up
Using 4-shafts for threading, the straight Twill threading is 1-2-3-4, repeat.

Your tie-up on 4 shafts for plain weave using the straight twill threading will be:
Treadle 1: 1–3
Treadle 2: 2–4

Note that every other thread is raised with this tie-up. Rep Weave is warp-faced plain weave.

If you have more than 4 shafts on your loom, you can still use the straight twill threading and plain weave tie-up to spread out the warp threads across more shafts. This is very handy for smaller looms. Using my placemat example to spread out the 384 warps ends on more shafts:

6 shafts:
Threading is 1-2-3-4-5-6.
384 warp threads spread across 6 shafts = 64 heddles/shaft

Tie-up for 6 shafts for plain weave on the straight twill threading is:
Treadle 1: 1-3-5
Treadle 2: 2-4-6

8 shafts:
Threading is 1-2-3-4-5-6-7-8.
384 warp threads spread across 8 shafts = 48 heddles per shaft

Tie-up for 8 shafts is:
Treadle 1: 1-3-5-7
Treadle 2: 2-4-6-8

PROFILE DRAFTS FOR REP WEAVE

When using profile drafts for Rep Weave, I find it easiest to think of the profile draft blocks as "Which

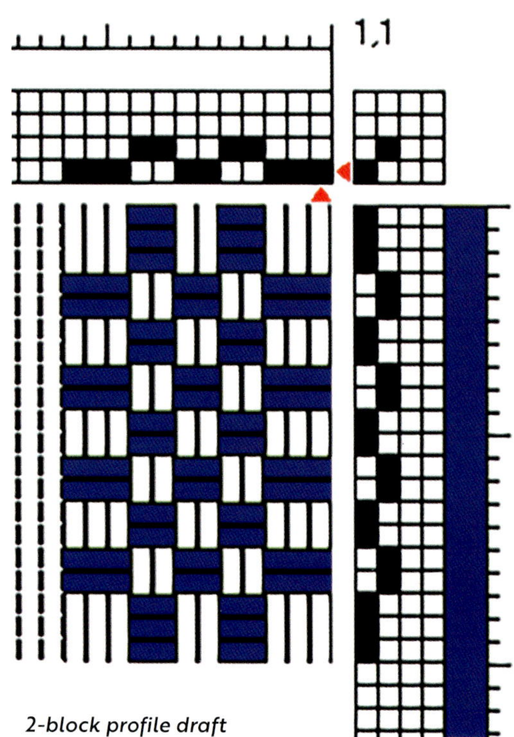

2-block profile draft

color warp yarn do I want on top versus the bottom in each block of threading." It's quite amazing how many design options you have by simply changing the warp colors in blocks and the order you thread the colors within the blocks.

Looking at the 2-block profile draft in the profile draft at left, I have two blocks of pattern laid out and will be using two warp colors: Block A and Block B. For rep weave, I think of these as Color A on top (Block A) versus Color B on top (Block B).

Before I wind my warp, I need to decide (a) which color I want on top in Color A blocks vs. Color B blocks and (b) whether or not I want only one color for an entire block for a solid-color stripe the length of the piece. Looking at the draft, for example, the first and last sections of Block A could be a solid stripe, with the center section alternating between Color A / Block A and Color B / Block B.

For this example, I'm going to use the profile design for placemats. The profile draft allows me to see the proportions of each pattern block within the piece. I want the placemats to be 12 inches across and have decided that each threading square represents 1 inch of warp width. I've decided to use 5/2 cotton yarn sett at 32 ends per inch for rep weave (see Steps 1–3 earlier in this chapter).

I'm going to use the same two colors of yarns in the two blocks but plan to have the colors change sides of the fabric when I weave.

CALCULATING WARP WIDTH AND LENGTH

Warp width: Count the number of colored-in squares for the threading. For this example, each square represents 1 inch worth of warp. There is a total of 12 colored-in squares in the threading, and I will be alternating the two colors of warp yarn between the different blocks across the warp.

I determined earlier that my sett is 32 ends per inch; 32 ends per inch times 12 inches = 384 total warp ends bundled in 1-inch (32 ends) increments. Each 1-inch warp bundle has 16 warp threads of Color A and 16 warp threads of Color B.

Warp length: Referring to the profile draft, if I weave each of the treadling blocks to square, the placemat would be about 20 inches long or 1-inch woven length for each colored-in treadling square. Most placemats are about 17–18 inches in length, so allowing a standard shrinkage / take-up allowance of 10% equals 2 inches added per placemat to allow for shrinkage off the loom. Adding the take-up/shrinkage allowance, each placemat would need 20 inches of warp plus 3 inches for hem allowances (1.5 inches on each end) per placemat for a total of 23 inches of warp per placemat.

However, there is a wild card in Rep Weave, which is the size of the large weft you plan to use. If the warp has a longer distance to travel over a large weft, you need more warp length. As a rule of thumb, I figure 15% warp take-up per placemat to accommodate for the large wefts that create the ribs. If you want to hedge your bets, add 20% of warp length for each placemat. It's far better to have extra warp than to run out of warp before the end of the last placemat!

USING TWO COLORS OF YARN WITHIN THE BLOCKS

I'm using the same two colors of yarn across the warp. Color A will be on top side of the fabric in Block A, with Color B on the bottom in the same block of threading. Color B will be on top in Block B, with Color A on the bottom.

To create this pattern where the colors change within the blocks, I need to wind both warp colors at the same time. To do this, I need a cone of Color A yarn and a cone of Color B yarn. I tie the two yarn color ends together with a slipknot loop and place the loop on the warping board peg for the end of the warp. I place my pointer finger between the two colors of yarn and wind both colors at the same time. Placing my finger between the yarns keeps the yarns from twisting around each other as I wind the warp. If you allow the yarns to twist together while you're winding the warp, you will have tensioning and tangling problems!

Winding two yarns at the same time means that two yarns will be next to each other on the same layer at the cross. One full circuit on the warping board gives you four threads (two from the starting peg to the end peg and two more from the end peg back to the starting peg). As you wind onto the warping board, the colors will likely shift sides with each other. This is not a problem because you can just move the threads in the pair over into proper position when you are threading the heddles.

For this exercise, we are only using two yarn colors and two blocks for pattern. Without changing the profile draft, you could (a) create solid-color stripes in the Block A borders and alternate the colors in the center section blocks only, (b) create solid stipes of color across the entire placemat by using only one color yarn per block, or (c) use one yarn color combination for the borders and then use new yarn color combination for the center. So many options, so much potential!

THREADING THE WARP FOR CHANGING COLORS WITHIN THE BLOCKS

I'm going to show the threading based on using 4 shafts threaded 1-2-3-4 and two colors of warp threads in each block of threading. Remember, we are weaving plain weave on a straight twill threading to distribute warp threads on 4 shafts. You do not need to add floating selvedges.

Important! You will alternate threading the two warp colors that you wound, depending on which color you want on the surface when you weave with the large weft: Color A or Color B.

For the Block A threading squares, Color A is on the top surface when we weave with the large weft, and at the same time Color B is on the bottom surface of the fabric. Therefore, when you thread squares for Block A / Color A, the threading is:
Shaft 1: Color A
Shaft 2: Color B
Shaft 3: Color A
Shaft 4: Color B

Now, you may be asking, "Why do I have to alternate the colors as I thread?" We raise odd- vs. even-numbered shafts with the tie-up for plain weave on the twill threading. So when Shafts 1 and 3 (Color A) are up, Shafts 2 and 4 (Color B) are down.

Our profile draft threading begins with three colored-in squares on Block A / Color A on the top layer of fabric. Each threading square represents 1 inch of warp at 32 e.p.i. Therefore, you repeat the above threading for a total of 96 threads. 32 threads per inch / square × 3 squares = 96 total threads for the first section of pattern.

Now the profile draft has two blocks of Block B / Color B on top. The threading for these two blocks is:
Shaft 1: Color B
Shaft 2: Color A
Shaft 3: Color B
Shaft 4: Color A

The profile draft has two Block B squares colored in, for a total of 64 warp ends (32 warp ends per square).

Note that Color B is now threaded on Shafts 1 and 3, and Color A is threaded on Shafts 2 and 4. When we raise Shafts 1 and 3 with a treadle: In Block B, Color B is raised, and at the same time in Block A, Color A is raised because, in Block A, Color A is threaded on Shafts 1 and 3.

Next, you repeat the Block A / Color A threading for 2 squares (64 ends).

Next, you repeat the Block B / Color B threading for 2 squares (64 ends).

Last, you repeat the Block A / Color A threading for 3 squares (96 ends).

You have a total of 384 warp ends.

Tie-up:
When we weave plain weave on a twill treadling, we tie up:
Treadle 1 to Shafts 1 and 3
Treadle 2 to Shafts 2 and 4

This tie-up raises every other warp thread across the warp.

Since we alternated threading the colors within each block of threading, this tie-up also lifts alternating colors within the threading blocks.

Referring back to the threading above:

Treadle 1: Shafts 1 and 3 (threaded with Color A in Block A and Color B in Block B)
Treadle 2: Shafts 2 and 4 (threaded with Color B in Block B and Color A in Block A)

Therefore, with the two blocks of threading, when you press Treadle 1, you raise Color A in Block A and Color B in Block B because of the way we thread each block. If you skipped that section, go back to the section on threading the warp just before this tie-up section.

Treadling
You will be alternating treadling Treadle 1 with Treadle 2 for the entire length of the placemat.

The key to Rep Weave is that you alternate weaving a pick of the large weft thread, using Treadle 1, and the next pick, using Treadle 2, will use a small weft thread. Repeat for the size of block desired.

When you want to change the warp color in a block, you weave two consecutive picks of the small weft, still alternating between Treadle 1 and Treadle 2. Then you continue alternating the large weft with the small weft for the desired length of the block.

To switch colors again in the blocks, you again weave two picks of small weft to change the warp colors, then continue alternating large weft with small weft.

PUTTING IT ALL TOGETHER

The number of picks for each weft in a block will be determined by the size of large weft you are using. The bigger the large weft, the bigger the ribs created and the fewer picks per inch are needed.

For example, I want the center blocks pattern to be as close to square as possible. Due to the size of the large weft, I really won't know how many picks of large weft will make a square until I actually weave. For our example, let's say 3 picks of large weft alternating with 3 picks of small weft give me the closest to square that I can get. Once I establish this, it's simply a matter of counting the number of large warp picks in a section.

Here are the threading, treadling, and tie-up all in one thread-by-thread mini-draft with notations on thick or thin weft and what colors will be on the top surface in each block to help visualize how this all works.

As you can see from the chart, you are lifting the same shafts, but the change in threading between the blocks means a different color warp is lifted within a block.

The thick vs. thin weft picks create the overall fabric pattern, with the thick weft creating larger ribs and the thin weft picks nestling between the thick weft picks.

Yes, you can create the appearance of more blocks by changing warp colors in each block's threading across your design.

Yes, you can create more blocks of pattern (think diamonds or curves) by using more shafts. Just remember that you need four shafts for each additional block of pattern. The threading for additional blocks could be:

Block C: Thread on shafts 5-6-7-8
Block D: Thread on shafts 9-10-11-12

Your tie-up will determine which to shafts to lift for the additional blocks at the same time as the other blocks. Oh, the possibilities!

Block B Threading				Block A Threading					Tie-Up		Treadling with thick vs. thin weft picks
4				4				■		4	
	3				3			■	3		
		2				2		■		2	
			1				1	■	1		
	3		1		3		1		■		Thick weft: Blue up in Block A, orange up in Block B
4		2		4		2				■	Thin weft: Orange up in Block A, blue up in Block B
	3		1		3		1		■		Thick weft: Blue up in Block A, orange up in Block B
4		2		4		2				■	Thin weft: Orange up in Block A, blue up in Block B
	3		1		3		1		■		Thin weft repeat: Blue up in Block A, orange up in Block B
4		2		4		2				■	Thick weft: Orange up in Block A, blue up in Block B

◆ PROJECT ◆

REP WEAVE RUG

2 BLOCKS ON 4 SHAFTS

This 2-block rug can be woven on 2 shafts; however, you would need 400 heddles on each shaft for all the warp threads. Spreading the warp over four shafts reduces the number of heddles per shaft to 200. This will likely mean you don't need to move as many heddles between shafts. (Refer to "Threading" in the Rep Weave section, page 80.) It will also be easier to lift the shafts with fewer threads on each shaft.

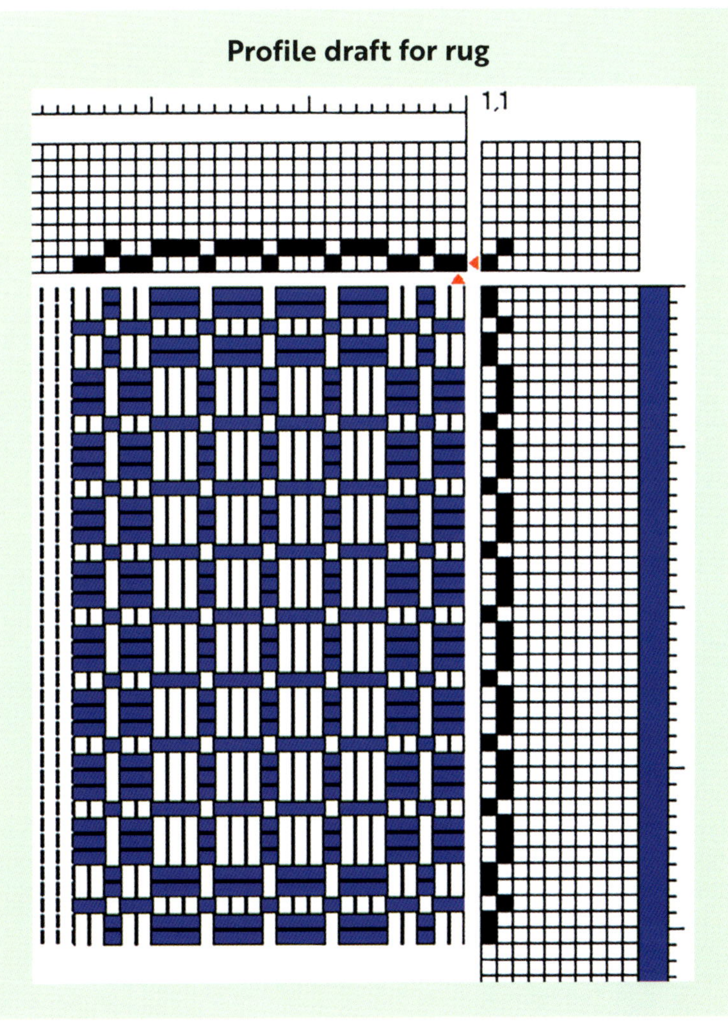

EQUIPMENT NEEDED

4-shaft loom

8-dent reed—sleyed at 4 threads/dent for sett of 32 e.p.i.

2 shuttles—one shuttle for the thin weft and one shuttle for the thick weft

Yarns:
Warps: 5/2 Tubular Spectrum mercerized cotton by Lunatic Fringe Yarns
Forest Green
#10 Blue-Green
Burnt Umber

Wefts: Large weft—2 strands of 1/2 cotton in dark green wound on a ski shuttle as one yarn
Small weft—5/2 cotton in forest green—single strand

Sett: 32 e.p.i.

Calculate the number of warp ends: Wrap your warp yarn around a ruler or sett gauge for 1 inch. Count the number of wraps. The number of wraps per inch equals your sett for rep weave. (See "Calculating the Sett" in the Rep Weave Structure section, page 77.)

I used 5/2 perle cotton that wraps out to 28 wraps per inch, which could be the warp ends per inch. However, I was concerned about warp coverage of the large weft, so I decided to increase the number of warp ends to 32 warp ends per inch. This means that with each press of the treadle, half of the warp threads (16 ends per inch) will weave on the top layer and the other 16 ends per inch will weave on the bottom layer. More warp threads per inch = better large-weft coverage.

I decided that each colored-in square in the threading grid equals 1 inch of warp. There are 25 colored-in threading squares for a rug 25 inches wide.

If you wanted to make placemats out of this same profile draft and yarn, you could decide that each colored-in threading square equals ½ inch of weaving width. For placemats, 25 squares × 0.5 inches = 12.5 inches wide, which is a nice size for placemat depth. You would then need half of the total number of warp ends used for a rug, since you are using half the size of the threading squares. See how convenient a profile draft can be?

For the rug, multiply 25 squares / inches times 32 warp ends per inch = 800 warp ends total.

Warp length: 84 inches
Here are my calculations based on the size of the large weft I used:
Planned finished length of the rug = 38 inches, not including hems
Calculated 30% take-up allowance for additional warp length for take-up over the large wefts in addition to shrinkage allowance of 10%
38-inch finished length + 11.5 inches of take-up allowance + 4 inches of shrinkage allowance + 3 inches for hems (1.5 inches of plain weave hems on each end) + tie-on allowance of 6 inches plus loom/thrum waste of 18 inches = 80.5 inches warp length

I decided to wind the warp to 84 inches and wound up with 18 inches of thrum waste after weaving the rug.

Wind the warp: There are two colors of yarn in the borders and two more colors in the center panel of the rug.

The borders are the first 5 threading squares and the last 5 threading squares on the profile draft.

Border #1: Use 2 cones of yarn, one in forest green and the other in burnt umber. Wind both yarns at the same time until you have 5 squares/inches worth of warp at 32 ends per inch (keep your pointer finger between the yarns to keep them from twisting).
5 threading squares = 5 inches of warp width.
5 squares × 32 ends/inch/square = 160 warp ends for first border (half in green / half in Umber)

Center panel: Wind the center panel, using 2 cones of yarn, this time using forest green and blue-green. The center panel section is 15 colored-in threading squares.
15 inches / threading squares × 32 ends per inch / square = 480 warp ends

Border #2: Wind this border the same as border #1 with forest green and burnt umber
5 inches / threading squares x 32 ends per inch / square = 160 warp ends for second border

Check your work:
160 ends (first border) + 480 ends (center panel) + 160 ends (second border) = 800 total warp ends

Calculate the number of heddles: You will be evenly distributing the warp ends over 4 shafts.
800 warp ends divided by 4 shafts = 200 heddles per shaft

Threading units: Thread straight twill 1-2-3-4 and alternate colors of warp yarn depending on the block/colors desired in the blocks. I used three different yarn colors; note the colors on each shaft in the blocks of pattern.

Borders threading units:
Both borders have the same threading.

Block A—Borders: Thread 1-2-3-4 with the following warp yarn colors sequence:

This threading will give you block patterning in the borders. If you want single color stripes in the borders, use only one color of yarn.

Shaft 1: Color A / Forest Green
Shaft 2: Color B / Burnt Umber
Shaft 3: Color A / Forest Green
Shaft 4: Color B / Burnt Umber

Block B—Borders:
Shaft 1: Burnt Umber
Shaft 2: Forest Green
Shaft 3: Burnt Umber
Shaft 4: Forest Green

Center panel threading units:

Block A—Center panel
Shaft 1: Forest Green
Shaft 2: Blue-Green
Shaft 3: Forest Green
Shaft 4: Blue-Green

Block B—Center panel
Shaft 1: Blue-Green
Shaft 2: Forest Green
Shaft 3: Blue-Green
Shaft 4: Forest Green

Tie-up
Treadle 1: Shafts 1 and 3
Treadle 2: Shafts 2 and 4

Treadling sequence:
Start with weaving 1.5 inches, using only the small weft for hems, alternating Treadle 1 with Treadle 2.

Pattern/body of rug:
Alternate Treadle 1 with Treadle 2 and at the same time alternate between picks of large weft and small weft To get you started:
Treadle 1: Pick of large weft
Treadle 2: Pick of small weft
Repeat until you have the block length you desire for the first block of pattern (I did 6 pairs of picks large weft / small weft).

Once you reach the blocks length desired, to change the positions of the colors in the blocks:

Treadle 1: Pick of small weft. (This gives you 2 picks of small weft next to each other, including the final small weft pick, to complete the first sequence above.)
Treadle 2: Pick of large weft
Treadle 1: Pick of small weft
Treadle 2: Pick of large weft
Treadle 1: Pick of small weft
Treadle 2: Pick of large weft

To transition to the next block of pattern, weave two picks of small weft next to each other.
Treadle 1: Small weft
Treadle 2: Small weft
Treadle 1: Large weft
Treadle 2: Small weft

Continue alternating large and small wefts and Treadles 1 and 2 until you reach the length of block you desire. Then transition to the next block with 2 picks of small weft next to each other.

End the rug weaving 1.5 inches, using the small weft for the hem.

Width in reed: 25 inches

Woven length on loom (measured off-tension): 38 inches long (Rep Weave section only; does not include hems)

Hem allowance: 1.5 inches woven with small weft only on each end of the rug

Finished size after washing: 36 inches long without hems (38 inches including finished hems)

Finishing: Cut the rug off the loom and zigzag stitch the raw ends. Trim the warp ends next to the zigzag stitching. Turn under the raw ends ¼ inch and press. Turn the hem so the fold matches the start of the Rep Weave section. Press. Machine-stitch hems.

WEAVE STRUCTURE

Doubleweave

Doubleweave is weaving magic. Seriously, the weaver (lost to history) who figured out how to weave two layers of fabric on the same warp was a true problem solver. Is the loom too narrow to weave a blanket? Doubleweave to the rescue. Want to weave two separate lengths of cloth on one warp? Doubleweave. Want to create a pillow cover without having to cut the fabric and sew seams? Doubleweave. Need extra-thick cloth for garment? Weave two layers that are stitched together with Doubleweave. You can spend a lifetime exploring the wonders of Doubleweave.

Since this is a book about profile drafting, we are going to do a little exploration of Doubleweave on both 4 and 8 shafts. The 4-shaft project is double-width cloth, using the profile draft to lay out a plaid/stripe fabric design. The 8-shaft project explores patterned Doubleweave. Patterned Doubleweave allows you to create designs that are two layers of cloth with one color combination on one side of the fabric and another combination on the reverse side—without the warp and weft yarn colors blending in the blocks; that is, unless you want the blending, and then you can do that too!

Doubleweave is easiest to thread using a straight twill threading, due to the large number of threads required to weave two layers of cloth at the same time. Twill threading is such a marvelous, versatile threading! We played a bit with Turned Twill blocks and Rep Weave earlier. Now we will use the twill threading to weave plain weave blocks in Doubleweave.

Yes, you can weave twill designs in Doubleweave blocks. It's all in the tie-up, the number of shafts you have on your loom, and the number of treadles you have on your loom. Warning: Playing with Doubleweave can lead to shaft envy, but it's amazing what you can weave on a 4-shaft loom.

With just 4 shafts, you can weave double-width cloth and tubes (cloth layers connected on each selvedge), switch the cloth layers from top to bottom and back again, and weave two separate layers of cloth that are not connected

at all. You can also play with pick-up sticks to weave blocks of design literally anywhere on the fabric. (See "Resources" on page 190 for books dedicated to Doubleweave.)

But I'm getting ahead of myself. Let's get back to Doubleweave on 4 shafts.

The straight twill threading is threaded 1-2-3-4, repeat. To weave plain weave on a twill threading, you raise/lower every other thread/shaft.

The tie-up for weaving plain weave for a single layer of cloth using a straight twill threading is:
Treadle 1: tied up to Shafts 1 and 3
Treadle 2: tied up to Shafts 2 and 4

For plain weave on a single layer of cloth, simply alternate treadling between Treadle 1 and Treadle 2.

To weave plain weave in two layers of cloth, think of the shafts as weaving a top layer and a bottom layer. Since there are two layers of cloth, you need to have twice the number of warp threads when you wind the warp than you would for a single layer of cloth. The warp threads can be the same color or different colors of yarn in the layers.

For example, if both layers of fabric will be the same color of yarn and the sett for the yarn is 10 ends per inch, you wind a warp that has 20 ends of warp per inch of fabric width—10 warp ends for the top layer of fabric and 10 warp ends for the bottom layer of fabric.

If you want the top fabric layer and bottom fabric layer to be different colors, you will wind both warp colors at the same time. This will give you 10 ends of Color 1 (top layer) and 10 ends of Color 2 (bottom layer) for a total of 20 ends at 10 e.p.i. for the top layer and 10 e.p.i. for the bottom layer.

When winding the warp using two yarn colors or two cones of the same color of yarn, be sure to place your pointer finger between the two yarns so the yarns don't twist around each other as you wind the yarns on the warping board or warping reel.

Winding two yarns at the same time means that two yarns will be next to each other on the same layer at the cross. One full circuit on the warping board gives you four threads (two from the starting peg to the end peg, and two more from the end peg back to the starting peg). As you wind onto the warping board, the colors will likely shift sides with each other. This is not a problem because you can just move the threads in the pair over into proper position when you are threading the heddles.

DOUBLEWEAVE ON 4 SHAFTS

Doubleweave works really well on 4 shafts. However, unlike Doubleweave on 8 shafts, where you can get the individual blocks of color to change sides of the fabric, 4-shaft Doubleweave can use profile drafts to lay out colors by blocks. This is really handy for laying out stripes and plaids in fabric. To help you wrap your head around how Doubleweave works, I'm going to start with weaving on 4 shafts. Then we will move on to the 8 shaft (and more) possibilities.

THREADING FOR TWO LAYERS OF FABRIC

One of the beauties of Doubleweave is that you can weave a wide piece of cloth on a narrow loom by weaving two layers connected/hinged on one side of the warp. The first Doubleweave project uses 4 shafts and several colors of yarn to create plaid napkins based on a profile draft. The width of the double-layer warp on the loom is only 6.8 inches. By weaving the fabric as Doubleweave hinged on one edge, off the loom I unfold the fabric and get napkins almost 14 inches wide. This is awesome if you have a narrow table or floor loom.

When threading the straight twill threading using one color of yarn, you simply thread Shafts 1-2-3-4 and repeat for the width of the stripe/plaid that you desire. Shafts 1 and 3 are assigned to weave the top layer of fabric. Shafts 2 and 4 are assigned to weave the bottom layer of fabric.

If you are weaving two layers of fabric of different colors, you will still thread 1-2-3-4 but alternate the warp colors as you are threading the shafts. Color A is threaded on Shafts 1 and 3 (top layer), and Color B is threaded on Shafts 2 and 4 (bottom layer). Since you wound both colors at the same time on the warp, the yarns will present in the same order as you plan to thread them. If the yarns have shifted, simply move the color you need over in the pair of threads when threading. This is not a problem.

For example, your top layer of fabric is blue (Color A) and the bottom layer of fabric is yellow (Color B), and you wound both colors at the same time onto the warping board.
Threading is:
Shaft 1: Color A (blue)
Shaft 2: Color B (yellow)
Shaft 3: Color A (blue)
Shaft 4: Color B (yellow)

Now, some books will use D for "dark yarn" (top layer) and L for "light" (bottom layer). That doesn't mean that you must use dark and light threads. It's simply another way to say alternate threading your colors. Use whichever designation makes sense to you.

Now you may be thinking, "Why can't I just thread Color A on Shafts 1 and 2 and Color B on Shafts 3 and 4? It would still make plain weave." Ah, yes it will, but the top and bottom fabric layers won't line up on top of each other at the selvedges of the fabric! Some very clever weaver in the past discovered that already.

SLEYING THE REED

Because you are weaving two layers of fabric, you have double the warp threads per inch. So when you sley the reed, you will have double the number of warp threads per dent to obtain the correct sett for your fabric.

For example: You have a warp sett of 16 e.p.i. For a single layer of fabric, you would use an 8-dent reed sleyed with 2 warp ends per dent to achieve 16 warp ends per inch.

For Doubleweave, you are weaving two layers that are each sett at 16 e.p.i., so you sley 4 warp ends per dent—2 warp ends for the fabric top layer, 2 warp ends of the fabric bottom layer per dent.

If you are using a sett that doesn't divide evenly into the number of dents in your reed, match the number of warp ends per dent of each color/layer of cloth. For example, if you need a sett of 14 e.p.i. and are using an 8-dent reed, for one layer of cloth the sleying order is 1-2-2-2 (1 thread in the first dent and 2 threads in each of the next 3 dents). For Doubleweave, you sley 2-4-4-4 to double the number of warp threads in each dent to get the 14 e.p.i. in each layer you are weaving.

TIE-UPS

The tie-up is dependent on what type of Doubleweave you are weaving. To determine tie-ups, it is helpful to ask yourself, "what do I want to happen with the warp threads?"

TWO LAYERS HINGED ON ONE SELVEDGE

Let's start with weaving two layers hinged on one edge to make a double-wide fabric where both layers are the same color of yarn. Use one shuttle wound with the weft color to weave. If you are using two colors in your warp, with Color A (blue) on the top layer and Color B on the bottom layer (yellow), and weave with Color A on the Color B side of the fabric, it will be a blend of blue and yellow. When you open the fabric there will be two broad stripes the entire length of the fabric—one large stripe of solid blue, the other stripe a blend of yellow and blue. Keep this in mind, because this is very handy for planning stripes or plaid double-width fabric.

For this example, we are going to use one yarn color in the warp.

Here's the sequence to determine the tie-up.

Shafts 1 and 3 are threaded for the top layer of fabric. **Shafts 2 and 4** are threaded for the bottom layer of fabric.

1) I want to start weaving on the top layer, which means I want to raise Shaft 1 and throw the first pick of the top layer. My first treadle is tied up to Shaft 1 only.

2) Now I need to weave the first pick of the bottom layer to establish my hinge at the selvedge. I need to raise Shaft 2 (first pick of bottom layer) and move the top layer warp threads out of the way. So I want to raise Shafts 1 and 3 (top layer threads out of the way) and Shaft 2 for the first pick of the bottom layer. Treadle 2 is tied up: Shaft 1 (top layer), Shaft 2 (bottom layer), and Shaft 3 (top layer).

3) Now my shuttle is at what will be the open selvedge edge of the fabric. Since my last pick wove the bottom layer, I need to weave a second pick of the bottom layer, which means this edge of the fabric will be open. I need to raise Shaft 4 (second thread

on the bottom layer) and Shafts 1 and 3 for the top layer, so those threads are out of the way again. Treadle 3 is tied-up Shaft 1, Shaft 3, and Shaft 4.

4) Now for the last pick on the top layer. I raise only Shaft 3. Because I alternate weaving the top vs. bottom layers, the hinge/connection between the two layers is created on the selvedge edge.

Tie-up grid for weaving double-width fabric connected on one selvedge:

		4	
	3	3	3
	2		
1	1	1	
Top Layer Pick #1	Bottom Layer Pick #1	Bottom Layer Pick #2	Top Layer Pick #2

I prefer to tie up the treadles in this order, so I can simply treadle 1-2-3-4 in order without having to think further about which layer of fabric I am weaving.

As you repeat the treadling sequence, you will have two layers of fabric connected together on one edge and not connected together on the opposite edge. When you take the fabric off the loom, it opens into double the width it was on the loom.

WEAVING TUBES

Tubes are created when you weave so the fabric layers are hinged on both selvedges. You use one shuttle to weave. You use the same tie-up shown above for weaving double width but change the treadling sequence.

Here's the treadling sequence for weaving tubes when using the same tie-up as above.

Note that you are alternating weaving the top vs. bottom layers of cloth.

1) **First pick of the top layer.** Press Treadle 1. (Shaft 1 is up; all other shafts down.)

2) **First pick of the bottom layer.** Press Treadle 2. (Shafts 1 and 3 are up for top layer, and Shaft 2 for bottom layer is up.) This connects/hinges the layers of fabric on one selvedge.

3) **Second pick of the top layer.** Press Treadle 4. (Shaft 3 is up for top layer.) The weft connects the layers of fabric on the fabric selvedge opposite the first hinge.

4) **Second pick of the bottom layer.** Press Treadle 3. (Shafts 1 and 3 for top layer are up, and Shaft 4 for bottom layer is up.)

Here's the treadling sequence for weaving tubes if you want to Treadle 1-2-3-4 in sequence. Note that the tie-ups for Treadles 3 and 4 have swapped places from the double-width tie-up.

Tie-up grid for weaving fabric layers connected on both selvedges:

			4
	3	3	3
	2		
1	1		1
Top Layer Pick #1	Bottom Layer Pick #1	Top Layer Pick #2	Bottom Layer Pick #2

WEAVING TWO SEPARATE LAYERS

You need 2 shuttles to weave two separate layers. The warp layers can be different colors or the same color of yarn. Regardless of the warp colors, you need to weave with two shuttles, so the selvedges do not get attached. Each shuttle can contain the same weft colors as the warp yarn, or each can have a different color of weft for color blending.

You use the same tie-up and treadling as double- width cloth and will press the treadles in the 1-2-3-4 sequence, but this time, you use 2 shuttles each assigned to a layer of the fabric.

1) **First pick of top layer.** Press Treadle 1; weave with Shuttle 1 / Color 1.

2) **First pick of bottom layer.** Press Treadle 2; weave with Shuttle 2 / Color 2.

3) **Second pick of bottom layer.** Press Treadle 3, weave with Shuttle 2 / Color 2.

4) **Second pick of top layer.** Press Treadle 4; weave with Shuttle 1 / Color 1.

SWITCHING THE TWO LAYERS

To switch which color weaves on top, you change the treadling, so the bottom layer of warp comes to the top and the top layer of warp goes to the bottom. At the transition, the layers interweave together across the width of the fabric, and the edges are open at both selvedges. You still need 2 shuttles, and you still weave each layer with the corresponding color of yarn/shuttle.

Use the same tie-up and treadling as for two separate layers of cloth. When you are ready to have the layers change sides, you need to change the treadling sequence.

Let's say the top layer, threaded on Shafts 1 and 3, is blue (Shuttle 1 has blue thread), and the bottom layer, threaded on Shafts 2 and 4, is yellow (Shuttle 2 has yellow thread).

To switch the layers, you need to bring the yellow warp threads on Shafts 2 and 4 to the top and move the blue warp threads on Shafts 1 and 3 to the bottom.

Looking at the tie-up you've been using, you can see you don't have any treadles tied up to raise just the bottom layer warp threads on Shafts 2 and 4, which means you need an additional treadle tied up. Let's walk through this.

1) Threading on Shafts 2 and 4 started as our bottom layer, and warp threads on Shafts 1 and 3 are threaded for our top layer. That means if you want the threads on Shafts 2 and 4 to raise alone, you need to add 2 treadles to our original tie-up, one for Shaft 2 and one for Shaft 4. That gives us 6 treadles.

2) However, we also need to be able to raise Shafts 2 and 4 up out of the way whenever we weave on the bottom layer, which now is Shafts 1 and 3. That means 2 more treadles, which brings us to 8 treadles. If you have an 8-shaft loom, you have enough treadles. However, 4-shaft looms generally come with only 6 treadles.

If you have a 4-shaft loom, you have two options: do a new tie-up or use a skeleton tie-up. A skeleton tie-up is very nice on a jack (rising shed) loom because you can press 2 (or more) treadles at the same time without having to change the tie-up. However, skeleton tie-ups don't work for countermarche looms, because you can't press two treadles at the same time.

Here's how to configure a skeleton tie-up:
Top Layer: Treadle tied up to Shaft 1
Top layer: Treadle tied up to Shaft 3
Bottom layer: Treadle tied up to Shaft 2
Bottom layer: Treadle tied up to Shaft 4
Treadle tied to **Shafts 1 and 3** (gets them out of the way)
Treadle tied to **Shafts 2 and 4** (gets them out of the way)

Refer to the table on page 91 for the skeleton tie-ups that work for changing layers, hinged double width and Tubes (hinged on both edges).

8-SHAFT DOUBLEWEAVE

When we move into 8 or more shafts for Doubleweave, the possibilities really start to expand. Here are the threading units for Doubleweave blocks, also known as Patterned Doubleweave.

Block A: 1-2-3-4 (thread dark, light, dark, light, or you can think of it as Color A, Color B, Color A, Color B).
Block B: 5-6-7-8 (DLDL or Colors ABAB)
Block C: 9-10-11-12 (DLDL or Colors ABAB)
Block D: 13-14-15-16 (DLDL or Colors ABAB)

To get two distinct blocks of color in a design, you need 8 shafts—Shafts 1–4 are weaving Block A, and Shafts 5–8 are weaving Block B. To add more blocks, you need 4 shafts per added block of pattern.

DESIGNING FOR PATTERNED DOUBLE-WEAVE BLOCKS

Referring back to the 4 shaft designs earlier, we were limited to two layers of plain weave. Now by adding more shafts, we can add more plain weave blocks and can set up our warps/tie-ups/treadling so that you get solid blocks of color that appear on the top surface or bottom surface to create the overall fabric design. You are weaving both layers at the same time. Two shuttles are required to get solid-color blocks of pattern.

Here's how this works. Take a deep breath. If you are a visual learner (like I am), this may not make sense by just reading it. However, if you put on a small sample warp and follow the steps, it will likely make more sense when you can see what the threads are doing. I know that helped me immensely.

SKELETON TIE-UPS ON 4 SHAFTS

B	B	Y	Y	BB	YY	Blue on Shafts 1 & 3 (top layer), yellow on Shafts 2 & 4 (bottom layer)
			4		4	
	3			3		
		2			2	
1				1		
						Weaving 2 layers with bottom (yellow) layer moving to top
		X				Pick 1: Raises yellow on Shaft 2; weave yellow on top layer
X					X	Pick 2: Raises both yellows, plus blue on shaft 1; weave on bottom with blue
		X				Pick 3: Raises yellow up on Shaft 4; weave yellow on top
	X				X	Pick 4: Raise all yellow and the other blue; weave with blue
						Colors: Blue moves to bottom layer; yellow moves to top layer
						Weaving 2 layers with blue on top, yellow on bottom
X						Pick 1: Blue on Shaft 1 weaves on top; weave with blue
		X		X		Pick 2: Raises both blues on 1 & 3, plus 1st yellow in shaft 2; weave with yellow
	X					Pick 3: Raises other blue on shaft 2 on top; weave with blue
			X	X		Pick 4: Raises both blues plus yellow in shaft 4; weave with yellow
						Two layers hinged on one side for double width—use 1 shuttle
X						Pick 1: Top layer—raises first warp on top
		X		X		Pick2: Bottom layer—raises both top warps plus one warp of the bottom
			X	X		Pick 3: Bottom layer—raises second warp in bottom, both top warps
	X					Pick 4: Top layer—raise second warp on top
						Tubes closed at both selvedges—use 1 shuttle
X						Pick 1: Top layer
		X		X		Pick 2: Bottom layer
	X					Pick 3: Top layer
			X	X		Pick 4: Bottom layer

2 BLOCKS ON 8 SHAFTS

Now, let's go step by step with 2 blocks on 8 shafts.

Create your own 2-block profile draft design, or you can use this one that I will use to outline the threading, tie-up, and treadling.

Figure 1: Profile Threading

Now I'll add the treadling "as drawn in," which means I will use the same number of blocks of treadling as I do for the threading.

First, I note my blocks in the tie-up. Blue is Block A, and yellow is Block B. Then I add my treadling and color in the drawdown. When I treadle for Block A, the Block A color is on the top layer. Treadle for Block B, the Block B color is on top. But what about those white squares in the drawdown? Here's when the fun begins. It depends on the yarn colors used in the threading (see figure 2).

When weaving a single layer of fabric, those white squares on the profile draft would be a blend of blue and yellow. Block A threading is blue. Block B is threaded yellow. For the first Block A treadling and weaving with blue, the Block A sections will be solid blue, but the Block B sections would be a combination of blue weft / yellow warp. Block B is threaded yellow, and when the weft is yellow, Block B sections are solid yellow and Block A sections are a blend of blue warp and yellow weft.

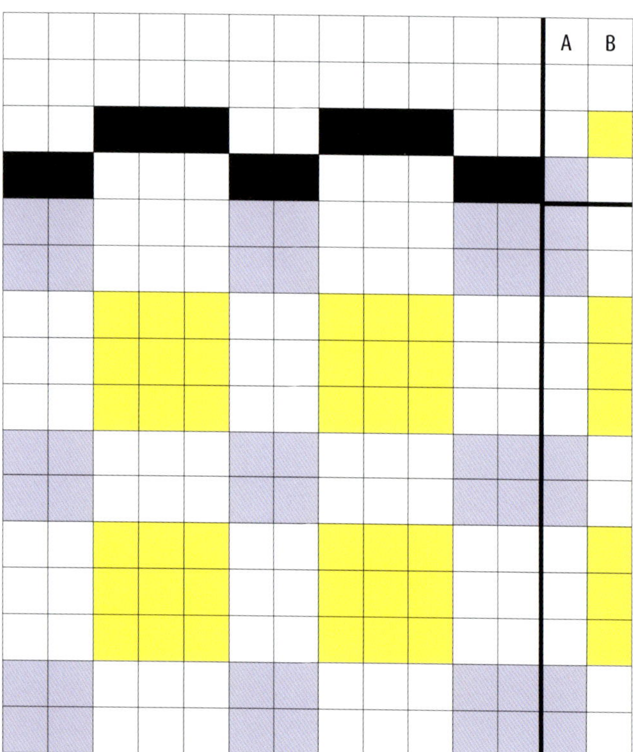

Figure 2: Adding the profile treadling/drawdown

However, if I weave two layers of fabric, I can get solid blocks of each color. The key is what color of yarn is on top in each block, based on the threading and treadling.

First, I need to wind my warp so that I wind both warp colors at the same time using two cones of yarn. I alternate threading the blue vs. yellow warp threads depending on which block I am threading.

I weave with two shuttles; one shuttle for each color of weft yarn. I also alternate weaving with blue or yellow weft regardless of which block of pattern I am treadling. (More on that in a bit.)

The profile draft in figure 3 shows the color combination in the drawdown that we are aiming for when we treadle / tie-up the shafts for weaving two layers of fabric.

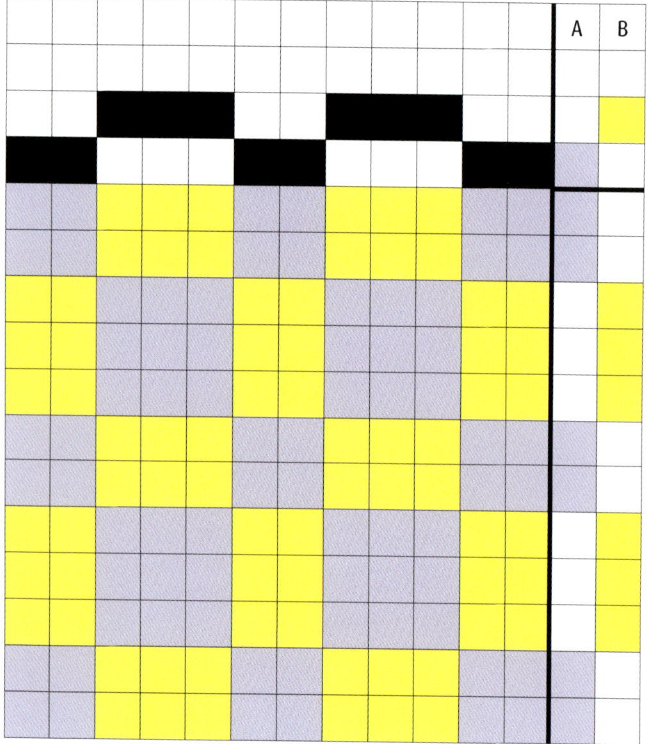

Figure 3

THREADING EACH BLOCK FOR DOUBLE LAYERS

Block A threading is 1-2-3-4, with Shafts 1 and 3 threaded with blue and Shafts 2 and 4 threaded in yellow.

Block B threading is 5-6-7-8, with Shafts 5 and 7 threaded in yellow and Shafts 6 and 8 threaded in blue.

Each colored-in square on the profile threading represents one threading unit repeat for a block.

The profile threading begins with 2 colored-in squares in Block A.

Block A threading unit / colors:
Shaft 1: Blue (top layer)
Shaft 2: Yellow (bottom layer)
Shaft 3: Blue (top layer)
Shaft 4: Yellow (bottom layer)

With my two layers of fabric, this threading represents 2 threads of blue on the top layer of fabric and 2 threads of yellow on the bottom layer for the first threading square in Block A.

I have 2 threading squares in Block A. So I repeat the threading unit for a total of 4 blue threads for the top layer and 4 yellow threads for the bottom layer.

Now the profile draft has 3 threading squares colored in on Block B. We want yellow to be on the top layer in Block B, so now we start threading with a yellow thread.

Block B threading unit is 5-6-7-8.
Shaft 5: Yellow
Shaft 6: Blue
Shaft 7: Yellow
Shaft 8: Blue

Repeat this threading sequence 3 times—one repeat for each Block B profile threading square. We will have a total of 6 threads in yellow and 6 threads in blue.

Here's what the thread-by-thread looks like for the first two A blocks and the first three B blocks.

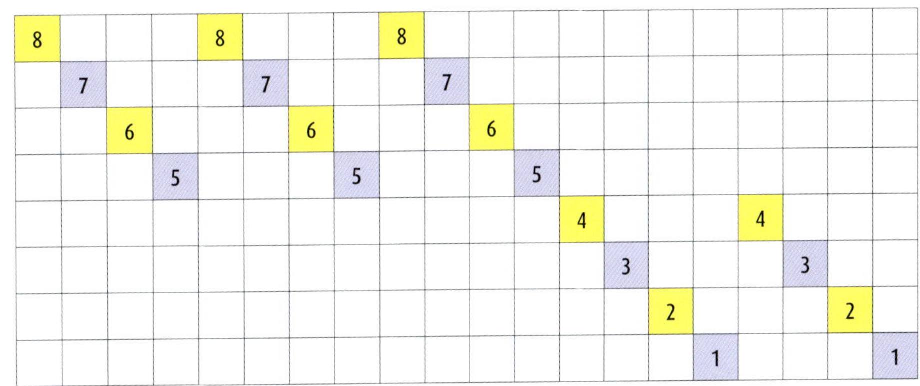

Figure 4

Wait just a minute! Let's look again at the Block A threading. There will be only 2 threads on the top layer (blue) and 2 threads on the bottom layer (yellow) per block of threading. This would be a very tiny block of pattern!

For example, if you are using a yarn with a sett of 16 e.p.i., 2 threads would only be about ⅛ inch wide. For our 2 repeats of the Block A sample, we have only 4 threads of blue on top, which is only ¼ inch!

Here's the key: *You* decide how many repeats of threading each colored-in square on the profile draft represents.

There are two ways of looking at the threading repeats per block.

1) Each block represents two layers of fabric—the top layer and the bottom layer. If you want a wider block, you determine how many threads you need on each surface of the fabric. For a wider band of pattern, you can decide each block represents 8 threads on the top surface and 8 threads on the bottom surface. To get 8 threads on both the top and bottom layers, repeat the threading 4 times. This equals 8 threads of each color, and my block size would be ½ inch across on the top and bottom layers. Keep repeating the threading units for each block until I achieve the size of fabric pattern block that I want.

2) You decide that each colored-in square in a block of threading equals 1 inch of woven width. If both layers of the fabric are plain weave, then you simply calculate the ends per inch for yarn for plain weave. Then double the number of warp ends in one inch.

For example, if the warp sett is 16 ends per inch for one layer, then for two layers of fabric, you would have 32 ends in 1 inch of wound warp. The top layer has 16 ends and the bottom layer has 16 ends in the same 1-inch worth of warp.

Then you simply repeat your threading units in a block until you have the correct number of warp ends on each layer of fabric.

Once you decide how many warp ends a colored-in square represents, you need to be consistent with that repetition across the draft to maintain the block proportions in the profile draft.

TREADLING

Once you determine the number of repeats of threading, to maintain the proportions of the blocks with the draft, you can weave the same number of treadling repeats as you have threading repeats.

In the text box example, I determined that each threading square represent 16 warp threads in each layer of fabric. Therefore, each treadling block square represents 16 picks of each color/layer for each square of treadling. Yes, you can decide to treadle more or fewer treadling repeats.

Two important points to keep in mind: (1) You must complete at least 4 picks of weft, two picks for the top layer (over and back) and two picks for the bottom layer, to complete the plain weave on each layer of fabric, and (2) changing the number of treadling repeats will change the proportions of your blocks.

TIE-UP

When setting up your tie-up, Shafts 1–4 are for Block A and Shafts 5–8 are for Block B. You will be weaving with two colors of yarn and alternate between weaving the top layer of cloth and the bottom layer of cloth. You will be weaving both sides of the cloth with each pick. Your tie-up makes this happen, so the correct color of weft weaves with the correct color of warp in the block you are weaving.

Figure 5 shows a standard tie-up for alternating 2 blocks of color in patterned Doubleweave. I'm going to walk you through how to recognize what each treadle is doing, so you can translate this tie-up to more shafts, if you have them available on a loom. The tie-up instructions are for a rising shed loom.

Figure 5

								Block B Shaft 8—Yellow
								Block B Shaft 7—Blue
								Block B Shaft 6—Yellow
								Block B Shaft 5—Blue
								Block A Shaft 4—Yellow
								Block A Shaft 3—Blue
								Block A Shaft 2—Yellow
								Block A Shaft 1—Blue
Treadle Block A				Treadle Block B				

This tie-up uses 8 treadles on 8 shafts. I've divided the grid between weaving Block A and Block B. The first four treadles (columns) are for Block A. The second four treadles are for Block B. As you go up the grid, the first four shafts (1–4) are for Block A, and the next four shafts (5–8) are for Block B. I have noted what color of yarn is threaded on each shaft.

Step 1: We are weaving plain weave. We want solid blue on the top surface in Block A and solid yellow on the bottom surface in Block A. In Block B, we want solid yellow on the top surface and solid blue on the bottom surface of the fabric.

Block A: The blue warp threads are on Shafts 1 and 3, so we want to raise the first thread in this plain weave pair, which is Shaft 1. At the same time, we want to raise the first blue thread in Block B, so we get blue on the bottom side of Block B threading, which is on Shaft 5; plus, we want to get all the yellow threads in Block B out of the way for this first pick of blue on the top surface in Block A, so we raise Shafts 6 and 8 (see figure 6).

Figure 6

8								Block B Shaft 8—Yellow
								Block B Shaft 7—Blue
6								Block B Shaft 6—Yellow
5								Block B Shaft 5—Blue
								Block A Shaft 4—Yellow
								Block A Shaft 3—Blue
								Block A Shaft 2—Yellow
1								Block A Shaft 1—Blue
Treadle Block A Blue on top/ Yellow on bottom				Treadle Block B Yellow on top/ Blue on bottom				

For the second pick/treadle, we will weave the bottom layer of fabric, which will be solid yellow on the backside of Block A and yellow on top in Block B. We need all the blue threads raised out of the way on Shafts 1 and 3 in Block A, plus the first yellow thread for the plain weave on the back layer. In Block B, we want to leave the first blue thread down (because it was raised on the previous pick) and raise the first yellow thread on Shaft 6 (see figure 7).

Figure 7

8								Block B Shaft 8—Yellow
								Block B Shaft 7—Blue
6	6							Block B Shaft 6—Yellow
5								Block B Shaft 5—Blue
								Block A Shaft 4—Yellow
	3							Block A Shaft 3—Blue
	2							Block A Shaft 2—Yellow
1	1							Block A Shaft 1—Blue

Now we need to weave the second pick of blue in Block A to complete the plain weave. In Block A, we raise the second blue thread on Shaft 3, and at the same time, we need to get all the yellow threads on the underside out of the way and raise the second thread in the blue sequence on Shaft 7, so the blue weaves on the underside of the fabric in Block B threading (see figure 8).

Figure 8

8		8						Block B Shaft 8—Yellow
		7						Block B Shaft 7—Blue
6	6	6						Block B Shaft 6—Yellow
5								Block B Shaft 5—Blue
								Block A Shaft 4—Yellow
	3	3						Block A Shaft 3—Blue
	2							Block A Shaft 2—Yellow
1	1							Block A Shaft 1—Blue

Now for the final pick with yellow yarn. We want to raise all the blues out of the way in Block A plus the remaining yellow threads to complete the plain weave in yellow on the backside (see figure 9).

The treadling sequence for blue on the top in Block A, and yellow on the bottom vs. yellow on the top in Block B / blue on the bottom is:

Treadle 1: Blue weft
Treadle 2: Yellow weft
Treadle 3: Blue weft
Treadle 4: Yellow weft

Figure 9

8		8	8					Block B Shaft 8—Yellow
		7						Block B Shaft 7—Blue
6	6	6						Block B Shaft 6—Yellow
5								Block B Shaft 5—Blue
			4					Block A Shaft 4—Yellow
	3	3	3					Block A Shaft 3—Blue
	2							Block A Shaft 2—Yellow
1	1		1					Block A Shaft 1—Blue

Repeat until you have the block size desired.

Step 2: Now it's time to have the colors switch sides of the fabric within the blocks so that, in Block B, solid blue will be on top and, in Block A, the yellow will be on top.

You still throw your two shuttles in the same sequence.
Treadle 5: Blue weft shuttle
Treadle 6: Yellow weft shuttle
Treadle 7: Blue weft shuttle
Treadle 8: Yellow weft shuttle

You will use only Treadles 5–8 and repeat the treadling sequence of 5 through 8 until you have woven the block length desired.

Figure 10 shows the full tie-up. Based on the steps we did in step 1, look at which shafts are being

Figure 10

8		8	8				8	Block B Shaft 8—Yellow
		7			7	7	7	Block B Shaft 7—Blue
6	6	6			6			Block B Shaft 6—Yellow
5				5	5		5	Block B Shaft 5—Blue
			4	4		4	4	Block A Shaft 4—Yellow
	3	3	3			3		Block A Shaft 3—Blue
	2			2	2	2		Block A Shaft 2—Yellow
1	1		1	1				Block A Shaft 1—Blue

Treadle Block A Blue on top in Block A / Yellow on top in Block B | Treadle Block B Yellow on top in Block A / Blue on top in Block B

raised in each block. I have colored the squares to help identify which colors are being raised with each treadle.

If you are like me, what happens in each block makes more sense when I see it happen on the loom. I encourage you to put on a small sample to experiment.

FRAME AROUND A BLOCK OF COLOR

You may have seen woven fabrics that have a frame of a solid color around a square of a different color of yarn. These are also two blocks of Doubleweave, but the tie-up is slightly different so that you are weaving two layers of fabric for the horizontal lines of the frames. This tie-up is also handy if you want to weave two layers of fabric at the start and finish of your project for hems.

			8	8		8	8	Block B Shaft 8—Yellow
	7	7	7			7		Block B Shaft 7—Blue
	6			6	6	6		Block B Shaft 6—Yellow
5	5		5	5				Block B Shaft 5—Blue
			4			4	4	Block A Shaft 4—Yellow
	3	3	3		3	3	3	Block A Shaft 3—Blue
	2				2			Block A Shaft 2—Yellow
1	1		1	1	1		1	Block A Shaft 1—Blue
Block A				Block B				

The threading is the same as for the two blocks above, and you alternate two colors. I've used our blue and yellow with the blue as the "frame" and yellow as the "windowpane." Here's the tie-up for the framed windows / two layers:

To weave the frame / two layers, repeat the Block A treadling (Treadles 1–4) and weave with two colors of yarn, starting with the color you have assigned for the frame. The second pick of the treadling sequence will be the color you have assigned to the windowpane. Odd-numbered shafts weave the frame, and even-numbered shafts weave the pane.

Treadle 1: Weave with "frame" weft color.
Treadle 2: Weave with "pane" weft color.
Treadle 3: Weave with "frame" weft color.
Treadle 4: Weave with "pane" weft color.

To weave the windowpane in Block B threading, use treadles 5–8 and again start with the color of weft assigned to the frame, followed by the color assigned to the pane. The odd-numbered shafts are the frame, and even-numbered shafts are the pane.

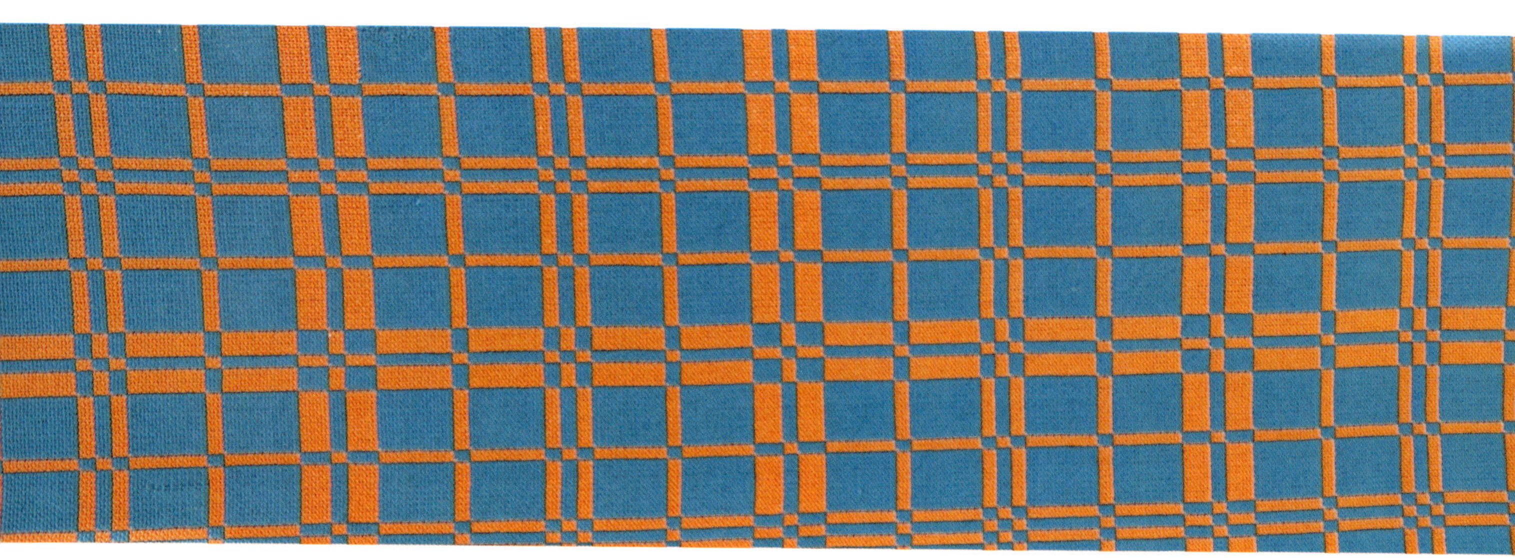

◆ PROJECT ◆

DOUBLEWEAVE PLAID NAPKINS

DOUBLE-WIDTH FABRIC ON 4 SHAFTS

Technically speaking, you can only weave one block of Doubleweave pattern on 4 shafts. But Doubleweave on 4 shafts is such a versatile weave for double width, tubes, and two separate layers of cloth that I just had to include a project.

EQUIPMENT NEEDED

4-shaft loom
1 shuttle
6 bobbins—one for each color of weft
10-dent reed—sley at 4 ends per dent

Profile draft for creating the stripes in the napkins

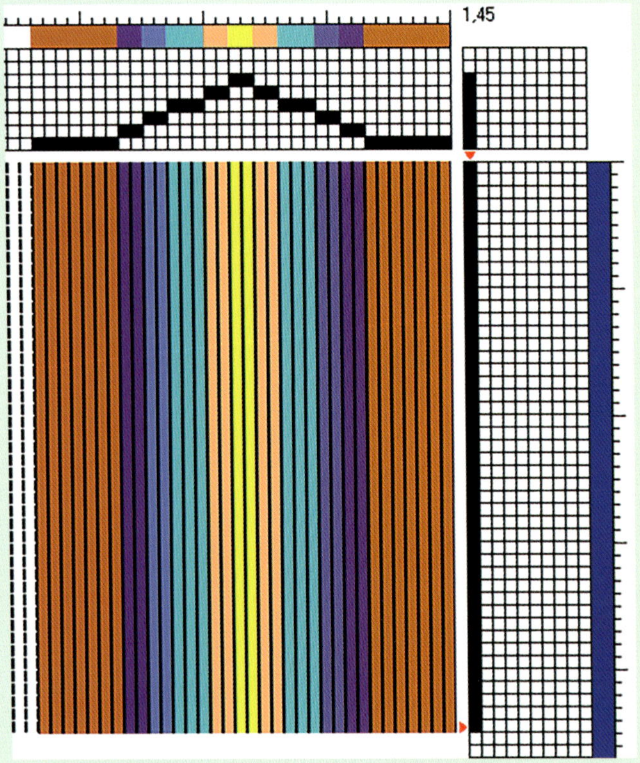

1,45

Profile draft for double width weaving

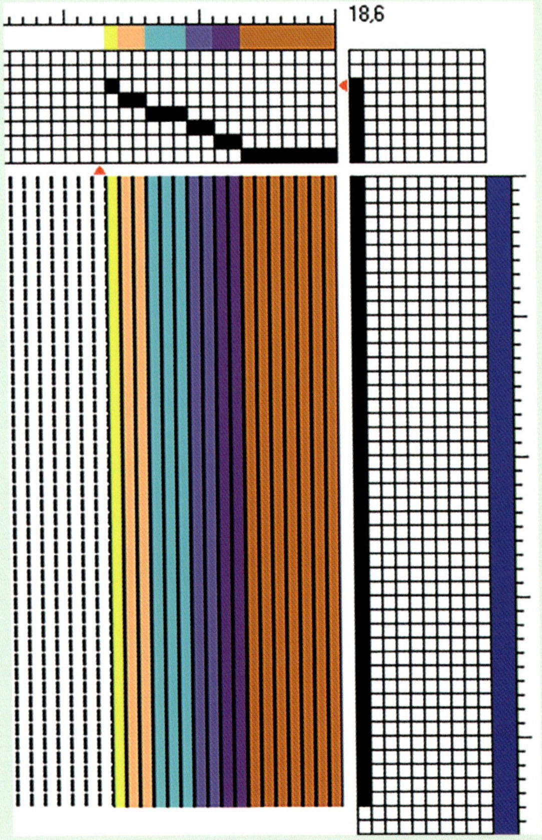

18,6

There are six colors of weft for the plaid napkins, and weaving goes faster if you wind individual bobbins for each color of weft. Then you can still use one shuttle and simply swap out the bobbins to weave the next color section.

I use the profile draft and assign a different color to each block. Then I "trick" my weaving program by pretending that the tie-up area on the profile draft engages every block—which is true because I weave every stripe of color across the warp. Boom, I can get proportionally pleasing stripes, which I make into plaid by weaving the same color progression with the wefts.

To use this same draft as a double width draft, I use only half of the draft, stopping the middle yellow section as one square of color. Each stripe of color will have double the warp ends, so I can open the fabric into a full-width napkin off the loom and both sides match exactly. You can weave napkins on a narrow loom by weaving double-width fabric on 4 shafts. Or you could go bigger and create a double-width blanket, using the same profile draft but using a larger yarn. Or you could create towels simply by assigning more warp ends per square in a block to create wider fabric and still maintain the proportions in the profile draft.

Yarns:
WEBS 10/2 cotton (Please note: I wove this out of my stash of 10/2 WEBS cottons. At the time I wove the napkins, not all the colors from my stash matched the color numbers at WEBS. They may change again in the future.)
Borders (Copper): Saddle #7125
Section 1 (Purple): Deep Periwinkle #6277
Section 2 (Blue): Mediterranean Blue #2448
Section 3 (Teal Green): Porcelain Green #5421
Section 4 (Burnt Orange): Burnt Sienna #7198
Section 5 (Yellow): Daffodil #1325

Sett: 20 e.p.i.

Warp: I wound the warp, starting with the wide outside border, and ended the warp width with the single of the center band of yellow. If you thread so the yellow band of color is on your right-hand side when sitting at the front of the loom, you will start weaving from the left selvedge with your first pick of weft. This will create the hinge in the yellow stripe that will be the center of the napkin when you follow the treadling sequence.

Remember, you are weaving 2 layers of fabric, so with each stripe you will wind twice the number of warp threads calculated per color section and threading each color section only once.

Calculate the number of warp ends: I used 10/2 cotton with a sett of 20 e.p.i. for each layer of cloth. To get the desired napkin finished width of 12 inches after washing, I decided that each square of the profile draft represents 8 ends of warp. If I were doing this piece flat, there are 33 colored-in squares for the warp times 8 warp threads/square = 264 warp threads.

However, I am doing double layers so I look at the number of squares for half of the design and calculate the following starting from the tie-up:
Border: 7 squares × 8 ends/square = 56 ends × 2 layers = 112 warp ends for borders
First color stripe: 2 squares × 8 ends/square = 16 ends × 2 layers = 32 warp ends
2nd stripe: 2 squares × 8 ends/square = 16 ends × 2 layers = 32 warp ends
3rd stripe: 3 squares × 8 ends/square = 24 ends × 2 layers = 48 warp ends
4th stripe: 2 squares × 8 ends/square = 16 ends × 2 layers = 32 warp ends
5th stripe (center band of color): 1 square × 8 ends/square = 8 ends × 2 layers = 16 warp ends. This is the section that will be hinged, and I want there to be a square in the center of the napkin. If I left it at 8 ends for the single square, I would have a very narrow center color band of only 4 warp ends per layer.

Total warp ends: 112 (Border)+32 (Stripe 1)+32 (Stripe 2)+48 (Stripe3) +32 (Stripe 4)+(Center) 16 = 272 warp ends
272 warp ends divided by 20 e.p.i. (when opened) = 13.6 inches width off the loom
13.6 divided by 2 (folded at center) = 6.8-inch width in reed

Calculate the number of heddles: The warp threads are distributed evenly on 4 shafts.
272 warp ends divided by 4 = 68 heddles per shaft

Threading units: Thread warp 1-2-3-4, repeat. The blocks in the profile draft threading represent a stripe color.

Shafts 1 and 3 weave the top layer of fabric.
Shafts 2 and 4 weave the bottom layer of fabric.

Tie-up: This project weaves two layers, hinged on one side to create double-width fabric off the loom. The hinge occurs in the center color stripe (yellow in my napkins). The tie-up is for weaving double-width fabric. This order of tie-up allows you to treadle in order of 1-2-3-4. (See "Treadling sequence" below.)

		4	
	3	3	
	2		3
1	1	1	

Treadling sequence:

		4		
	3	3	3	
	2			
1	1	1		
■				First pick of top layer—lifts only first warp thread of top layer-bottom layer on 2 & 4 stay down
	■			First pick of bottom layer—lifts top layer (1 & 3) out of the way and 2 for 1st thread of bottom
		■		Second pick of bottom layer—lifts top layer (1 & 3) out of the way and 4 for 2nd thread of bottom
			■	Second pick of top layer—lifts second thread of top layer on Shaft 3

Reminder: Thread the warp so the center stripe of the napkin is on your right-hand side, then start weaving with your shuttle entering from the left side of the shed, using the treadling sequence.

Warp length: Allow 15 inches of woven length per napkin (includes shrinkage and hem allowances) plus tie-on and thrum (loom waste) allowance that is appropriate for the loom you are using.

For my 4 napkins, the warp length was 94 inches.

Width in reed: 6.8 inches

Weft: Same colors as the warp stripes of color woven in the same order as the colors appear in the warp.

Weaving: Start by weaving 4 inches in border color = 3 inches for the border plus additional inch for the hem. Weave each color section to square. End with another 4 inches for the border.

Weave 2 picks of thrums / contrasting yarn between each napkin. Once it's off the loom, you can cut the napkins apart between these 2 picks for a perfectly straight cut.

Woven length on loom per napkin (measured off-tension): 15 inches per napkin—this allows for 1 inch on each end for hems plus a little extra.

Finished size after washing: 12 inches square after narrow hems on each end

Shrinkage: 16%

Finishing: Zigzag stitch along all napkin ends. Soak in warm water and then lay flat to dry to block the napkins to size. This step also helps reduce shrinkage when napkins are machine washed / dried in the future. Cut napkins apart (remove divider thrums yarns after cutting the napkins apart). Measure the width of the outside borders and turn under the raw ends of the napkins so the borders on each napkin end match the width of the side borders. Press.

Now turn under the raw edges so they are between the body of the napkin and the hem. Machine- or hand-hem.

◆ PROJECT ◆

PATTERNED DOUBLEWEAVE TABLE RUNNER

ON 8 SHAFTS

This two-block table runner features blocks of color that switch from top to bottom sides of the fabric to create the overall fabric design. By simply changing the sizes of the blocks, the overall pattern looks far more complicated than it is.

Your first decision when weaving this project is to select the yarns. I used 5/2 mercerized cotton from Lunatic Fringe. Due to the double layers and the yarn size, the runner has great body and has enough weight that it lies nicely on a table.

The next decision is whether you want to have fringe on the ends of the runner or if you want to weave two separate layers to turn the edges to the inside of the piece for hems. If you want fringe, calculate the amount of fringe into the warp length for both ends. I finished my runner by tying knots using the Damascus edging from Peter Collingwood's *The Techniques of Rug Weaving* book, page 485. I also found videos online by searching "Damascus rug finishing techniques," which you can do if you can't locate a copy of Collingwood's book. Damascus edging creates a lovely finish with a decorative ridge of knots on one side of the fabric. Overhand knots will also work well, but the large number of warp threads can make for tying a lot of knots. Whatever knots you decide to use, I found that using 4 warp threads from the top layer and tying them with 4 threads from the bottom layer works well. Hem stitching will also make a lovely finish for fringe.

If you decide to weave two layers separately and then turn the ends under, you need to first tie up your loom, using the tie-up at the end of the Doubleweave Weave Structure section on page 94. After weaving about 2 inches for hemming, you will then have to retie your treadles for the patterning of the runner unless you have a loom with enough treadles.

EQUIPMENT NEEDED

8-shaft loom with minimum 18-inch weaving width

2 shuttles (one for each color of weft)

8-dent reed (sley 4 ends per dent / 2 ends per dent of each color)

Here's the tie-up for the runner with the two blocks of color switching sides of the fabric. Page 94 has an in- depth discussion on this tie-up.

8		8	8				8	Block B Shaft 8—Yellow
		7			7	7	7	Block B Shaft 7—Blue
6	6	6			6			Block B Shaft 6—Yellow
5				5	5		5	Block B Shaft 5—Blue
			4	4		4	4	Block A Shaft 4—Yellow
	3	3	3			3		Block A Shaft 3—Blue
	2			2	2	2		Block A Shaft 2—Yellow
1	1		1	1				Block A Shaft 1—Blue

Block A
Blue on top in Block A / Yellow on top in Block B

Block B
Yellow on top in Block A / Blue on top in Block B

When you want Color A (blue in our example / blue-green in the project) on the top fabric layer in Block A and Color B (yellow in our example/copper in the project) on the bottom layer, press treadles 1 through 4 and repeat until you have the size of block desired/indicated by the profile draft.

To have the colors switch sides of the fabric so Color B (yellow/copper) is on top in Block A and blue/blue-green is on top in Block B, press treadles 5 through 8 in sequence until you have the desired size of the blocks.

Yarns:
Lunatic Fringe Yarns Tubular Spectrum 5/2 mercerized cotton in #10 blue-green
Lunatic Fringe Yarns Tubular Spectrum 5/2 mercerized cotton in copper

Warp:
260 ends blue-green
260 ends copper
Total warp ends: 520

Sett: 16 e.p.i.

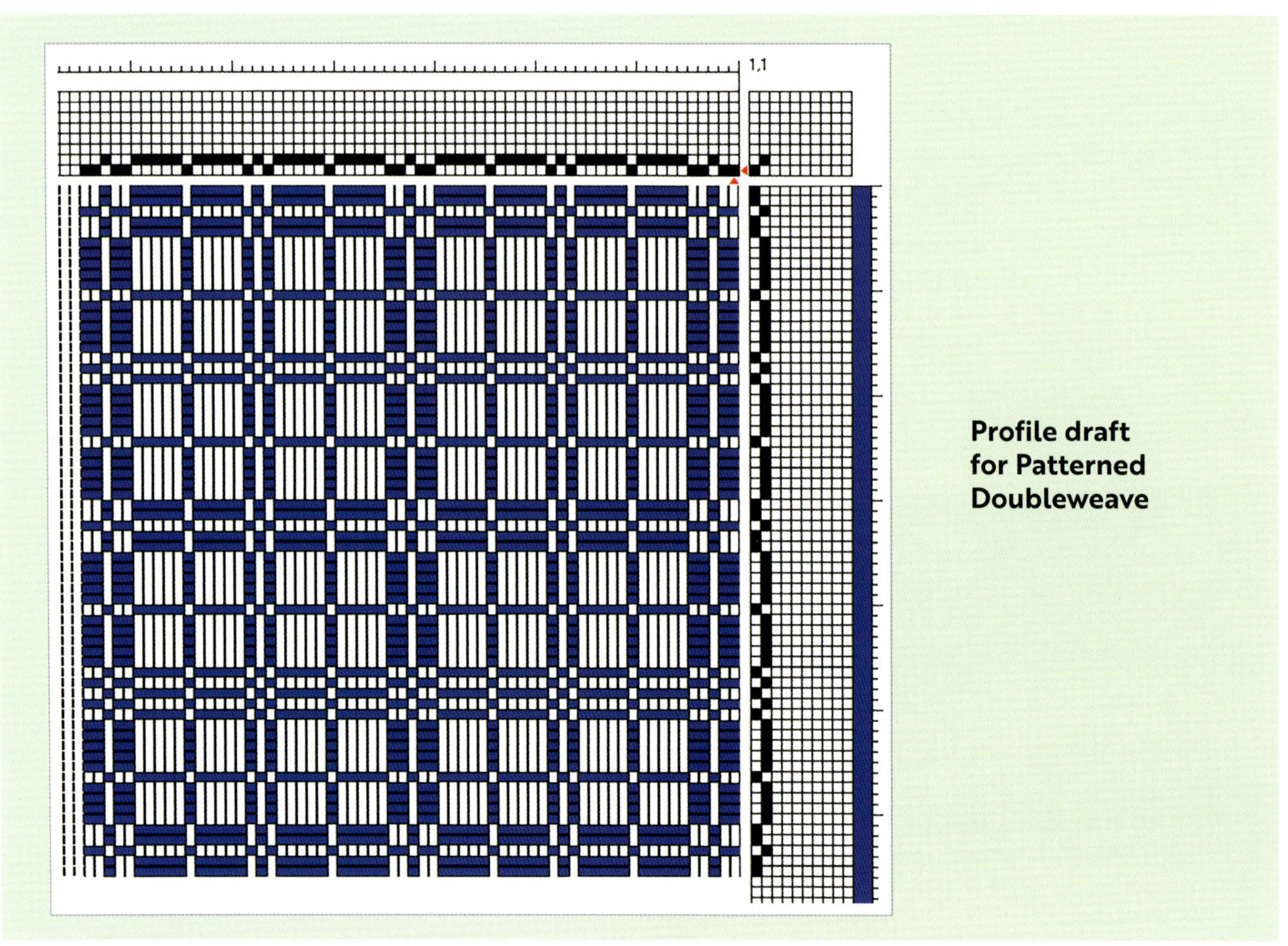

Profile draft for Patterned Doubleweave

Calculate the number of warp ends: There are 65 total threading squares on the draft. My first step was deciding how wide I wanted the runner to be and how many warp ends each threading square represents.

The 5/2 yarn is sett for plain weave at 16 e.p.i. For one layer of fabric, if each colored-in threading square represents 16 warp ends, the profile draft square also represents 1 inch of warp width. With 65 total threading squares, that would give me a runner 65 inches wide. That's much wider than I wanted for a runner.

I decided that each colored-in square represents 4 threads in a layer. My sett is 16 e.p.i. To see if this is a more realistic runner width, I multiplied:
65 squares × 4 threads per square in a layer = 260 warp threads
Divide 260 threads by 16 e.p.i. = 16.25 inches wide on the loom.

Since this is Doubleweave, I need to multiply the number of warp threads in 1 layer of fabric times 2 to get the warp thread needed for two layers of fabric.

Multiply 260 warp ends × 2 (layers of fabric) = 520 total warp threads (260 ends for the top layer, 260 ends for the bottom layer).

The runner uses two colors of warp yarn, so we need a cone of each color of yarn. Wind the warp holding both colors together with your pointer finger between the threads as you wind to keep the threads from twisting around each other. Winding both yarn colors at the same time means each inch of wound warp has 32 ends (16 of Color A and 16 of Color B).

If you bundle your warp ends in 1-inch increments at the cross, you will have 16 bundles of 32 warp threads each, plus one bundle of 8 warp ends, to equal 520 total warp threads.

Calculate the number of heddles: Once I decide the number of warp ends represented per square, I can calculate the number of heddles per shaft. Since the warp thread colors alternate with each other when threading, each square of threading repeat represents 2 threads of a color. Refer back to the tie-up earlier.

Block A / Color A is on Shafts 1 and 3 and Shafts 5 and 7 (odd numbered shafts).
Block B / Color B is on Shafts 2 and 4 and Shafts 6 and 8 (even numbered shafts).

I count the number of squares for Block A threading, which on our draft is 20 squares. Each threading square represents 2 repeats of threading, for a total of 4 threads for the top layer and 4 threads for the bottom layer.

20 squares × 2 threading repeats/square = 40 threads/heddles on each of Shafts 1, 3, 5, and 7.
Total heddles or Block A = 40 threads per shaft × 4 shafts = 160 total warp threads for Block A threading.

There are 45 squares for Block B threading.
45 squares × 2 threading repeats/square = 90 threads/heddles on each of Shafts 2, 4, 6. and 8.
Total number of heddles: 90 × 4 shafts = 360 ends for Block B threading.

Check our work: We have a total of 520 warp ends (260 top layer, 260 bottom layer).
160 heddles for Block A + 360 heddles for Block B= 520 total warp ends.

Threading Units:
Block A: 1-2-3-4 Alternate warp colors: Shaft 1: Color A, Shaft 2: Color B, Shaft 3: Color A, Shaft 4; Color B
Block B: 5-6-7-8 Alternate warp colors: Shaft 5: Color A, Shaft 6: Color B, Shaft 7: Color A, Shaft 8: Color B

Note that your warp colors alternate across the warp, regardless of which block is being threaded. The appropriate warp threads within the blocks will be raised using the tie-up and treadling.

Repeat the threading units/colors in each block based on your sett/number of warp threads represented by each colored-in threading square. (Refer back to "Calculating the number of warp ends.")

Based on my desired size of runner, each threading square on the profile draft represents 4 threads of each color. In each threading unit, there are 2 threads for Color A and 2 threads for Color B. So each colored-in square of the threading represents 2 repeats of the threading for the block to give me a total of 4 threads of Color A on top layer and 4 threads of Color B on the bottom layer per threading square.

For example, the profile draft threading begins with 2 colored-in squares of Block A. Each of those squares represents 4 threads on top layer (Color A) and 4 threads on bottom layer (Color B). Each threading unit for Block A has 2 threads in Color A (one on Shaft 1, one on Shaft 3) and 2 threads of Color B (one on shaft 2 and one on Shaft 4). Therefore, to get to 4 total threads on the top layer and 4 total threads on the bottom layer, I need to repeat the threading unit 1-2-3-4 twice to get 4 threads of each color per threading square.

There are two threading squares in the first Block A on the profile draft. I need to repeat the Block A threading unit a total of 4 times for the two threading squares of Block A on the draft. This means I will have a total of 8 warp threads on each layer (4 threads of each color × 2 squares).

In case your brain just exploded, here's another way to approach threading.
Each colored-in square in the threading = 4 threads of each color. Keep repeating the block threading unit until you have 4 threads of each color threaded on Shafts 1-4 for Block A threading. Bundle those ends with a piece of thrum. This is one threading square on the profile draft.

Move on to the next square of threading in the draft. That's also Block A. Keep repeating Block A threading on Shafts 1–4 until you have 4 threads of each color. Now remove the thrum from the first bundle and bundle both threading blocks together. This tells me these threads are the first two blocks of threading.

TIP: Use two different colors of thrums to bundle the set of threads in the blocks—one color of thrum for Block A and one color of thrum for Block B. Once you complete threading for a full block of pattern, bundle those threading units together consistently using the same color thrum for a block of threading. For example, Block A is bundled with a red piece of yarn, and Block B is bundled with a green piece of yarn. Then you can tell at a glance what the last block of threading was that you did.

Tie-up: Use the tie-up in the Doubleweave introduction, pages 94-95.

Treadling sequence: You are weaving layers of fabric for both blocks at the same time. The weft travels from weaving the top layer in one block and then the bottom layer in the other block.

You will alternate the colors of weft in the same sequence regardless of what block you are weaving. I assure you, this looks more complicated when it's written out than it really is when you are weaving.

Block A treadling: Treadle 1-2-3-4, alternating Color A weft color / shuttle with Color B weft color/shuttle.
Block B treadling: Treadle 5-6-7-8, alternating Color A shuttle with Color B shuttle in the same order.

So, the Block A treadling sequences for blue-green on top Block A and copper on top in Block B is:
Treadle 1: Pick of Color A shuttle
Treadle 2: Pick of Color B shuttle
Treadle 3: Pick of Color A shuttle
Treadle 4: Pick of Color B shuttle
Repeat until you have the block sizes desired.

To switch for Block B treadling so the colors switch layers in both blocks, note that the order you throw the shuttles is the same, but you have changed which treadles are being used.

Treadle 5: Pick of Color A shuttle
Treadle 6: Pick of Color B shuttle
Treadle 7: Pick of Color A shuttle
Treadle 8: Pick of Color B shuttle

Warp length: 76 inches planning for a 45-inch-long runner maximum, allowing 11.5 inches of warp per pattern repeat. My runner wound up being 38 inches off loom, unwashed.

Width in reed: 17.5 inches

Weft: Same yarns as warp.

Woven length on loom (measured off-tension): 39 inches

Hem allowance: I allowed 5 inches of warp on each end to tie the fringes. If you decide to weave the double layer hems, allow 3 inches on each end for hems.

Finished size after washing: 36 inches long × 14.75 inches wide

Shrinkage: 10%

Finishing: Damascus edging knots (4 threads from top layer / 4 threads from bottom layer—see "Resources," page 190) or tie overhand knots with 2 ends from top layer/2 ends per bottom layer.

WEAVE STRUCTURE
Crackle Weave

I consider Crackle Weave to be the shape-shifter of weave structures. The term "crackle weave" was coined by Mary Meigs Atwater because the patterning reminded her of the crackling designs in pottery glaze. Crackle Weave likely arrived in the United States with Swedish immigrants. In Sweden, this same weave structure is called "Jämtlandsdräll," which translates to English as "a weave from Jamtland."

Crackle Weave is based on the three-end point twill threading, using a straight twill tie-up. A variety of treadling sequences borrowed from other weave structures changes the interlacement of the warp and weft yarns while maintaining the same overall design from the profile draft. This allows us to create strikingly different pieces using the same warp and threading. It's great fun!

THREADING UNITS

The Crackle threading blocks are:
Block A: 1-2-3-2
Block B: 2-3-4-3
Block C: 3-4-1-4
Block D: 4-1-2-1

Four blocks of pattern can woven using only 4 shafts.

There is an important rule to remember when threading Crackle Weave. You must have a transition thread between blocks of pattern. This transition thread acts as a tie-down thread between blocks of pattern/threading. Conveniently, the transitional thread on 4 shafts is the same as the first thread in the threading sequence for the block you are threading.

Look back at the threading blocks. If you thread Block A next to Block B, there would be 2 threads on the same shaft (in this case, on Shaft 2) next to each other between Block A and Block B. The same is true between Block B and C, Blocks C and D, and Blocks D and A. Using a transition thread between blocks of threading eliminates this doubled warp

thread problem. So, here's what the threading blocks look like with the transition threads added between blocks. The transition threads are in red for each threading unit.

Block A: 1-2-3-2-1 (1 being the transition thread between Block A and Block B
Block B: 2-3-4-3-2 (2 being the transition thread between Blocks B and C)
Block C: 3-4-1-4-3 (3 being the transition thread between Blocks B and C)
Block D: 4-1-2-1-4 (4 being the transition thread between Blocks D and A)

Note: Only use the transition thread between different blocks of threading. If you have a profile draft where you repeat the threading for another segment of the same block, you only use the transition thread at the end of an entire section of threading for the block.

To illustrate the use of the transition thread, I've created a threading profile draft that has several blocks that repeat (A, C, and D) and a block that doesn't repeat (B).

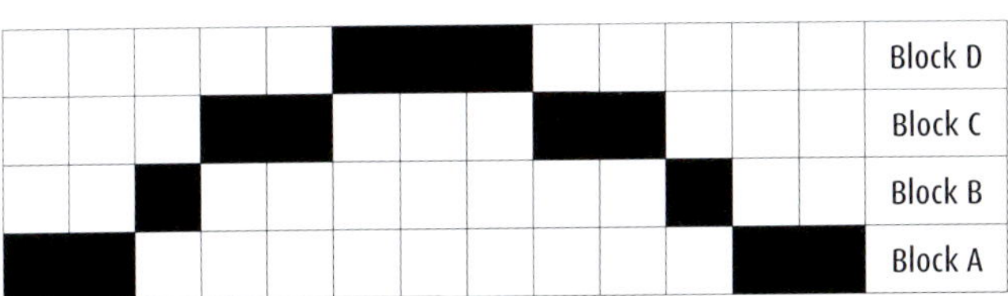

Figure 1

Here's the threading for the above profile threading draft (see figure 1). I have the transition threads in red type. Note that there is only one transition thread placed at the end of the threading unit repeats for a block of threading:

Start with a floating selvedge because this is a twill-based weave structure. A floating selvedge will ensure you catch the outermost warp thread with every pick.

Start with 2 blocks of threading for Block A:
1-2-3-2 (first square of A block threading)-1-2-3-2-1 (second A block square with transition thread on Shaft 1 at the end of threading sequence) The total threading sequence for the 2 threading squares is: 1-2-3-2-1-2-3-2-1.

1 Block of threading for Block B:
2-3-4-3-**2** (only 1 block so you need to have the transition thread at the end of the threading sequence)

2 Blocks of Block C:
3-4-1-4 (first C block)-3-4-1-4-3 (second C Block with transition thread in red)

3 Blocks of Block D:
4-1-2-1 (First Block D) 4-1-2-1 (second Block D)
4-1-2-1-4 (third Block D with transition thread in red)

2 Blocks of Block C:
3-4-1-4 (first block)-3-4-1-4-3 (second block with ends with transition thread in red)

1 Block of Block B:
2-3-4-3-2 (only one block, so include the transition thread at the end in red)

2 Blocks of Block A (end of profile draft):
1-2-3-2 (first block) 1-2-3-2 (second block A threading ends without a transition thread because we are at the end of threading and don't need to transition to another block)

End threading with another floating selvedge.

Do you have an 8-shaft loom? You can get a total of 8 blocks on and 8 shaft loom. The threading blocks for 8 blocks of pattern with the transition threads in red added between blocks are:
Block A: 1-2-3-2-**1** (1 is transition between Block A and Block B)
Block B: 2-3-4-3-2 (2 is transition between Block B and Block C)
Block C: 3-4-5-4-3 (3 is transition between C and D)
Block D: 4-5-6-5-4 (4 is transition between D and E)
Block E: 5-6-7-6-5 (5 is transition between E and F)
Block F: 6-7-8-7-6 (6 is transition between F and G)
Block G: 7-8-1-8-7 (7 is transition between G and H)
Block H: 8-1-2-1-8 (8 is transition between H and A)

With 8 shafts, just like in the 4-shaft instructions, if you have multiple colored-in squares for the threading in the same block, you repeat the threading without the transition for the number of squares and add the transition only on the last repeat of threading.

TIE-UP

The tie-up for 4 shaft Crackle is a straight twill tie-up (see figure 2). Treadles 1–4 are the twill tie-up, and treadles 5 and 6 are plain weave for hems and tabby pick treadling in some weave structures.

Figure 2: 4-shaft tie-up

		4	4		4
	3	3		3	
2	2				2
1			1	1	

Figure 3 is the standard tie-up for 8-shaft Crackle for twill form. There are other tie-up options available when you have 8 or more shafts. (See "Resources," page 190.) You need 10 treadles. The first 8 treadles weave pattern. The last 2 treadles on the right-hand side of the tie-up are plain weave. Notice how the tie-up is a straight twill progression on the first 8 treadles for the pattern. I've used two different colors to aid in seeing the tie-up progression. And yes, you can play with this tie-up for different warp/weft interlacement patterning.

Figure 3: 8-shaft tie-up

		8		8		8	8		8
	7				7	7		7	
6		6		6	6				6
	5		5	5			5	5	
4		4	4		4				4
	3	3			3		3	3	
2	2			2		2			2
1			1		1		1	1	

TREADLING

I used the 4-shaft tie-up and threading when I wove a sample to play with the structure. The treadling is where the fun really happens with Crackle. By using treadling sequences from different weave structures, you get the same overall fabric design but with thread interlacements that are different to give you a completely different appearance to the fabric design due to the interlacements of the warp and weft. The tie-up and threading remain the same for the entire sample.

For my sample, I used the profile draft for the Crackle project.

The tie-up is the straight twill tie-up on 4 shafts in the "Tie-Up" section above.

The threading is the twill threading on 4 shafts / 4 blocks of pattern earlier in this chapter.

Here are a few treadling options to get you started on exploration. All of these samples were woven on the same warp of WEBS 8/2 Tencel in "Straw" sett at 20 e.p.i. I also used different wefts in the samples to examine the way the warp and weft colors play together. The blue pattern weft is 5/2 Bamboo from WEBS, and the red weft sections are WEBS 8/2 Tencel. Both wefts worked well, and the 5/2 Bamboo gives a firmer hand to the fabric than using the 8/2 Tencel as weft. I also found that the red and gold Tencel wefts did not give as strong of an overall pattern due to being fairly close in color value. But it was worth the sampling!

OVERSHOT BLOCKS TREADLING

The treadling in this section is based on Overshot blocks, where you alternate a pick of supplemental pattern weft that is larger in grist than your warp yarn with a pick of tabby (plain weave) weft that is the same yarn as your warp thread. Each colored-in square of treadling on your profile draft represents a certain number of pattern picks that you determine based on weaving pattern blocks to square or not. Your sett should be calculated for the plain weave sett for the warp yarn you select.

For my sample, I used 8/2 Tencel for the warp sett at 20 e.p.i. and 5/2 Bamboo for the pattern weft with the 8/2 Tencel for the tabby/plain weave weft. I decided that each colored-in square of the profile draft equals 5 pattern picks. (That's a total of 10 picks

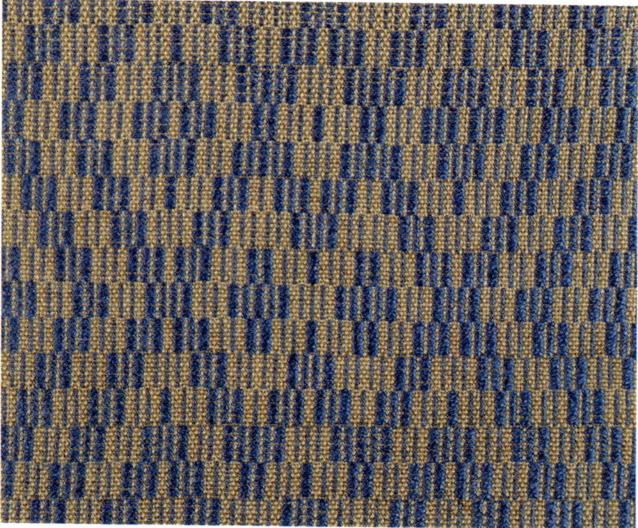

Crackle using Overshot treadling. 5/2 Bamboo pattern weft, 8/2 Tencel tabby weft

alternating 1 pattern pick with 1 plain weave base cloth pick.) You can change the size of the blocks however you want.

TIP

When I treadle any weave structure that uses a pattern weft and a plain weave / tabby weft, I start weaving from the right-hand selvedge with both shuttles, so my first picks of weft are going left.

The first pick is pattern weft. Press the treadle for the first pattern pick, throw pattern weft, then beat.

The next pick is the first pick of plain weave, which I set up as the left-hand plain weave treadle (because my shuttle is going left) in the pair of treadles for plain weave.

The third pick in the sequence is the second pick of pattern weft.

Then, the last pick in sequence is the second plain weave pick, which is the treadle on the right-hand side (the shuttle is going right) of the pair of plain weave/tabby treadles.

Here are the treadling sequences for each block of pattern. Notice that you repeat pressing the same block pattern treadle within the block, alternating the pattern pick with a plain weave pick:

Block A:
Treadling sequence: 1-5-1-6 repeat
Treadle 1 tied up to Shafts 1 and 2. One pick with pattern weft.
Treadle 5 tied up to Shafts 1 and 3 for first pick of tabby weft.
Treadle 1 tied up to Shafts 1-2. One pick pattern weft.
Treadle 6 tied up to Shafts 2 and 4 for second pick of tabby weft.

Block B:
Treadle 2 (tied up to Shafts 2 and 3), alternating with Treadles 5 and 6 for tabby weft.
Treadling sequence: 2-5-2-6 repeat.

Block C:
Treadle 3 (tied up to Shafts 3-4) alternating with Treadles 5 and 6 for tabby weft.
Treadling sequence: 3-5-3-6, repeat

Block D:
Treadle 4 (tied up to Shafts 1-4), alternating with Treadles 5 and 6 for tabby weft.
Treadling sequence: 4-5-4-6, repeat

Continue treadling the blocks as they are laid out on the profile draft in the project with 5 pattern picks/5 tabby picks per square on the profile draft. If you would like shorter blocks, reduce the number of pattern/tabby picks per block. For longer blocks, simply increase the number of pattern/tabby picks per block.

Here are the treadling sequences for each block using the tie-up and treadling (see figure 4). P is pattern pick, and T1 and T2 are the alternating tabby picks.

		4	4		4	Tie-Up
	3	3		3		
2	2				2	
1			1	1		

P						Block A Treadling sequence
				T1		
P						
					T2	
	P					Block B Treadling sequence
				T1		
	P					
					T2	
		P				Block C Treadling sequence
				T1		
		P				
					T2	
			P			Block D Treadling sequence
				T1		
			P			
					T2	

Figure 4

The table in figure 4 has only two pattern picks/ tabby picks. Just imagine how long a thread-by-thread treadling draft would be! The profile draft has the same information in a lot less space.

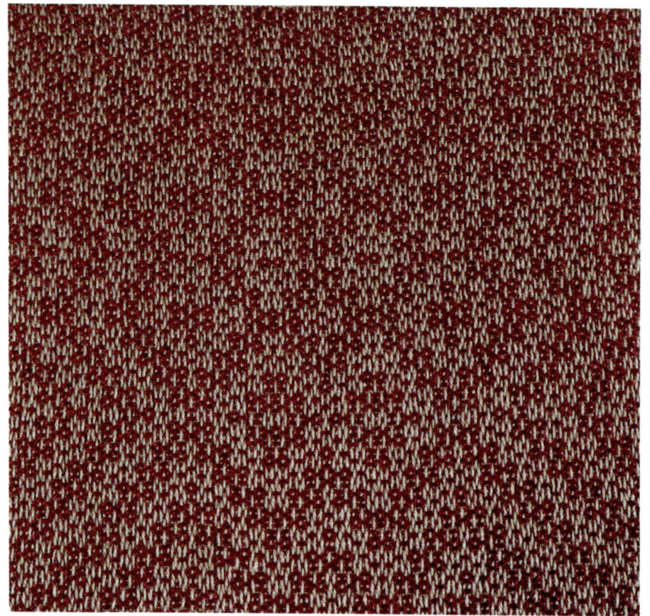
Crackle using Twill treadling with 5/2 Bamboo weft

TWILL TREADLING

Since Crackle is a 3-end point twill threading, twill treadling is a logical selection. However, the fabric pattern created doesn't look anything like point twill. It's delightful!

You use one shuttle with a weft that is a contrasting color to the warp, so the woven pattern shows up better.

The twill treadling sample pictured was woven on the same warp as the other samples. However, the sett of 20 e.p.i. with 8/2 Tencel was a bit open for the twill treadling. As an experiment (because that's another role that sampling can fill), I used Rust 5/2 Bamboo for the weft and wove a second sample section. The fabric with the 5/2 Bamboo has better body, and the sett of 20 e.p.i. works well for the pattern. The sample using Tencel for the weft convinced me to sett the Crackle Scarf project at 24 e.p.i.

Twill treadling is "tromp as writ," which means the treadling sequence is the same as the threading sequence. The tie-up is still the straight twill tie-up.

Tie-up:
Treadle 1: 1-2
Treadle 2: 2-3
Treadle 3: 3-4
Treadle 4: 1-4

Block A Threading: 1-2-3-2, with Shaft 1 added as transition thread to the next block
Block A Treadling: 1-2-3-2, with Treadle 1 added when transitioning to the next block

Block B Threading: 2-3-4-3, with Shaft 2 added as transition thread to the next block
Block B Treadling: 2-3-4-3, with Treadle 2 added when transitioning to the next block

Block C Threading: 3-4-1-4, with Shaft 3 added as a transition thread to the next block
Block C Treadling: 3-4-1-4, with Treadle 3 added when transitioning to the next block

Block D Threading: 4-1-2-1, with Shaft 4 added as a transition thread to the next block
Block D Treadling: 4-1-2-1, with Treadle 4 added when transitioning to the next block

I find that it's easier to keep track of my treadling for Crackle if I create a list next to the profile draft that has the treadling sequence for each block of pattern.
For the twill treadling, my list would be:

Block A: 1-2-3-2-1
Block B: 2-3-4-3-2
Block C: 3-4-1-4-3
Block D: 4-1-2-1-4

I use a magnetic board to hold my patterns when weaving. These are metal boards with magnetic strips that are usually sold for counted cross stitch embroidery or knitting patterns. I use the boards for weaving, and they work great! The boards are very handy to keep track of where I am when threading. Once I've threaded, I use the magnets to track my treadling.

SUMMER AND WINTER TREADLING

This 4-shaft sample uses the same straight twill tie-up but is woven using Summer and Winter treadling, weaving a pick of pattern weft followed by a pick of tabby / plain weave yarn that matches your warp yarn.

Weaving Crackle using the Summer and Winter treadling, the pattern picks alternate between two pattern treadles for pattern picks, with tabby picks alternating between each pattern pick.

Crackle using Summer and Winter treadling. 5/2 Bamboo pattern weft, 8/2 Tencel tabby weft

To ensure the Crackle pattern blocks touch each other at the corners, you need a total of 5 pattern picks per block. Yes, my "going left, press left / going right, press right" for the treadles still works for both the pattern and the tabby picks!

TREADLING SEQUENCE

Using the straight twill tie-up, your treadling sequences are using the treadles in the same order as the threading sequence, alternating with a plain weave pick for the base cloth. Pattern treadles are red in the treadling sequences.

Unlike Crackle which uses the twill treadling where you have to worry about transition threads between blocks, the use of tabby/plain weave picks between blocks eliminates worrying about transition treadles.

Block A: Pattern picks alternate between Treadle 1 (tied up to Shafts 1 and 2) and Treadle 2 (tied up to Shafts 2 and 3) for 5 picks ending with Treadle 1. Between each pattern pick, you alternate the tabby/plain weave picks between Treadle 5 and Treadle 6.

Block A Treadle: 1-5-2-6-1-5-2-6-1-5 (total of 5 pattern picks/5 tabby picks per Block A square in profile draft)

Block B: Pattern picks alternate between Treadle 2 (Shafts 2 and 3) and Treadle 3 (Shafts 3 and 4) for 5 pattern picks ending with Treadle 2. Alternate tabby Treadles 5 and 6 between each pattern pick.

Block B Treadle: 2-6-3-5-2-6-3-5-2-6

Block C: Pattern picks alternate between Treadle 3 (Shafts 3 and 4) and Treadle 4 (Shafts 1 and 4) for 5 pattern picks ending with Treadle 3. Alternate tabby Treadles 5 and 6 between each pattern pick.

Block C Treadle: 3-5-4-6-3-5-4-6-3-5

Block D: Pattern picks alternate between Treadle 1 (Shafts 1 and 2) and Treadle 4 (Shafts 1 and 4) for 5 pattern picks ending with Treadle 4. Alternate tabby Treadles 5 and 6 between each pattern pick.

Block D Treadle: 1-5-4-6-1-5-4-6-1-5

I don't know about you, but I find that following that fully written out treadling sequence for each block would be very tiring after a while!

It's so much simpler to use tabby between pattern picks alternating Treadle 5 and Treadle 6:
Block A: Treadle 1-2-1-2-1
Block B: 2-3-2-3-2
Block C: 3-4-3-4-3
Block D: 1-4-1-4-1

Did you notice a pattern in the treadling? The treadling pairs are the same as the threading pairs and the tie-up for each block of the straight twill threading and tie-up.

Block A: Shafts 1-2 tie-up and Treadle 1-2 repeated treadling pair
Block B: Shafts 2-3 tie-up and Treadle 2-3 repeated treadling pair
Block C: 3-4 tie-up and 3-4 and Treadle 3-4 repeated treadling pair
Block D: 1-4 tie-up and Treadle 1-4 repeated treadling pair

As you can see by comparing the photos of the three samples, the overall fabric design is similar in each sample, but by changing the treadling sequences, the interlacements of the warp and weft create patterns that look very different within the blocks.

These are just three variations of many possibilities you can use to "crackle" a weave structure. Put a sample warp on your loom and just start trying different treadling sequences used in various weave structures. Some may turn out less successful than you'd hoped, but many will be so much more than you anticipated! Have fun.

◆ PROJECT ◆

CRACKLE WEAVE SCARF

WITH TWILL TREADLING

After weaving my samples, I decided that the twill threading / treadling would be fun in a scarf woven with Tencel. However, I discovered when weaving the sample that a sett of 20 e.p.i. was too open to use 8/2 Tencel for both the warp and weft. Therefore, I decided to increase the ends per inch to 24, which makes a great fabric for a scarf with a lovely hand and drape. As a bonus, the scarf has amazing iridescence! To weave the scarf, the profile draft starts and ends with the border sections. The middle section of the draft is simply repeating weaving Blocks D, C, B, A, B, C, D, until you reach the scarf length you want. Be sure to leave enough warp after the middle section for a repeat of the border.

Yarns: 8/2 Tencel Valley Yarns from WEBS

Warp: Lemongrass, 600 yards

Weft: Navy Blue: 600 yards

Sett: 24 e.p.i. sleyed 2 ends/dent in 12-dent reed

Threading units: The profile draft has one colored-in square for each block of pattern. This means you need to add a transition thread at the end of each block of threading. The transition threads are in parenthesis at the end of the threading units for each block.
Block A: 1-2-3-2-(1)
Block B: 2-3-2-3-(2)
Block C: 3-4-1-4-(3)
Block D: 4-1-2-1-(4)

Tie-up: Straight twill tie-up
Treadle 1: Shafts 1 and 2
Treadle 2: Shafts 2 and 3
Treadle 3: Shafts 3 and 4
Treadle 4: Shafts 1 and 4
Treadle 5: Shafts 1 and 3 for plain weave hems if desired
Treadle 6: Shafts 2 and 4 for plain weave

EQUIPMENT NEEDED

4-shaft loom
12-dent reed (sley 2 ends per dent)
1 shuttle

Treadling sequence: Because each block of pattern is treadled one time, the treadling sequences include the transition treadle at the end of each block of treadling.
Block A: 1-2-3-2-1
Block B: 2-3-4-3-2
Block C: 3-4-1-4-3
Block D: 4-1-2-1-4

Calculate the number of warp ends: Each colored-in square of the threading represents 5 warp threads, because each block of pattern needs the transition thread for the next block.

There are 43 threading blocks. 43 blocks × 5 ends per block = 215 warp threads plus 2 floating selvedges (one on each selvedge) for a total of 217 warp ends.

Profile draft for Crackle

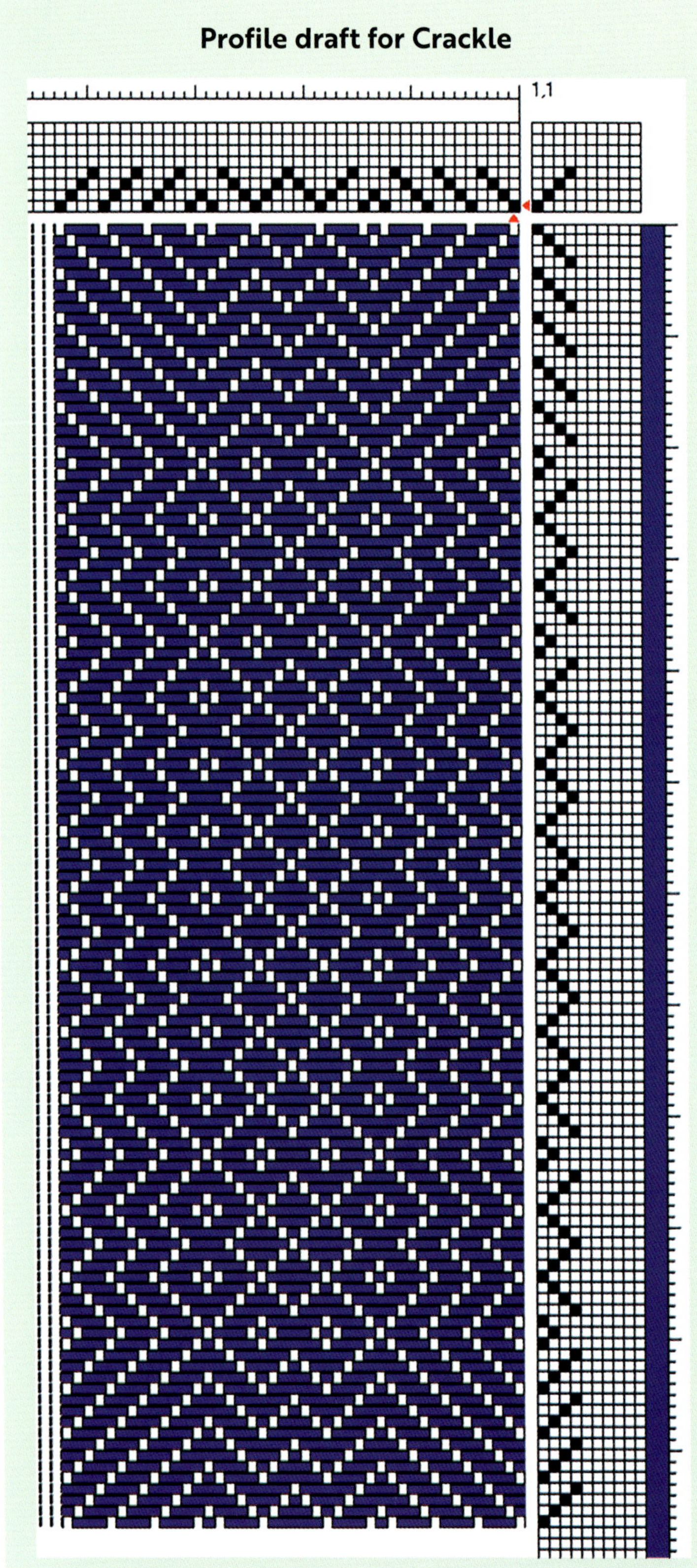

Calculate the number of heddles: To calculate the number of heddles on each shaft, you have to break down the threading units for each block. Since each block has a different combination of the 4 shafts, you need to figure out the threads per block by shaft and then add together the shaft totals used in each block for the total heddles on a shaft.

For this profile draft:
(1) There is only one colored-in square per threading block across the profile draft.
(2) Each profile draft threading block (colored-in square) represents 1 threading unit for that block.
(3) Because each threading unit is repeated one time, we need a transition thread at the end of every block of threading.

Block A: Threaded on Shafts 1, 2, and 3
There are 12 Block A's threaded as one unit 1-2-3-2-1 with the final thread in the unit being the transition thread between new blocks of pattern, for a total of 5 threads per threading unit/threading square.

Shaft 1: 12 blocks × 2 threads/block = 24 heddles (2 threads/block for pattern including transition)
Shaft 2: 12 × 2 threads/block = 24 heddles (2 threads/block for pattern)
Shaft 3: 12 × 1 thread/block = 12 heddles (1 thread/block for pattern)
Shaft 4: 0 threads/heddles threads/heddles per block threading

Block B: There are 12 squares of Block B threaded 2-3-4-3-2 (final thread on Shaft 2 is transition thread).
Shaft 1: 0 threads/heddles per block threading
Shaft 2: 12 × 2 threads/block = 24 heddles (2 threads/block for pattern including transition thread)
Shaft 3: 12 × 2 threads/block = 24 heddles
Shaft 4: 12 × 1 thread/block = 12 heddles

Block C: There are 10 squares of Block C threaded 3-4-1-4-3 (final thread on Shaft 3 is transition thread).
Shaft 1: 10 × 1 thread/block = 10 heddles
Shaft 2: 0 threads/heddles per block threading
Shaft 3: 10 × 2 threads/block = 20 heddles
Shaft 4: 10 × 2 threads/block = 20 heddles

Block D: There are 9 squares of Block D threaded 4-1-2-1-4 (final thread on Shaft 4 is transition thread).
Shaft 1: 9 × 2 threads/square = 18 heddles
Shaft 2: 9 × 1 thread/square = 9 heddles
Shaft 3: 0 threads/heddles per block threading
Shaft 4: 9 × 2 threads/square = 18 heddles

Now, to get the total number of heddles per shaft, add together the matching shafts in each block.

Shaft 1: Block A = 24, Block B = 24, Block C = 10, Block D = 18 ,for a total of 76 heddles
Shaft 2: Block A = 24, Block B = 24, Block C = 0, Block D = 9, for a total of 57 heddles
Shaft 3: Block A = 12, Block B = 24, Block C = 20, Block D = 0, for a total of 56 heddles
Shaft 4: Block A = 0, Block B = 12, Block C = 20, Block D = 18, for a total of 50 heddles

Check your work:
Shaft 1 = 52 heddles
Shaft 2 = 57 heddles
Shaft 3 = 56 heddles
Shaft 4 = 50 heddles
Total = 215 warp ends plus 2 floating selvedges equals 217 total warp threads

Weaving:
Hem allowance: Weave ½-inch plain weave at beginning and end of the scarf (alternate Treadle 5 tied-up Shafts 1-3 with Treadle 6 tie-up Shafts 2-4).

Pattern area: Weave according to the profile draft. The border treadling ends with Block A, Block B, Block A. Measure the length of this section and note the measurement so that you will have at least that amount of warp available for the border section on the other end.

Weave center length:
Block D
Block C
Block B
Block A
Block B
Block C
Repeat

Treadling sequences: Since the blocks are single repeats, each block ends with the transition treadling.
Block A: 1-2-3-2-1
Block B: 2-3-4-3-2
Block C: 3-4-1-4-3
Block D: 4-1-2-1-4

Warp length:
94 inches
60 inches of finished length after washing + 6 inches for take up/shrinkage + 6 inches fringe/tie-on + 20 inches thrum waste

Width in reed: 9 inches

Woven length on loom (measured off-tension): 65 inches without hems.

Finished size after washing:
62 inches long (pattern area only)
8 inches wide

Shrinkage: 10%

Finishing: Tie fringe in overhand knots of 8 ends per knot. Soak the scarf in warm water, and lay flat to dry. Tencel feels very stiff just off the loom and after washing. However, it softens up nicely when dry. Trim fringe to desired length.

WEAVE STRUCTURE
Satin, Sateen, and Damask

Satin uses a broken twill threading to create a warp-faced weave on one side (satin side of the fabric) and a weft-faced weave on the reverse side (sateen side of the fabric). True Satin requires a minimum of 5 shafts to weave the broken twill and creates warp and weft length floats over 4 threads. Traditionally, Satin is woven with very fine threads, so the satin side (warp length floats) of the fabric is very shiny and the tie-downs on each end of float are virtually invisible. The broken twill threading gives the fabric its characteristic shine, drape, and resistance to wrinkling.

Satin fabric originated in Quanzhou, China, during the early medieval time period (500 CE –1500 CE) and was woven exclusively with silk yarn. As the Silk Road trade routes expanded into the Middle East, the port of Quanzhou was called "Zaitun" in Arabic, and eventually the fabric produced in Quanzhou became commonly known as "Satin." Trade along the Silk Road eventually brought the fabric to Europe, first appearing in Italy in the 1100s.

You can weave a broken twill Satin on 4 shafts, but this is considered "false satin." Why? It has to do with the float length, appearance of the fabric, and industry standards created around Satin fabric. I have found that the shorter floats produced on 4 shafts break up the surface of the fabric more often, and the sheen is not as pronounced using 4 shafts as it is with the longer floats produced on 5 shafts.

Traditionally, Satin fabric is woven with long staple fibers such as silk that can be spun into very fine threads. As a handweaver, you can weave satin fabric using yarns with any fiber content. I've used yarns as large as 5/2 mercerized cotton for a lovely warp-prominent fabric on one side/weft-prominent fabric on the reverse side. However, you technically shouldn't call it "Satin," but rather "Satin Weave."

Damask is basically turned Satin woven in two or more blocks of pattern. The fabric pattern

is created by weaving warp-faced fabric in one block of pattern vs. weft-faced fabric in another block. There are some references that say Damask fabric must be woven on a draw loom or jacquard loom to be considered true Damask. True, the intricate patterning we usually associate with Damask textiles needs to use the flexibility provided by these looms to raise individual threads to create the patterns in the cloth. However, you can weave two blocks of Damask on 10 shafts. For those who have a computer driven dobby loom, the Damask world is your oyster!

If you have a 4-shaft loom, I have included information on weaving "False Satin." I have also included weaving "False Damask" on 8 shafts. This information is toward the end of the chapter, but I recommend reading the instructions for Satin and Damask, so you've studied all the tools in your toolbox.

SATIN WEAVE

As noted earlier, true Satin requires 5 shafts so the warp floats (satin side) and weft floats (sateen side) both float over 4 threads between tie-down/binder threads. You can use the same color of yarn for warp and weft for a solid color fabric. A particularly delightful use of Satin Weave is creating stripes of color. (See the Satin project on page 124.)

I'm going to start by explaining how to create the broken twill interlacement in the fabric, using the threading vs. using the tie-up.

There are two ways of creating the broken twill necessary for weaving satin:
(1) Thread the warp in broken twill and tie up the treadles as straight twill, or
(2) thread the warp as straight twill and use the tie-up to create the broken twill.

Some weaving references insist that the broken twill must be created in the threading. This is not "cast in stone."

I am a fan of using the straight twill threading and creating the broken twill with the tie-up. This makes threading so much easier. And in my book, easier is better.

SATIN COUNTER

Due to the broken twill structure, each warp thread interlaces with the weft at a different interval, depending on what shaft(s) are being lifted. The weft threads hold down the ends of the warp floats on the satin side of the fabric. The weft threads that hold the ends of the warp floats on the satin side of the fabric are called "stitchers" or "binders."

We want to make sure that the stitchers that hold each end of the warp floats are separated from neighboring stitcher threads, so we create the broken twill patterning for Satin. This separation is called the "Satin Counter."

The Satin Counter is a simple formula for determining how to create the broken twill in the tie-up, so the warp (satin side) and weft floats (sateen side) travel the same distance, but the tie-down stitcher threads don't create a diagonal line in the fabric when we press the treadles in order.

There are two rules for determining the Satin Counter based on the 5 shaft Satin threading unit of 1-2-3-4-5:

1) The Satin Counter can never be 1, or the interlacement of warp and weft creates straight twill. This leaves 2, 3, 4, 5.
2) The counter also can never be 1 less than the total number of shafts used in the threading unit or it creates twill going in the opposite direction. We are using 5 shafts. 5–1 = 4. That leaves us with 2 and 3.

This means that the shafts that are tied up must be separated by 2 or 3 shafts when you tie up the next treadle.

This may make more sense in seeing it laid out on tie-up grids comparing straight twill with broken twill for satin. These tie-ups are for rising shed looms, and you are raising one shaft per treadle. Why only one shaft? Because it's easier to raise one shaft than it is to raise four shafts with one treadle, especially if you have a large loom.

When weaving satin on a rising shed loom, the side of the fabric that you are looking at while weaving will have the weft floats (sateen side). The reverse side of the fabric will have the warp floats for the satin side of the fabric.

The draft in figure 1 shows 5 shafts with a straight twill threading and a straight twill tie-up for a rising shed loom. We get diagonal lines with 4 end weft floats (blue) tied down by warp threads (white), because we are raising one warp thread as a binder/stitcher with each treadle/pick of weft. Remember, we are looking at the sateen side of the fabric when we weave, and the draft shows the sateen/weft floats side of the fabric.

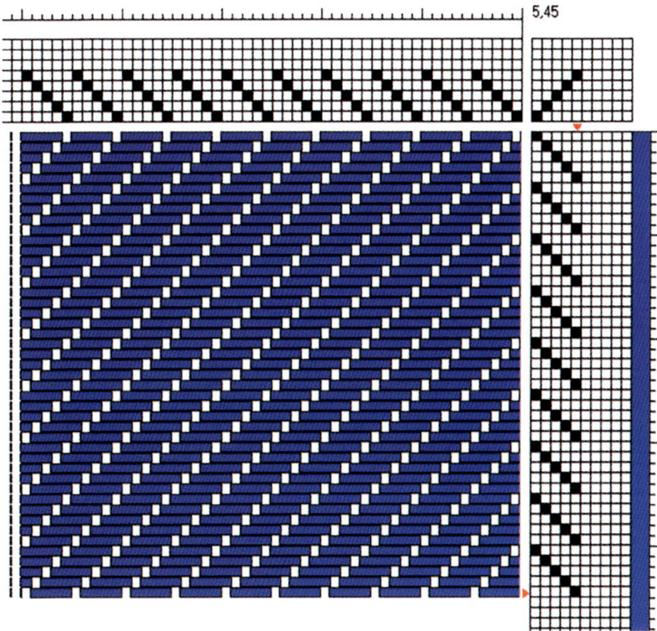

Figure 1: Straight twill threading, treadling, and tie-up

Step 1: The tie-up starts with Treadle 1 tied up to Shaft 1. Our Satin Counter stitcher intervals are 2 and 3. In the tie-up grids in figures 2–5, the separations for the Satin Counter are colored yellow. Note that, when counting the separation, you include the position of the thread on the previous treadle when counting the separation of shafts for the stitcher warp tie-downs.

Step 2: For Treadle 2, you want it to leave at least 2 warp threads down and lift the next warp thread in the broken twill sequence. So leave Shaft 1 and 2 down (colored yellow) and lift Shaft 3 (see figure 2). There's the separation of 2 from our Satin Counter formula.

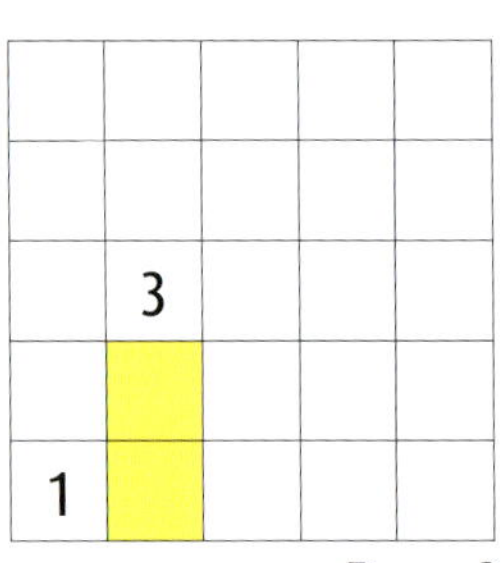

Figure 2

Step 3: Now you want to separate the next warp thread on Treadle 3 by two threads from the thread on Treadle 2, so Treadle 3 is tied up to Shaft 5 (see figure 3).

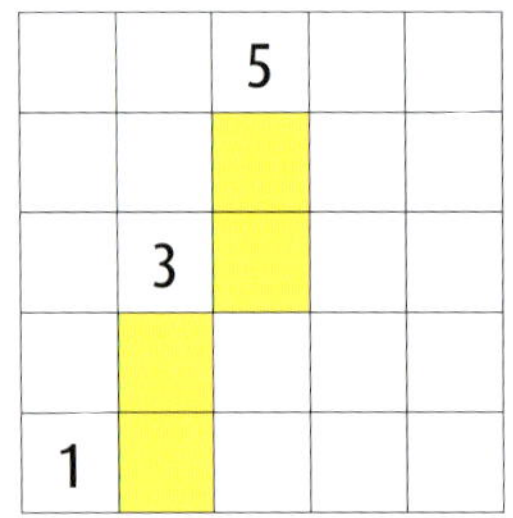

Figure 3

Step 4: For Treadle 4, Shafts 2 and 4 still have not been tied up, so you can either tie up to Shaft 2 or 4. Remember, you need a 2 or 3 shaft separation for the broken twill. If you tie up Treadle 4 to Shaft 4, that means that, if you raise a warp thread on Shaft 4, this warp thread is right next to the warp thread on Shaft 5 on Treadle 3. So Treadle 4 is tied up to Shaft 2, which is a 3-thread separation from the thread on Shaft 5 (see figure 4).

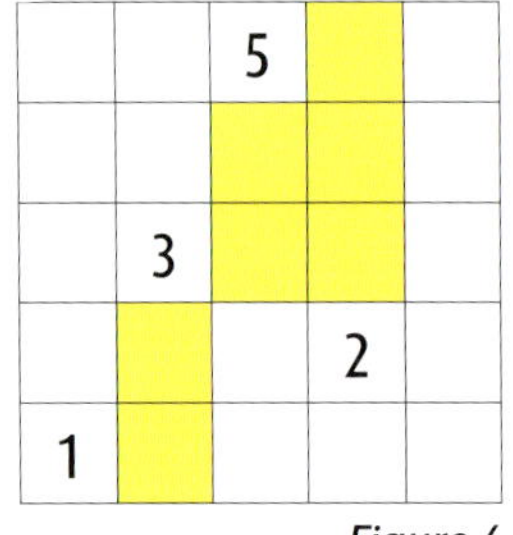

Figure 4

Step 5: Treadle 5 is tied up to the last available shaft, which is Shaft 4. You still get a 2-thread separation from the warp thread on Shaft 2, so you are good to go! (See figure 5.)

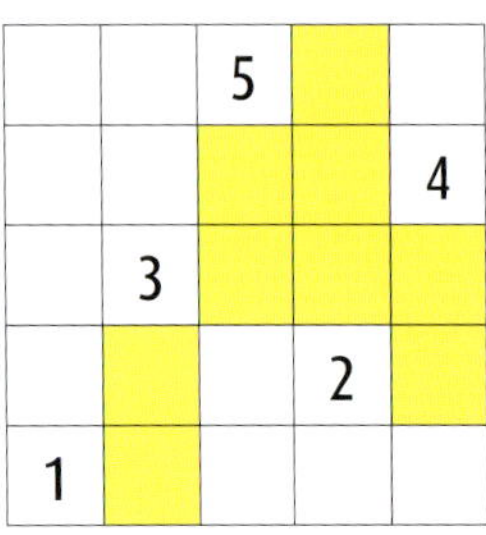

Figure 5

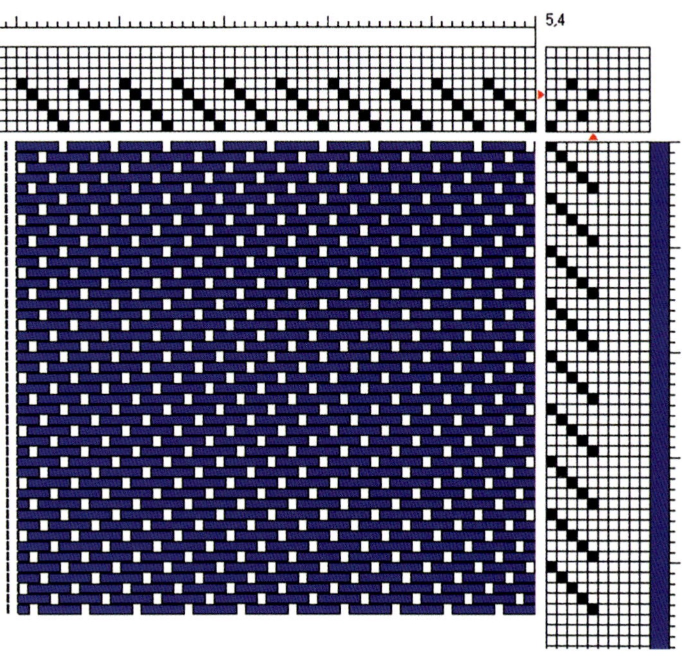

Here's what the drawdown looks like with the straight twill threading, broken twill tie-up, and treadling 1-2-3-4-5. The white threads in the drawdown are the stitchers/binders. The woven pattern is a broken twill where no two stitcher/binder threads are next to each other. Perfect.

A tie-up as follows also works to weave broken twill. Note that no two stitchers are next to each other in sequence, and you still maintain either a 2- or 3-thread separation:

Treadle 1: Shaft 1
Treadle 2: Shaft 4
Treadle 3: Shaft 2
Treadle 4: Shaft 5
Treadle 5: Shaft 3

OVERVIEW

1) **Satin** is a broken twill weave structure featuring warp floats on one side of the fabric. The other side of the fabric is considered **sateen** and features weft floats. The warp and weft floats do not change sides of the fabric. True Satin is woven on 5 shafts. The warp floats on the satin side are over 4 weft threads. The weft floats on the sateen side are over 4 warp threads.

Using the tie-up to create broken twill with straight twill threading and treadling

2) **Damask** is based on the Satin weave structure except the warp and weft floats change sides of the fabric depending on the threading in a block. You need 5 shafts per block of threading. For example: Block A is threaded on Shafts 1–5 and Block B is threaded on shafts 6–10.

3) **False Satin** is a broken twill woven on 4 shafts. The warp floats are over 3 weft threads, and the weft floats are over 3 warp threads.

4) **False Damask** is woven on 4 shafts per block of pattern threaded on a broken twill threading or straight twill threading with a broken twill tie-up. The blocks create pattern in the fabric with blocks that are warp float dominant blocks vs. weft float dominant blocks.

5) Since satin is based on broken twill, which technically uses a broken twill threading, the twill floats don't travel in a straight line in the fabric. However, it's easier to thread the warp using a straight twill threading and then break up the twill lines using the tie-up.

6) Tie up your loom so that you are raising one shaft at a time for the tie-down threads of the broken twill. It's easier to raise one shaft than it is to raise 4 shafts with one treadle on a jack loom. Using this single-shaft tie-up, you will be looking at the back/sateen side of the fabric. This is actually good! (See #7 below.)

Tie up the broken twill so you can press the treadles in order to achieve the broken twill patterning:
Treadle 1 tied up to Shaft 1
Treadle 2 tied up to Shaft 3
Treadle 3 tied up to Shaft 5
Treadle 4 tied up to Shaft 2
Treadle 5 tied up to Shaft 4

Refer to the section on the Satin Counter earlier to learn how to determine the order that the shafts are tied up to create the proper floats for satin.

7) Weaving with the sateen (weft floats) side on top makes it much easier to beat the fabric evenly and catch errors. Press the weft into place so that the weft threads lie next to each other. Use a shallow

Note the weft-faced (Sateen) and warp-faced (Satin) sides of the fabric.

weaver's angle. If your twill angle of the weft starts to go in the opposite direction, you are pressing the wrong treadle! This reversal of the twill will really show on the satin side by producing really long warp direction floats. No, I didn't do this on purpose, and I found the errors after I took the scarf off the loom. I decided a close-up photo of the mistake makes a good illustration of this easy-to-do error.

8) **Use floating selvedges!** Instead of adding two warp threads to the warp chain for the floating selvedges, simply use the first and last warp threads in the warp chain as the floating selvedges. Thread the straight twill, starting with the second warp thread in the chain. If it doesn't work out even at the last warp threads, it doesn't matter for pattern in satin. Just thread until you get to the last warp thread, then make the last warp thread a floating selvedge.

9) **Yarn selection:** Shiny yarns produce the dramatic color change satin is known for when light hits the fabric. Note the iridescence on the weft-faced side in the photo. You can use other fiber content such as wool, cotton, or linen to make striking stripe designs by taking advantage of the warp-dominant coverage of the weave structure.

Yarn size matters, but not as much as you might think. Keep in mind what the fabric will be used for and how long the float lengths will be, depending on the sett for the yarn you are using. Generally, you use the same size yarn for the warp and weft. However, you can use a finer yarn for the weft than you do for the warp. You can also use yarn with different fiber content. For example, use Tencel for the warp and weave with cotton.

10) You may need a closer warp sett for the warp than the "typical" twill sett for a yarn, especially if it's a slippery yarn like silk or Tencel. I've found that adding 4 more ends per inch than the "typical" twill sett when using slippery yarns works well. For example, if a yarn wraps to 16 e.p.i. for plain weave, the typical twill sett would be 20 e.p.i. However, for satin, I've found that 24 e.p.i. works better for satin. How to know for certain? Weave a sample!

Notice the two lines. These are two treadling errors created by not pressing Treadle 5 at the end of the sequence. If you do this, on the weft-faced side the twill progression starts to travel in the opposite direction. It's harder to see on the sateen side, but it shows up vividly on the Satin side.

MOVING TO 10 SHAFTS—DAMASK

The fabric is considered Damask when blocks of weft floats vs. blocks of warp floats create an overall pattern in the fabric. You can also think of this as warp-faced (Satin) vs. weft-faced (sateen) in the blocks of pattern. You need 5 shafts per block of pattern.

With 10 shafts, you can create two blocks of pattern—you can have satin (warp floats) in Block A and sateen (weft floats) in Block B. If you weave with a contrasting color of yarn, when the weft is dominant in a block, the block will be the color of the weft being used. The warp-faced blocks will be the color of the warp threads. For example: The entire warp is yellow yarn, and your weft is red. When the block is being treadled for Block A warp floats, the block will be yellow (with tiny spots of red). The Block B threading blocks are weft-dominant, and the color of Block B threading will be red with tiny spots of yellow. By changing the tie-up, you can change warp-faced to weft-faced over the surface of the fabric.

The warp is threaded in straight twill. Shafts 1–5 are assigned to Block A. Shafts 6–10 are assigned to Block B.

The tie-up is a broken twill on 5 shafts in each of the blocks. The key to the tie-up is that the opposite block is tied up as a reverse image of the other block of pattern. In other words, what goes up in Block A stays down in Block B, and what goes up in Block B stays down in Block A.

In figure 6, I have the tie-up for two blocks of Damask. In both tie-ups, I have colored in the squares that create the stitchers in each block. Note that when you treadle for Block A, the stitcher warp thread/shafts go up, so you will have the weft showing between each tie-down. At the same time, in Block B everything except the stitchers go up, so it creates warp floats between the stitchers.

The reverse happens when you treadle for Block B. When you treadle for Block B, the stitchers go up in Block B threading, creating weft floats, while in the Block A threading everything except the stitchers raise, creating warp-length floats.

Here's what the tie up looks like for two blocks of Damask (see figure 6). I have colored the stitcher warp threads yellow in each block simply as a reference. If there is not a number in the square, that means that shaft is not tied up. If you look at the tie-up, you can see that what goes up in Block A stays down in Block B on the first 5 treadles, and in the next 5 treadles, what goes up in Block B stays down in Block A.

Here's what the thread-by-thread draft looks like (figure 7):

Figure 6

10	10		10	10			10			Block B tie ups
9	9	9	9						9	
8		8	8	8		8				
7	7	7		7				7		
	6	6	6	6	6					
		5			5	5		5	5	Block A tie ups
				4	4	4	4	4		
	3				3		3	3	3	
			2		2	2	2		2	
1						1	1	1	1	
Weft floats in Block A/ warp floats in Block B					Warp floats in Block A/weft floats in Block B					

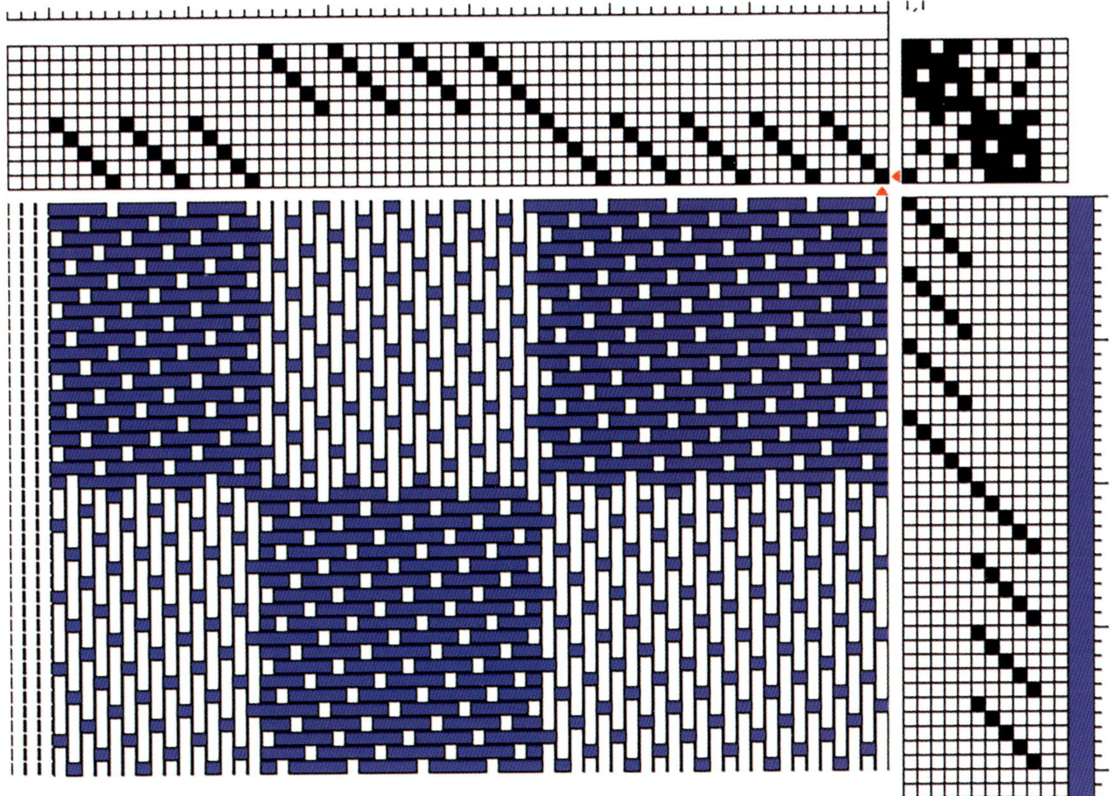

Figure 7: Thread-by-thread draft of two blocks of Damask

Figure 8

15	15		15	15	15	15		15	15			15			
14	14	14	14		14	14	14	14						14	
13		13	13	13	13		13	13	13		13				Block C tie ups
12	12	12		12	12	12	12		12				12		
	11	11	11	11		11	11	11	11	11					
10	10		10	10			10				10		10	10	
9	9	9	9						9	9	9	9	9		
8		8	8	8		8				8		8	8	8	Block B tie ups
7	7	7		7				7		7	7	7		7	
	6	6	6	6	6						6	6	6	6	
		5			5	5		5	5	5	5		5	5	
				4	4	4	4	4		4	4	4	4		Block A tie ups
	3				3		3	3	3	3		3	3	3	
			2		2	2	2		2	2	2	2		2	
1						1	1	1	1		1	1	1	1	

Weft floats in Block A, warp floats in Blocks B and C | Weft floats in Block B, warp floats in Blocks A and C | Weft floats in Block C, warp floats in Blocks A and B

MORE SHAFTS = MORE DESIGN FUN!

If you have 15 shafts, you can weave three blocks of pattern. Threading for Block A is on Shafts 1–5, Block B is Shafts 6–10, and Block C is Shafts 11–15. The tie-ups work the same, so you have weft floats in Block C and warp floats in the other two blocks (see figure 8).

Here's what a tie-up for 3 blocks of Damask looks like. Again, I have colored the squares in the tie-up that control the stitchers. When you treadle for a block, you are raising the stitchers for that block, and in the other blocks the stitchers stay down. You need 15 shafts and 15 treadles. Again, only the shafts that are tied up are marked in the tie-up boxes. If there's not a number in a box, don't tie up that shaft.

FALSE SATIN AND FALSE DAMASK ON 4 OR 8 SHAFTS

If you have a 4- or 8-shaft loom, you can weave what is considered False Satin on 4 shafts and False Damask on 8 shafts. The fabric will look very similar to the Satin/Damask weave structures, but they are considered "false" because you can't get a true Satin Counter-based separation between the shafts/threading repeats creating the broken twill like you can on 5 shafts. At each threading point, you will have two shafts that are next to each other between blocks, creating either 3/1 or 1/3 twill floats. The shorter floats result in less sheen than Satin, but you still get a weft-dominant vs. warp-dominant fabric.

4-SHAFT FALSE SATIN THREADING AND TIE-UP

As with 5-shaft Satin, on 4 shafts you will have weft floats on one side of the fabric and warp floats on the opposite side.

Thread the warp in a straight twill threading 1-2-3-4, then repeat.

Tie-up: You will only be raising the stitcher warps. When weaving, you will be looking at the weft-faced side of the fabric. As I mentioned earlier, it is easier to press the weft into place evenly when looking at the weft-dominant side. It's also easier to see a treadling error on the weft-dominant side of the fabric. If the twill line starts going in the opposite direction when you treadle, you pressed an incorrect treadle.
Treadle 1: Tied to Shaft 3
Treadle 2: Tied to Shaft 1
Treadle 3: Tied to Shaft 4
Treadle 4: Tied to Shaft 2

Treadling order: Treadle 1, 2, 3, 4 repeat

8-SHAFT FALSE DAMASK THREADING AND TIE-UP

You can create two blocks of False Damask pattern on 8 shafts. Shafts 1-4 are assigned to Block A and shafts 5-8 are assigned to Block B. I actually love False Damask—it makes very striking fabric especially if your weft thread is a different color than your warp threads. The weft-faced blocks are a completely different color than the warped faced blocks—it's almost like magic!

Thread each block in straight twill threading, repeating each threading until you have the width you desire for the block:
Block A: 1-2-3-4 (repeat until width of block is achieved)
Block B: 5-6-7-8 (repeat until width of block is achieved)

Tie-up a broken twill (see figure 9). The stitcher warps are highlighted in yellow. If there is not a number in a yellow box, that indicates the stitcher, but you don't raise the stitcher warp with that block. When you are raising the stitchers only in a block, you have weft-faced floats. In the opposite block, you raise everything except the stitchers to get warp-faced floats:

Figure 9: 8-shaft False Damask tie-up

8	8		8			8		Block B tie up
	7	7	7	7				
6	6	6					6	
5		5	5		5			
		4		4	4		4	Block A tie up
3					3	3	3	
			2	2	2	2		
	1			1		1	1	
Weft floats in Block A, warp floats in Blocks B				Warp floats in Block A, warp floats in Blocks B				

Once you determine the stitcher warps to create the broken twill, in one block (A), you will raise only the stitcher warps, but in the other block (B), you will raise everything but the stitcher warps. The reverse happens for Block B—you raise all the stitcher warps as opposed to Block A, where you raise everything that is not a stitcher warp. Read that again while looking at the tie-down.

Time to put all this information into practice on your loom!

◆ PROJECT ◆

SATIN WEAVE STRIPED SCARF

ON 5 SHAFTS

The project is woven on 5 shafts, so you need an 8-shaft loom. However, you can weave this on 4 shafts using the instructions at the end of the instructions for False Satin on page 123. You will still get satin stripes on one side of the scarf and sateen on the other side.

Profile drafts are an excellent way to lay out stripes in a project. You use the proportions of the blocks to create the stripe widths and assign a stripe color to each block. Simply decide the width in the warp each colored-in square of the threading draft represents.

When choosing your yarns, remember that Satin requires a closer sett than normal for twill threading so you will get warp-dominant on one side of the fabric and weft-dominant on the other.

To calculate the sett for Satin, I've found that determining the plain weave sett by doing the wrap test and adding 4 ends per inch for twill works well for yarns such as mercerized cotton that aren't terribly slippery. However, if I use a very slippery yarn such as silk or Tencel, adding 8 threads per inch to the plain weave sett works best. The only way to know for sure is to sample the yarn you are using!

For example: The 8/2 Tencel in the project wraps to 32 wraps per inch which equals a plain weave sett of 16 e.p.i. Normally, the twill sett would be 20 e.p.i. Tencel is slippery, and I found that a sett of 24 e.p.i. works best for Satin. However, Tencel yarn from one manufacturer can be very different from another manufacturer, even if the yarns are labeled as the same size. Once you pick your yarn, doing a small sample will confirm or disprove your decision for the warp sett.

EQUIPMENT NEEDED

8-shaft loom (for Satin) or 4-shaft loom (False Satin)
1 shuttle
12-dent reed sleyed 2 ends per dent for 24 e.p.i.

Profile draft to lay out stripes for the project

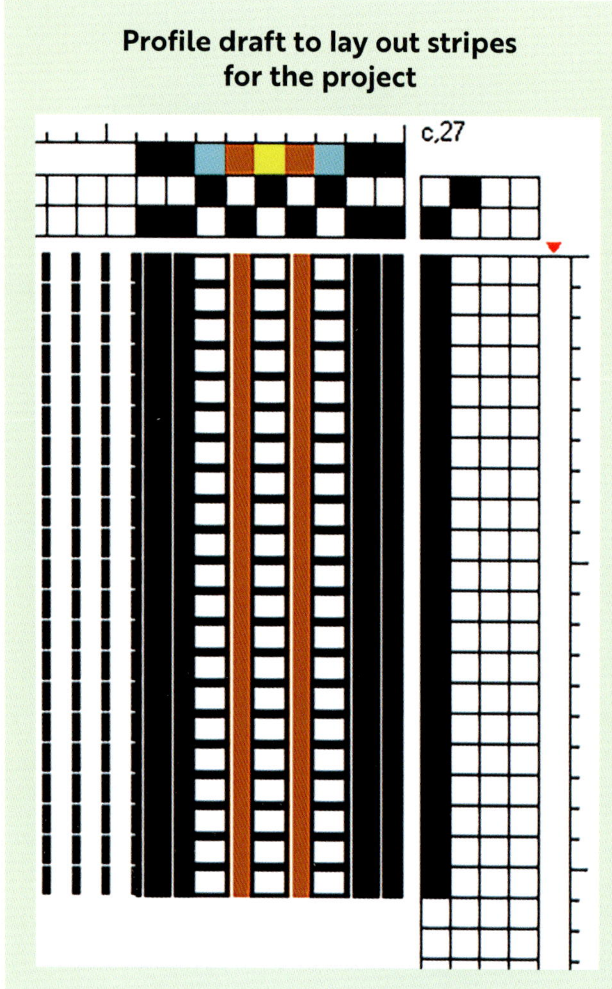

Using the profile draft to lay out the satin stripes, I decided that each threading square represents 1 inch of warp width.

Starting from the profile tie-up:
There are 2 blocks in Block A – that represents two inches of Stripe Color #1 (black).
The next square in Block B is 1 inch in Color #2 (spice).
The next square in Block A is 1 inch of Color #3 (teal).
The next square in Block B is 1 inch Color #4 (variegated fire).
The next square in Block A is 1 inch Color #3 (spice).
The next square in Block B is 1 inch Color #2 (teal).
The last two squares in Block A are 2 inches Color #1 (black).

If you have an 8-shaft loom, you can choose to weave this scarf as Satin stripes or as two blocks of False Satin pattern.

If you have 10 or more shafts available, you can choose to weave two blocks of Damask, which can be treadled as contrasting warp-faced with weft-faced stripes or as two blocks to create more pattern possibilities.

Equipment needed:
8-shaft loom (for Satin) or 4-shaft loom (False Satin)
1 shuttle
12-dent reed sleyed 2 ends per dent for 24 e.p.i.

Yarns: 8/2 Tencel by WEBS Valley Yarns for the warp and weft

Warp:
Black
Dark teal
Spice
Fire (variegated)

Weft: 8/2 Tencel in Spice

Sett: 24 e.p.i.

Threading Units: Thread in straight twill 1-2-3-4-5 when using 5 shafts. If you are weaving two blocks, please see pages 121-122 for 8 and 10 shaft threading.

Calculate the number of warp ends: Each square of the profile represents 1 inch of weaving width at 24 e.p.i.
9 squares × 24 e.p.i. = 216 warp ends
The first and last warp threads are used as floating selvedges. Due to the stripes, I did not add warp threads for the floating selvedges in the warp end count. The number of warp ends does not thread a complete threading unit at the end. This is fine. Simply thread as far as you can, and use the last warp thread for a floating selvedge.

Calculate the number of heddles: This is a straight twill threading over 5 threads, with one thread per shaft in each threading repeat. Each square of threading represents 1 inch of stripe width at 24 e.p.i.

There are 9 inches (squares) total = 216 warp ends. Divide 216 warp ends by 5 shafts = 43.2 heddles per shaft.

Or you could look at it as 24 divided by 5 = 4.8 threading repeats per square of threading. Well, that's pretty close to 5.

Since we are just checking for heddle count per shaft, to keep things simple, each block represents 5 threading repeats per shaft x 9 threading squares = 45 heddles per shaft.

Tie-up: This tie-up raises the stitcher ends only for the broken twill. With this tie-up, you will be looking at the weft-dominant (Sateen) side of the fabric when weaving. On the opposite (bottom) side of the fabric will be the warp-dominant Satin stripes.
Treadle 1: Shaft 1
Treadle 2: Shaft 3
Treadle 3: Shaft 5
Treadle 4: Shaft 2
Treadle 5: Shaft 4

Treadling sequence: Treadle 1-2-3-4-5 (repeat), weaving only with the color of yarn you have selected for the weft.

Warp length: 94 inches

Width in reed: 9 inches

Woven length on loom (measured off-tension): 65 inches

Finished size after washing: 8.25 inches wide × 62.5 inches long (plus fringe)

Shrinkage: 9%

Finishing: Tie the scarf fringe in overhand knots of 6 warp ends per knot. Soak scarf in cool water, then lay flat to dry. The scarf will feel stiff when wet, but once dry and handled, it softens up beautifully. Trim fringe to desired length.

WEAVE STRUCTURE

Overshot

Unlike many weave structures that were brought to North America by immigrants, Overshot is a weave structure that has its roots in North America dating back to the 1700's. Overshot's origins appear to be for use in coverlets.

Overshot is technically defined as a twill-derivative weave structure. The threading and tie-up are both based on straight twill. The twill-based threading allows for weaving a plain weave base cloth (sometimes referred to as the ground cloth) interlaced with supplemental pattern weft to create the overall fabric designs. It is a very versatile weave structure with an almost infinite number of design possibilities.

There are literally hundreds of drafts for Overshot, and once you understand the concept of plain weave base cloth with supplemental weft patterning, it's a very easy structure to weave. One of the first weaving projects I did independently as a new weaver was an Overshot pattern from *A Handweaver's Pattern Book*, a collection of 4-shaft drafts compiled by Marquerite Porter Davison.

I wove a lot of Overshot as my weaving life progressed. The more I wove, the more I contemplated how to create my own designs. To create my own designs, I needed to know more about how the weave structure works. In this section, I'll share with you how Overshot "works."

THREADING OVERSHOT

Overshot is a "twill derivative" weave structure. This means the threading and tie-up are based on twill.

Let's start by looking at straight twill on 4 shafts. For 4-shaft straight twill, the threading consists of 4 threads, threaded on shafts 1-2-3-4 repeat. Plain weave is woven with twill threading by raising every other thread with the tie-up.

The straight twill tie-up is:

Treadle 1: Shafts 1 and 2
Treadle 2: Shafts 2 and 3
Treadle 3: Shafts 3 and 4
Treadle 4: Shafts 1 and 4
Treadle 5: Shafts 1 and 3 for first pick of plain weave
Treadle 6: Shafts 2 and 4 for second pick of plain weave

TEN RULES FOR WEAVING OVERSHOT

Rule 1: The warp sett is based on the yarns used for the plain weave base cloth. See Rule #10.

Rule 2: The supplemental pattern weft is a larger grist yarn than the base cloth warp/weft, so the pattern weft covers the base cloth for a clean pattern. The rule of thumb is that your supplemental pattern weft should be approximately 2 times larger than the base cloth warp/weft. For example, you'll use an 8/2 cotton for the base cloth and a 5/2 cotton for the pattern weft.

Rule 3: Pay attention to the "squish-ability factor" (yes, I made up this term) of your pattern wefts. The more air in a yarn, the better it "squishes" into the intersections of the weft and warp interlacements. Think of it as compressing a feather pillow vs. a fiberfill pillow. The feather pillow has a lot of air between the feathers, and when you squeeze the pillow, you force the air out from between the feathers and can compress the pillow into a much smaller space. Compare this to a fiberfill pillow which has densely packed fiber without much air space between the fibers. You can't force much air out between the fibers, so the pillow does not compress as easily.

How does this relate to selecting yarns? When picking your pattern weft yarn, a softer, loftier yarn such as wool will compress and fit in the little spaces between the warp/weft intersections in the base cloth so you can use a larger grist of pattern weft yarn. However, if you use a pattern weft like mercerized cotton, the densely spun cotton yarn doesn't have much air incorporated in the yarn, and it won't compress as nicely into those little spaces between the warp and weft. This can distort your fabric at both the fell line and the selvedges. It's like packing a soft-sided duffel bag. The more you stuff into the bag, the more the sides bulge out. The same thing happens when stuffing too large or dense a pattern weft yarn between the plain weave warp/weft.

Rule 4: In a standard thread-by-thread Overshot draft, only the supplemental weft pattern picks are shown on the treadling. A profile draft treadling shows which block of the supplemental pattern weft shows on the top surface of the fabric to create the fabric pattern. (See information on Rising Shed vs. Sinking Shed looms on page 18.)

Rule 5: You must weave with two shuttles. One shuttle is wound with the base cloth weft which is the same size yarn as the warp yarn. The second shuttle contains the supplemental pattern weft yarn.

Rule 6: You alternate weaving one pick of pattern weft with one pick of base cloth weft. Because you are weaving plain weave with the base cloth weft, you must also alternate between the two treadles tied up for plain weave to weave the base cloth.

Rule 7: The pattern weft moves from the top side of the fabric to the back side of the fabric through the little holes created at the intersections of warp and weft of the base cloth. The pattern is created by floats of weft that travel over/under several warp threads. These pattern weft floats are built up with multiple picks of pattern weft to create blocks that make up the Overshot fabric designs. You need to be aware of how far those pattern weft floats travel on both the top and bottom sides of the fabric, so the floats don't get too long across the fabric surfaces. See Rule #8.

Rule 8: Pattern weft float lengths are dependent on how many warp ends traveled over or under and on the sett for a base cloth. For example, you may have a draft where the pattern weft goes over 10 base cloth warp ends and intend to use a base cloth sett of 24 ends per inch. When your pattern weft goes over 10 warp ends, the float will be just under ½ inch long. However, if you use a base cloth sett at 12 ends per inch, those pattern weft floats will be almost 1 inch long!

Rule 9: Shrinkage is your friend! Because the pattern weft moves between your top and bottom layers of fabric, you may need a bit more open base cloth sett than you might normally use for the base cloth yarn. When you take the fabric off the loom, the warp and weft threads will bend over and under each other, closing in the little holes at the warp/weft intersections. When you wet-finish the fabric, the warp and weft yarns will move even closer together, and the little holes in the base cloth will close up more. This moves your pattern wefts closer together as well to give you a more defined fabric pattern design.

Rule 10: Do a wrap test of your yarn to determine sett. Most sett charts are calculated for beating on an open shed, so the warp setts suggested in the charts are much closer than what a wrap test will give you for a yarn. When in doubt, weave a small sample to check the sett, pattern weft coverage, threading, tie-up, and treadling. You want to use the sett calculated by your wrap test so there is more space for the supplemental pattern weft to change sides of the fabric in the intersections between the warp and weft without distorting your fabric.

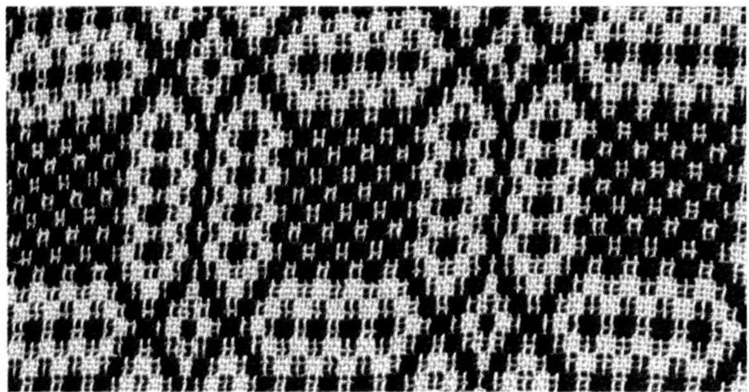

To weave straight twill, you treadle: Treadle 1, Treadle 2, Treadle 3, Treadle 4, repeat.
To weave plain weave on a twill threading/tie-up you alternate Treadles 5 and 6.

Now let's move on to Overshot.

The threading units for Overshot blocks are:
Block A: 1-2 (Shafts 1 and 2)
Block B: 2-3 (Shafts 2 and 3)
Block C: 3-4 (Shafts 3 and 4)
Block D: 1-4 (Shafts 1 and 4)

The Overshot block threading units are the same as the tie-up for weaving straight twill. And the tie-up for Overshot is the same as the tie-up for straight twill.

Now comes the tricky part: threading the blocks of pattern. Look at the threading units above. If you thread Block A next to Block B, then you have 2 threads next to each other that are on the same shaft. The same is true for Block B, next to Block C. If you have two threads next to each other on the same shaft, you get doubled warp threads between every block of pattern. This is a problem.

The solution to this problem is to eliminate one of those matching threads at the transition between the blocks. This means the two blocks share the same thread when transitioning between blocks.

Many books will show this sharing of the thread between blocks by circling the blocks of threading. I find this circling method very confusing.

Here's how I approach threading Overshot from a profile draft and dealing with the shared threads at the transitions to the new block of threading. When you thread Overshot, the general rule is a minimum of 2 repeats of the threading per block for a total of 4 threads per block. Yes, if you are using fine threads such as a 20/2, you can have each block of pattern represent more threading repeats, so your blocks of pattern are larger in the fabric design.

For the Overshot project, I used 2 repeats of threading per block and will do this for the example on page 131.

Let's start with a simple profile draft of 7 blocks.

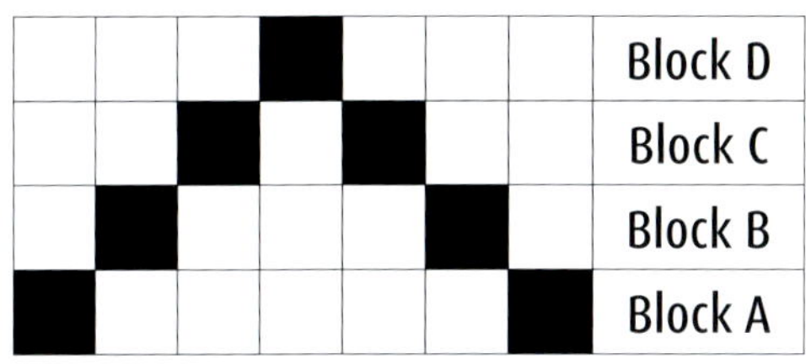

Figure 1

Important note! The blocks start in ascending order of A, B, C, D so you thread in ascending order and the pattern goes uphill. When the blocks change to descending order of D, C, B, A, the threading changes to descending order and the pattern goes downhill.

The threading for ascending order with 2 repeats of the threading per block is:
Block A: 1-2-1-2
Block B: 2-3-2-3
Block C: 3-4-3-4
Block D: 1-4-1-4

The threading for descending order is:
Block C: 4-3-4-3
Block B: 3-2-3-2
Block A: 2-1-2-1

Figure 2 shows what the profile draft looks like as a thread-by-thread draft doing a full threading of each block. I've marked the duplicated threads between blocks of threading in red. If I leave those duplicated threads between blocks, I have 2 warp threads on the same shaft next to each other that will give me doubled warp threads in those areas. That's not good.

To fix the doubled warp threads, I eliminate one of the extra threads on the same shafts between blocks. The threading now looks like figure 3.

The threads that are marked with yellow are now shared between the blocks. I have put arrows between the blocks to note block threading changes/shared warp threads.

Compare the threading in figure 2 and figure 3. Note that between Block C and Block D on the ascending side of the threading, the last thread in Block C is on Shaft 4 and the first thread in Block D is on Shaft 1. That means on the ascending side of the threading, Blocks C and D do not share a warp thread. However, on the descending side of the threading, Block D and Block C share a warp thread.

Figure 2

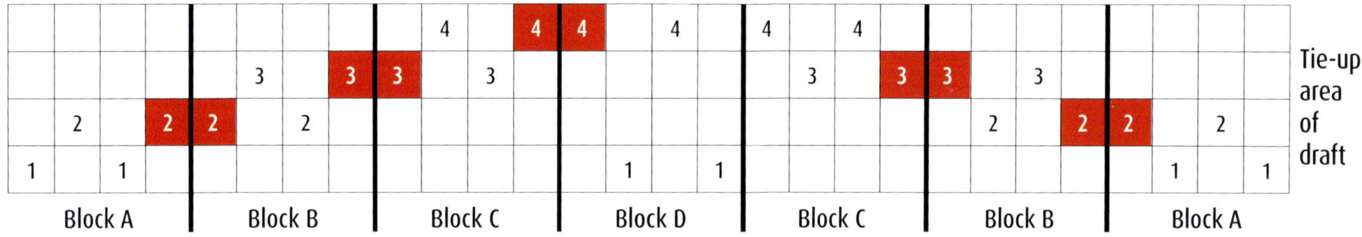

Figure 3

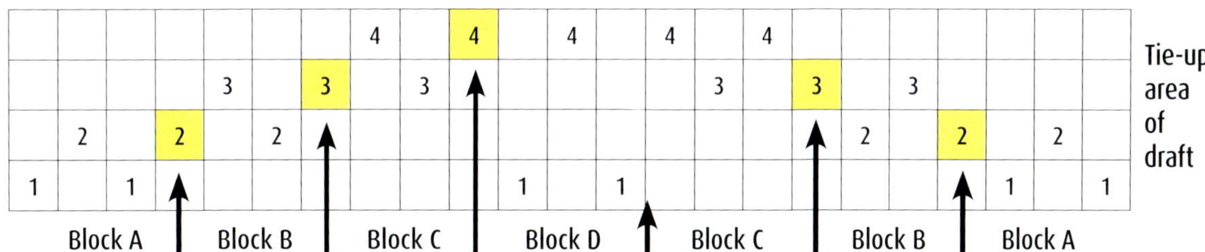

THREADING OVERSHOT DIRECTLY FROM A PROFILE DRAFT

You don't need to create a thread-by-thread draft to thread Overshot. You can thread directly from the profile draft as long as you remember about the shared threads between some blocks of threading.

Here's how I use profile drafts to thread Overshot. I'm using the profile draft in figure 1 and each colored-in square on the threading represents 2 repeats of the threading in a block.

1) I create the profile draft in my weaving software so I can see the overall design of the fabric. I print out the profile draft, and I write the threading unit repeats on the same paper in case I have a brain block while threading.

2) The tie-up is "home plate," and just like in baseball, everything starts at home plate.

3) The profile draft threading in figure 1 starts in ascending order. The first threading square is Block A, so I thread 1-2-1-2 for a single square of Block A.

4) The second threading square is on Block B, which is threaded 2-3-2-3. However, Block A ends on Shaft 2 and Block B begins on Shaft 2. I don't want two threads on the same shaft next to each other, so I skip the first thread in Block B on Shaft 2 and thread the rest of the sequence 3-2-3. The last thread in Block A is shared with Block B.

5) The next threading block is Block C which is threaded 3-4-3-4. However, Block B ends on Shaft 3, so I skip the first thread in the Block C threading unit and thread 4-3-4. Block B and Block C share the first thread on Shaft 3 in Block C.

6) The next threading block is Block D, which is 1-4-1-4. Block C ends on Shaft 4 and Block D starts on Shaft 1. So that I don't have to worry about a shared warp thread between the blocks, I thread Block D 1-4-1-4.

7) Now the profile draft is descending, so I switch my threading units to descending order. Block D ends on Shaft 4, and the descending threading order for Block C is 4-3-4-3. So, I skip the first thread in the Block C unit and thread 3-4-3.

8) Next is Block B descending, which is 3-2-3-2. Block C ends on Shaft 3, so I skip the first descending thread in Block B and thread 2-3-2.

9) Last is Block A descending which is 2-1-2-1. Block B ends on Shaft 2, so I skip the first descending thread in Block A and thread 1-2-1.

Written out step by step, this looks complicated, but you just must remember that if the threads between units are the same, skip the first thread in the next Block Unit threading.

TIE-UP

The tie-up for Overshot is a straight twill tie-up, shown in figure 4 as a profile tie-up.

			■	Block D
		■		Block C
	■			Block B
■				Block A
A	B	C	D	

Figure 4—Profile Tie-Up

Figure 5 shows the thread-by-thread tie-up for Overshot. The pattern block being treadled is listed on the bottom line (A, B, C, D). P1 and P2 are plain weave pick #1 and plain weave pick #2.

		4	4		4
	3	3		3	
2	2				2
1			1	1	
A	B	C	D	P1	P2

Figure 5—Thread-by-Thread Tie-Up

TREADLING

A profile draft only shows that the treadling is happening for the pattern picks in a block. You decide how many pattern picks each treadling square represents.

For example: If the profile draft has one square colored-in for treadling in Block D (figure 6), you can decide that square represents 3 picks of pattern weft. This means you throw the pattern weft for 3 total picks and at the same time alternate treadling the plain weave treadles between each pattern pick (figure 7).

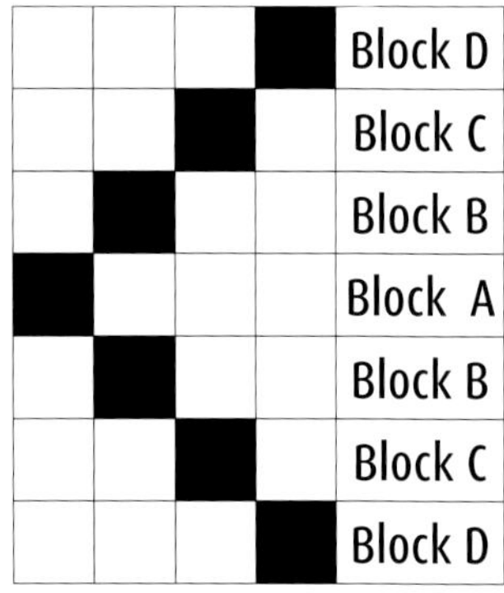

Figure 6—Profile Treadling

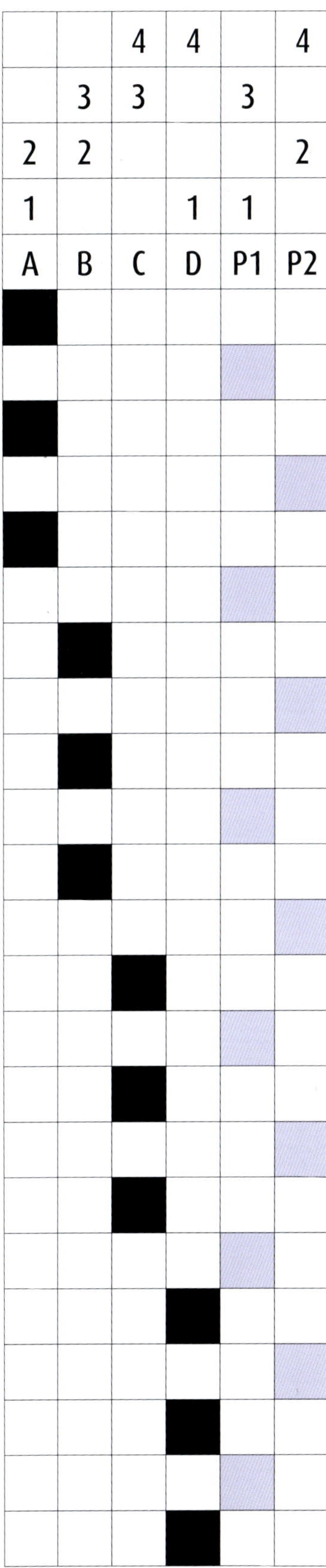

Figure 7—The ascending order of picks represented by the profile treadling in figure 6

The profile treadling is much easier to read. Once I decide how many pattern picks each colored-in treadling square represents, I can just treadle according to the treadling profile draft, with my left foot assigned to treadling to the pattern wefts and my right foot treadling the alternating plain weave picks between each pattern weft pick.

TIP! To help keep track of which treadle to press, I like to drop a treadle between the four pattern treadles and the two plain weave treadles. I have the first four pattern treadles tied up on the left side and treadle with my left foot. Then, I leave a treadle that is not tied up (dropped), then tie up the two plain weave treadles on the right-hand side that I treadle with my right foot. With this setup, I have less chance of mistakenly pressing the first plain weave treadle instead of the pattern treadle 4.

COMBINING PATTERN BLOCKS USING THE BLOCK TIE-UP FOR MORE PATTERN BLOCKS

You don't always have to treadle in the straight twill tie-up. You can change the order of treadling the blocks to get new fabric design. Or you can create larger pattern blocks by combining blocks with the tie-up. This is easily done with a profile draft, so you can quickly see the fabric design.

For example, you can create a profile draft using the straight twill tie-up.

Now change the order of the tie-ups! Here are some profile drafts where the design changes because I change the order of the tie-ups. It took me less than five minutes to create these three different fabric designs in my weaving software.

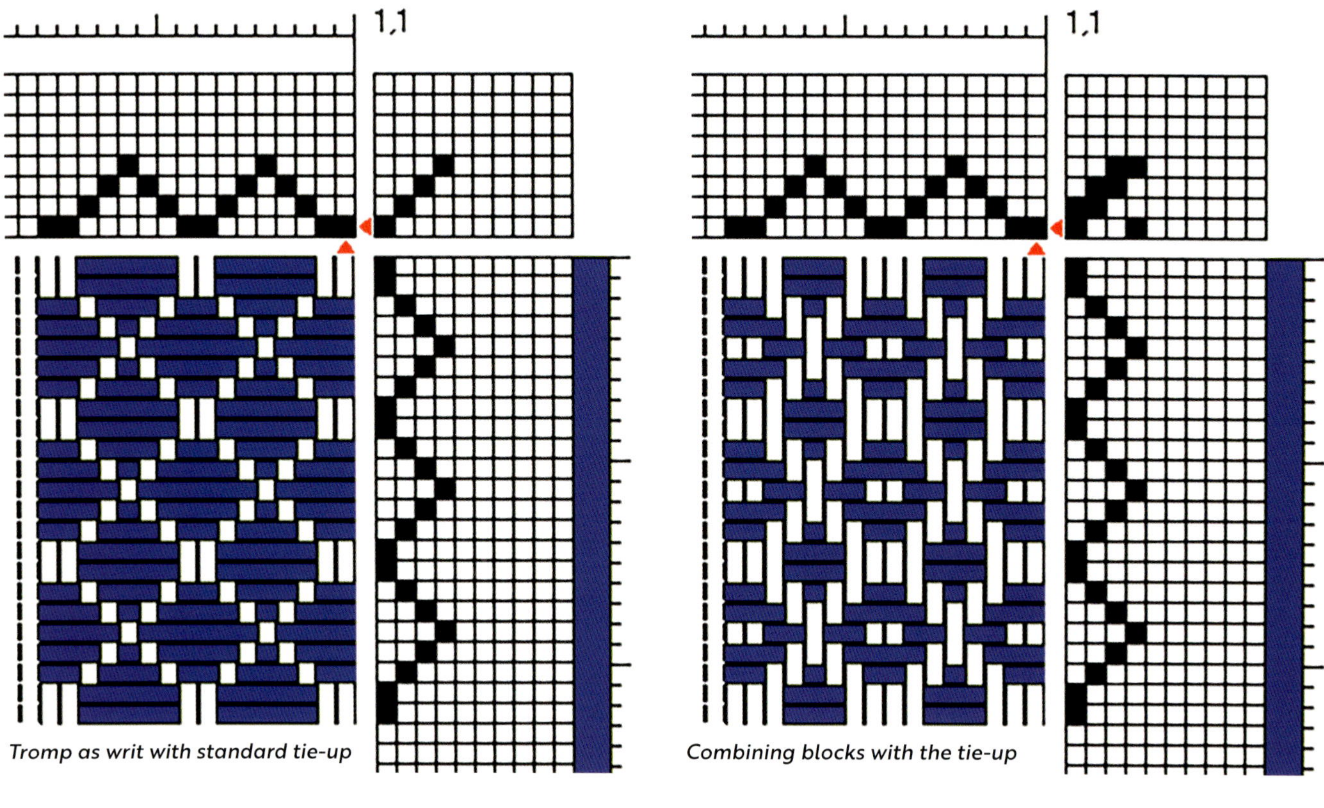

Tromp as writ with standard tie-up

Combining blocks with the tie-up

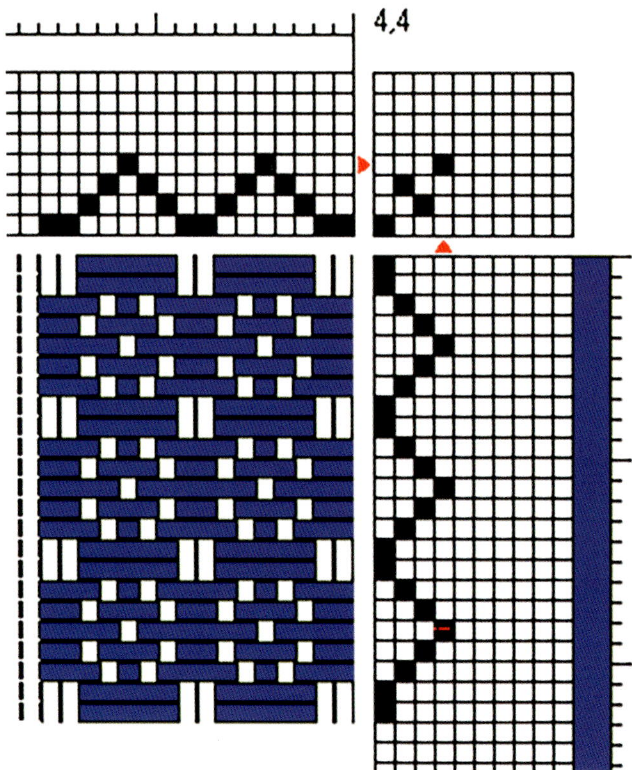

Changing the block order with the tie-up

ROSE VS. STAR TREADLING/TIE-UP

There are two more ways you can treadle Overshot—rose or star. Refer to figure 8.

Star treadling creates diagonal lines that connect each block and is treadled starting from the inner treadles to the outer treadles and back. I used the star treadling for the project sample. The tie-up starts with Block A and progresses to Block D. (See the top section of the profile draft in figure 8.)

The rose treadling makes rounder motifs and is treadled from the outer treadles to the inner treadles and back. Here's what the project profile draft looks like with the rose treadling. As you can see, the tie-up starts on Block D and progresses to Block A. (See the bottom section of the profile draft in figure 8.)

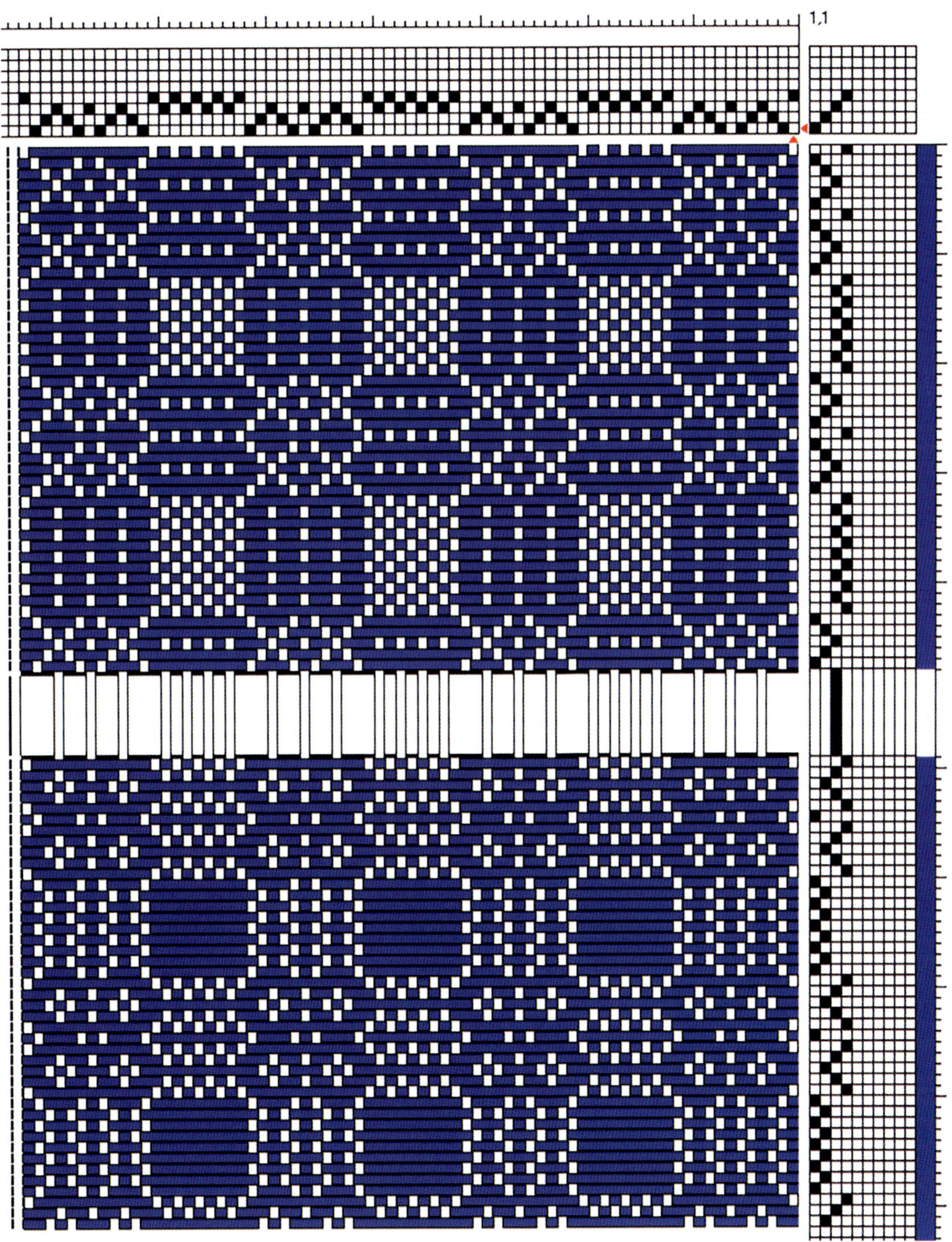

Figure 8: Star vs. rose treadling of the Overshot project profile draft

LISTENING TO ATHENA

I learned something new when I wove the sample for the Overshot project and was reminded to listen to that little voice in my head when it is trying to tell me that something isn't right. I affectionately call that voice "Athena" for the Greek goddess of weaving.

For the Overshot project sample, I threaded the blocks using my method of dropping a warp thread when the warp thread is shared between blocks. It went well, or so I thought at first.

When I weave Overshot, I check my threading by weaving a few picks of plain weave. If the plain weave is over/under all the way across, my threading is correct.

I wove about an inch of plain weave, and I noticed I had two warp threads next to each other right in the center of the warp. I assumed it was caused by threading a heddle on the wrong shaft. (Athena whispered, "Are you sure?") Since it was a sample, I decided to weave and see what happened.

Note the center motif of the pattern is not balanced one each side of the diamond shape due to the threading problem.

As I wove the pattern, the threading error caused one side of my pattern weft to consistently be on the wrong side of the fabric. This misplaced warp thread caused the edges of the diamond shape to be missing on the left side of the motif (note circled area on photo). After wet-finishing, the misplaced pattern weft was even more pronounced. Obviously, I would need to be much more careful threading the large sample.

I threaded up the project using only the profile draft, opened the first plain weave shed and had not one, but 4 doubled warp threads spaced evenly across the warp. (Athena actually said, "I told you so" in my head.) That was the bad news. The good news is there was a pattern to the errors, which actually makes it easier to find the problem.

I concluded it was a threading error, so to check my work, I used the Block Substitution tool in my weaving program to create a thread-by-thread draft from the profile draft. I then used the thread-by-thread draft to double-check my threading.

And according to the thread-by-thread draft, I had threaded correctly! What the heck was going on? I had never had this happen in years of weaving Overshot!

After much muttering, comparing the draft to the threading, and walking away to think about it, I had an epiphany. (Thank you, Athena!) The section of the warp with the error was where the profile draft goes from Block A to Block C and then back to Block A. The double warps error was in the transitions between the stand-alone Block C (3-4-3-4) and back to Block A (1-2-1-2). It was in the plain weave tie-up.

Plain weave Treadle 1 is tied up to Shafts 1 and 3. Plain weave Treadle 2 is tied up to Shafts 2 and 4. This is all correct except on the descending side of the threading going from Block C (threaded 4-3-4-3) to Block A (threaded 1-2-1-2) ascending section of the profile draft, I ended the Block C threading on Shaft 3 and started Block A on Shaft 1. This was logical in the "shared warp ends" method of threading because these threads are clearly not on the same shaft.

However, leaving a thread on Shaft 1 next to a thread on Shaft 3 meant that both threads are lifted with plain weave Treadle 1, and at this specific spot on the threading, those threads are next to each other in the threading. (I swear Athena said, "Well, duh.") The problem would also happen if I threaded Block C 3-4-3-4 and Block A 1-2-1-2, because the threads on Shafts 2 and 4 would be threaded next to each other and raised together by the plain weave treadle tied to Shafts 2 and 4.

So, my options were to rethread all 259 warp ends (argh) and to remember to remove those threads on Shaft 3 (argh) or to pull the threads on Shaft 3 where the doubling happened. Athena concurred that I could do this but reminded me I would have a density gap in my plain weave base cloth. I went for it and pulled the four threads across the warp and left them hanging off the back of the loom. I kept my fingers crossed that the gaps would "come out in the wash."

It worked beautifully! And the threading gaps closed up nicely when I wet-finished. Whew.

Lessons learned: (1) Check that my warp threads always alternate between the two plain weave treadles at the block intersections, and (2) don't assume that my weaving program threading conversion is always right!

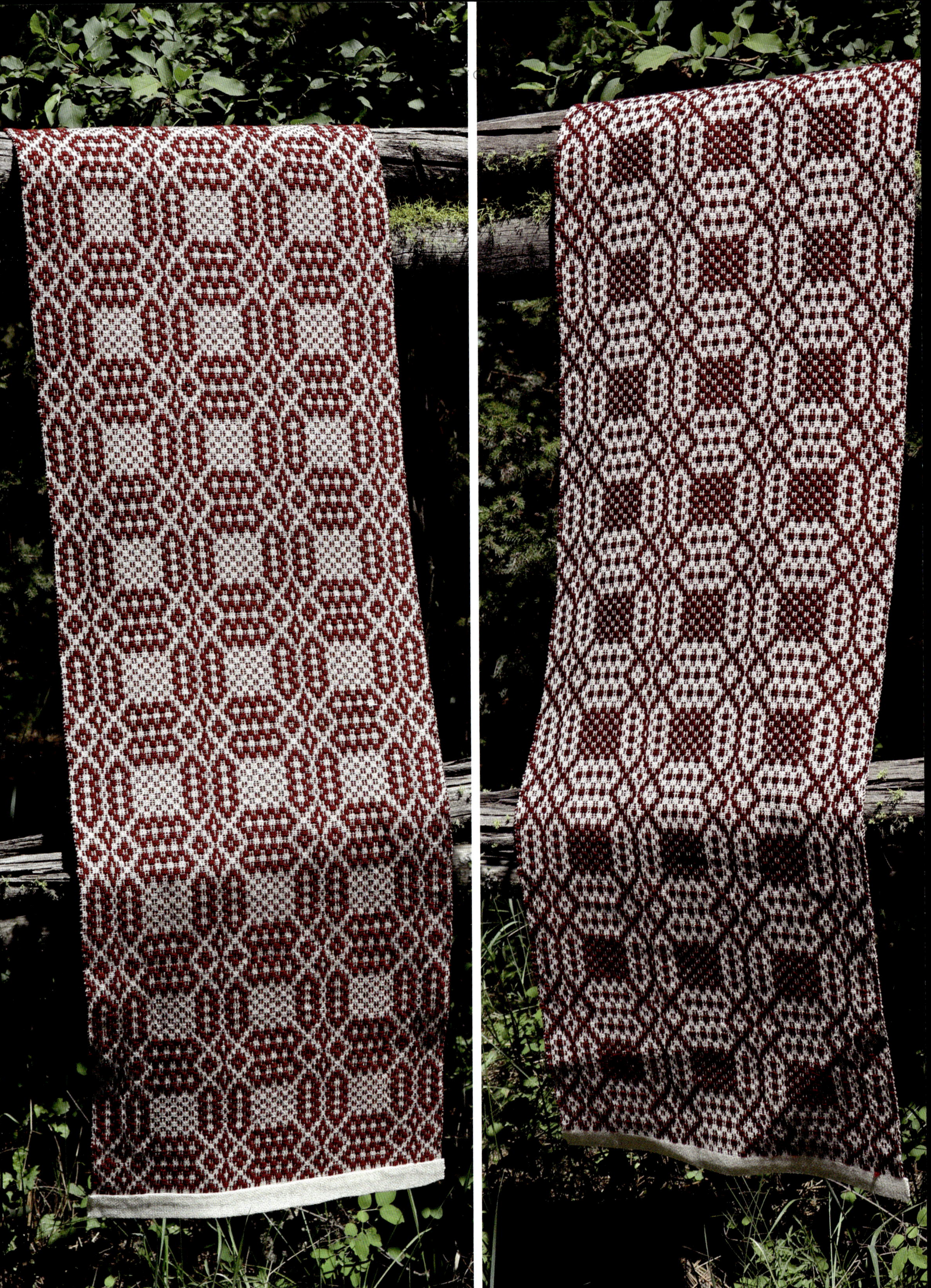

◆ PROJECT ◆

OVERSHOT RUNNER

I have a personal preference for the star treadling in Overshot. I like the diagonals of pattern that are created. However, you can easily change this to the rose pattern by changing the direction of the treadling or by simply changing the tie-up so the tie-up progression goes Block D, Block C, Block B, Block A. Changing the tie-up progression means you can still use the same profile threading and treadling in the draft for this project.

Profile draft for the project

EQUIPMENT NEEDED

4-shaft loom
2 shuttles
8-dent reed (sley 2 ends per dent)

Threading units:
Block A: 1-2
Block B: 2-3
Block C: 3-4
Block D: 1-4

Repeat the threading unit 2 times per block (total of 4 threads per block of threading).

Before threading, read the Overshot threading section on page 132 to make sure you don't have two threads on the same shaft at the block transitions. Also read the box on page 136 on the transition between stand-alone C Block to the next Block A in the middle of the pattern repeat. When transitioning from Block C back down to Block A in the pattern, you need to thread Block C in descending order (4-3-4-3) but eliminate the last thread on Shaft 3 in the sequence, so you thread 4-3-4 and then Block A 1-2-1-2.

Yarns:
8/2 White linen for the warp and base cloth weft
4/2 Ad Astra organic cotton in Garnet (color #54) from The Yarn Barn of Kansas for the pattern weft

Sett: 16 e.p.i.

Calculate the number of warp ends: Because of the shared transition threads between blocks, it can be a bit trickier to calculate warp ends from the profile draft. I have 2 methods: the long way and the short way.

The long way: For this runner, each colored-in square of the threading represents two repeats of the threading. So, the initial move is to count the number of squares and multiply by 4 threads. There are 73 threading squares × 4 = 292 warp ends.

Now, we need to subtract those transition threads that are shared between blocks. Looking at the threading units, Blocks A (1 and 2), B (2 and 3), and C (3 and 4) will share a transition thread when these blocks are next to each other on the profile threading.

The next step is to count the connections where these squares are threaded in sequence. There are 40 times where these blocks are next to each other. Take 292 (total number of threads) minus 40 intersections = 252 threads.

We need 2 floating selvedges to capture the pattern wefts neatly on each selvedge. 252 threads plus 2 floating selvedges = 254 warp ends.

The fast way: Put the profile draft into your weaving software and use the Block Substitution tool for Overshot. But before you get smug about software conversion, read the box on page 136 about my discovery when threading the runner project.

Calculate the number of heddles: Because of the transition threads, I decided to "ballpark" the heddle counts per shaft and count each square as 4 threads. It's better to have a few too many heddles on a shaft than too few, right?

Count the number of squares for each block across the profile draft and multiply by 4 (total threads in the block) and then divide by 2 for each shaft. Then add together the matching shafts in the different blocks.

Block A: 16 squares × 4 = 64 total threads.
Block A is threaded on Shafts 1 and 2 so divide 64 by 2 = 32 heddles per shaft
Shaft 1: 32
Shaft 2: 32

Block B: 16 squares × 4 = 64
Block B is threaded on Shafts 2 and 3 so divide 64 by 2 = 32 heddles per shaft for Block B
Shaft 2: 32
Shaft 3: 32

Block C: 24 squares × 4 = 96
Block C is threaded on Shafts 3 and 4 so divide 96 by 2 = 48 heddles per shaft for Block C
Shaft 3: 48
Shaft 4: 48

Block D: 17 squares × 4 = 68
Block D is threaded on Shafts 1 and 4 so divide 68 by 2 = 34
Shaft 1: 34
Shaft 4: 34

Now add together the number of heddles on the same shafts in the various blocks. Remember, this will be more than you need on each shaft due to the shared warp threads between blocks.

Shaft 1: 66 (32 in Block A and 34 in Block D)
Shaft 2: 64 (32 in Block A and 32 in Block B)
Shaft 3: 80 (32 in Block B and 48 in Block C)
Shaft 4: 82 (48 in Block C and 34 in Block D)

Total number of heddles: 292, which is more than we need for the total warp threads of 252 when we subtract the transition threads between blocks—see "Calculate the number of warp ends."

Tie-up: Straight twill tie-up
Treadle 1: Tied to Shafts 1 and 2 (Block A warp threads lifted)
Treadle 2: Tied to Shafts 2 and 3 (Block B warp threads lifted)
Treadle 3: Tied to Shafts 3 and 4 Block C warp threads lifted)
Treadle 4: Tied to Shafts 1 and 4 (Block D warp threads lifted)
Treadle 5: Tied to Shafts 1 and 3 (first pick plain weave base)
Treadle 6: Tied to Shafts 2 and 4 (second pick plain weave base)

Treadling sequence: Each colored-in treadling square represents 3 picks of pattern weft. Alternate treadles between pattern weft pick (Shuttle #1) and a plain weave pick (Shuttle #2) that is the same yarn as the base cloth warp thread. Also remember to alternate between the plain weave treadles.

For example, the treadling starts with Block D—plain weave treadles are in italics:
Treadling for one square of Block D:
Treadle 4: Throw pattern weft shuttle. Beat.
Treadle 5: Throw base cloth weft shuttle. Beat.
Treadle 4: Pattern weft shuttle. Beat.
Treadle 6: Base cloth weft shuttle. Beat
Treadle 4: Pattern weft shuttle. Beat.
Treadle 5: Base cloth weft shuttle. Beat.

This gives you 3 picks of pattern weft treadling for Block D.

Next up on the draft is one square of Block A:
Treadle 1: Pattern weft
Treadle 6: Base cloth weft (note that you continue alternating Treadles 5 and 6 to maintain the base cloth plain weave even though you are changing blocks)
Treadle 1: Pattern weft
Treadle 5: Base cloth weft
Treadle 1: Pattern weft
Treadle 6: Base cloth weft

Next up: Block B
Treadle 2: Pattern weft
Treadle 5: Base weft
Treadle 2: Pattern weft
Treadle 6: Base weft
Treadle 2: Pattern weft
Treadle 5: Base weft

Next up: Block C
Treadle 3: Pattern weft
Treadle 6: Base weft
Treadle 3: Pattern weft
Treadle 5: Base weft
Treadle 3: Pattern weft
Treadle 6: Base weft

Remember to alternate pattern picks with the base cloth picks and alternate between the two base cloth treadles! Since there are an odd number (3) picks of pattern, you also have an odd number of base cloth picks.

Warp Length: 84 inches (allowing total of 24 inches thrum and tie-on allowance)

Width in reed: 16 inches

Woven length on loom (measured off-tension):
Pattern area only = 48 inches

Hem allowance: 2.5 inches plain weave on each end

Finished size after washing: 14 inches wide × 43.5 inches long (pattern area only)

Shrinkage: 9%

Weaving:
Weave 2.5 inches for hem using the base cloth weft.
Weave pattern area to 48 inches (or until last pattern repeat is completed).
Weave 2.5 inches for hem using base cloth weft.

Finishing: Zigzag across both ends of the plain weave hems. Soak the runner in warm water and then lay it flat to dry.

Trim off excess warp ends next to the zigzag stitching. Turn the raw edge of hems under ¼ inch. Press. Now match the folded edge of the hem to the end edge of the pattern area. Press. Machine- or hand- hemstitch the hems.

chapter 6
TIED-UNIT WEAVES

Unit weaves are structurally the same within each block of pattern and are threaded and treadled in units (groups) of warp threads and treadling repeats. Changing the block threading units creates pattern in the fabric based on how the warp and weft interlace within the blocks. This change of interlacement creates pattern vs. background blocks that look different but are still structurally the same as the other blocks in the fabric design.

A Tied Unit Weave uses the warp threads to tie down a supplemental weft at the same intervals in each block of threading/treadling.

A familiar example of a Tied Unit Weave is Summer and Winter. Each block of threading uses a set of warp threads to tie down the supplemental pattern wefts. Weaving for a specific block, the pattern weft shows on top, while in all the other blocks, the pattern weft is on the other side of the fabric. The tie-down warp threads create a plain weave with little dots of color where the warps are catching the pattern weft.

The threading units for each block use the same tie-down warp threads, but each block uses different pattern shafts working in tandem with the tie-down shafts to create the pattern weft floats at regular intervals within the blocks.

All unit weaves are block weaves, but not all block weaves are unit weaves.

WEAVE STRUCTURE

Summer and Winter

The Summer and Winter weave structure has a long history. Many antique coverlets feature the Summer and Winter block patterning. However, the name "Summer and Winter" was first used by Mary Meigs Atwater in her book *The Shuttle-Craft Book of American Hand-Weaving* in reference to the two sides of the pattern—the "Summer" side, which is lighter and features more background/base cloth, and the "Winter" side, which is darker and features more pattern weft blocks. This may seem a bit curious until you remember that most of the early coverlets were woven of undyed linen or cotton with a wool pattern weft that was usually dyed. Summer is a season with more hours of light—thus the lighter Summer side dominated by the blocks of background / base cloth with the light colored linen or cotton predominant. Winter is the season with fewer hours of sunlight, so the dark Winter side is dominated by the dyed wool supplemental pattern weft.

Another theory from the Smithsonian Museum is that the Winter side of the coverlet with the floats of wool pattern weft predominant would be next to the body in the winter as the wool would help trap body heat. Conversely, the Summer side would be mainly linen or cotton, so in the summer, the cooler linen or cotton side would be next to the body.

Summer and Winter is a unit weave. Each unit weave block of pattern is independent of the other blocks in the design, but the threads are interlacing identically to the other blocks. This interlacement is what makes Summer and Winter a unit weave. The warp threads are your base cloth yarn and are sett for plain weave for the yarn you have chosen. (See the box on page 10 for calculating sett.)

Summer and Winter requires two shuttles to weave. Shuttle #1 is wound with the supplemental pattern weft. This supplemental pattern weft is usually a little larger in grist than the yarn used for

the base cloth. A general rule of thumb is to have the supplemental weft one or two steps larger than the base cloth warp/weft. For example, if I'm using an 8/2 yarn for the base cloth warp and weft, I would use a 5/2 yarn for the supplemental pattern weft. If the pattern weft yarn is easily compressed as with a wool yarn, you can use a larger yarn for better coverage because the wool yarn has a good squish-ability factor and will compress into the little space between the warp / base cloth weft intersections. (See Rule #3 in "10 Rules for Overshot" on page 129.)

Shuttle #2 is wound with the base cloth weft and is the same yarn as you are using for your warp. If you are using an 8/2 cotton for the warp, use the same 8/2 cotton for the base cloth weft.

An important note! When weaving plain/balanced weave, your aim is to have the same number of weft picks per inch as you have warp ends per inch. For Summer and Winter, you will also have the same number of supplemental weft picks per inch.

In other words, in 1 inch of woven fabric in Summer and Winter sett at 16 e.p.i. (the base cloth yarn sett), there will also be 16 supplemental pattern weft picks in the same inch! This means that you need to keep in mind the use of the textile when selecting your yarns so that the hand/weight/drape of the fabric will work successfully for its final use.

Summer and Winter is a two-tie unit weave. Each block uses the same two warp threads to tie down the pattern wefts at regular intervals. These tie-down warp threads are always threaded on Shafts 1 and 2, and these shafts weave the plain weave base cloth as well. The other shafts are used to create the pattern weft floats between the tie-down warps. You need only one pattern shaft assigned per block of pattern. The pattern shafts work with the base cloth shafts to make up the different blocks of pattern across the fabric.

Vital Info!! When looking at a Summer and Winter fabric, when the pattern weft floats are on the surface, this is referred to weaving pattern in that block. Looking across the same side of the fabric, where you see the plain weave base cloth in the other block(s), this is referred to as weaving background in those blocks.

For Summer and Winter, the pattern weft creates floats on either the top side of the fabric or the backside of the fabric depending on the threading for the block. When pattern warp threads are threaded on the same pattern shafts, weft floats are created in the blocks where the same pattern warp threads are assigned.

Because the same two tie-down threads on Shafts 1 and 2 are engaged with every treadle, when the background plain weave base cloth shows, there will be little spots of color/pattern weft where the pattern weft on the other side of the fabric is being tied down by the warp threads.

When pattern is woven in a block on one side of the fabric, the opposite side of the fabric in the same block is weaving background.

I know all this "pattern" talk can be a bit confusing. We need to remember that "fabric pattern design" is the big picture and "block pattern design" is the little picture. Think of it as a jigsaw puzzle—each individual puzzle piece has a part of the picture (pattern block), and by putting the puzzle pieces together, we get the entire picture (fabric pattern design).

THREADING THE BLOCKS

In Summer and Winter, the background/tie-down shafts are always Shafts 1 and 2 and are used in every block of pattern.

The pattern shafts are assigned as follows:
Block A: Shaft 3
Block B: Shaft 4
Block C: Shaft 5
Block D: Shaft 6
Block E: Shaft 7
Block F: Shaft 8

If you have a 4-shaft loom, you can weave two blocks of pattern: Shafts 1 and 2 are the plain weave base cloth/tie-down shafts, and Shafts 3 and 4 weave pattern in the blocks they are assigned to.

If you have an 8-shaft loom, you can weave 6 blocks of pattern. However, you may run into the situation of not having enough treadles. I'll discuss a solution to this in the 8-shaft / 4-block Summer and Winter project.

When weaving to have pattern in a particular block, the pattern weft will be on top wherever the warp threads are threaded for that particular block while the pattern weft for all the other blocks will be on the reverse side of the fabric. This means that all blocks are performing the same warp/weft interlacement in each block but, depending on which pattern shafts are raised, will determine which blocks have pattern weft floats on the top of the fabric.

Summer and Winter can be woven at different ratios of tie-down warps to pattern warps. The most common ratio used is the 1:1 ratio—which means threading 1 tie-down thread to 1 pattern thread in each threading unit. See the text box for the threading units for the other threading ratios.

The threading key for Summer and Winter 1:1 ratio is:
Block A: 1-3-2-3
Block B: 1-4-2-4
Block C: 1-5-2-5
Block D: 1-6-2-6
Block E: 1-7-2-7
Block F: 1-8-2-8

SUMMER AND WINTER THREADING RATIOS KEY

Shafts 1 and 2 (red type) are always the tie-down shafts in each threading unit.

Threading

Ratio	Block A	Block B	Block C	Block D
1:1 Ratio	1-3-2-3	1-4-2-4	1-5-2-5	1-6-2-6
1:2 Ratio	1-4-3-2-3-4	1-6-5-2-5-6	1-8-7-2-7-8	1-10-9-2-9-10
1:3 Ratio	1-3-4-3-2-3-4-3	1-5-6-5-2-5-6-5	1-7-8-7-2-7-8-7	1-9-10-9-2-9-10-9
1:4 Ratio	1-4-3-4-3-2-3-4-3-4	1-6-5-6-5-2-5-6-5-6	1-8-7-8-7-2-7-8-7-8	1-10-9-10-9-2-9-10-9-10
2:4 Ratio	1-2-3-4-3-4	1-2-5-6-5-6	1-2-7-8-7-8	1-2-9-10-9-10

Each colored square in your profile threading equals 4 warp threads. Note in the threading units that the threads on the two base cloth shafts (Shafts 1 and 2) always alternate in the threading with the pattern shafts (Shafts 3 through 8).

THREADING 2 BLOCKS OF PATTERN

Figuring out the tie-up and treadling all starts with the threading. I will be using one color of warp and threading for two blocks of pattern on a 1:1 ratio. Shafts 1 and 2 are the tie-down shafts. Shafts 3 and 4 are to create pattern weft floats. Block A threading is on Shafts 1, 2 and 3. Block B threading is on Shafts 1, 2 and 4.

Each colored-in square on the profile draft threading represents one threading repeat of 4 warp threads.

For example, one profile threading square is colored in for Block A: Thread 1-3-2-3 one time. Next on the profile threading, there are 4 colored-in squares for Block B—Thread 1-4-2-4 for a total of 4 repeats for a total of 16 warp ends.

TIE-UP

We are going to continue with a 2-block pattern to explore the tie-up using a rising shed (jack) loom:
Block A is threaded 1-3-2-3.
Block B is threaded 1-4-2-4.

To weave plain weave all the way across the warp, we need to raise every other warp thread. Shafts 1 and 2 alternate in the threading across the warp regardless of what block we threaded. Thus, we tie up a treadle to those two shafts that will raise every other warp thread of the warp to create the first pick of plain weave.

The other warp threads are on Shafts 3 and 4, and the threading of these shafts alternates with the tie-down shafts. Therefore, to raise every other thread that remains to be raised in the warp, we raise all of the pattern shafts across the warp for the second pick of plain weave. I have marked these treadles P1 and P2 for plain weave Pick 1 and plain weave Pick 2.

Thus your tie-up for plain weave base cloth across the fabric without any pattern weft thrown is:

	4				
	3				
2					
1					
P1	P2				

Figure 1: Tie-up for plain weave base cloth

Now to tie up the pattern weft pick treadles so we are weaving both pattern and base cloth at the same time with the tie-up. Keep in mind, your threading alternates between a tie-down warp thread and a pattern warp thread. Therefore, when you raise the pattern warp threads, your pattern weft thread floats will be on the bottom side of the fabric in the block you are treadling for. The top side will show background for the block you are treadling for.

Looking at our threading in each block, a warp threaded on the tie-down shafts alternates threading with a warp thread on the pattern shafts.

It's time to add the tie-up for the pattern blocks of the fabric design. Let's think this through for a moment. What do you need the yarn to do when you press a pattern treadle? First, you must raise one of the tie-down shafts, and with the next pick, you have to raise the second tie-down shaft. With this in mind, I have filled in the first part of Treadles 3 and 4, alternating those tie-down shafts only.

	4				
	3				
2			2		
1		1			
P1	P2				

Figure 2: Adding the tie-down shafts to the treadles to be used for pattern picks

Now you need to add the pattern weft shafts for the particular block of pattern.

Start with Block A. The pattern shaft assigned to Block A is Shaft 3. Therefore, to create warp floats on the bottom side of the fabric in Block A, you need to raise all the threads on Shaft 3 to create pattern weft floats on the backside of the fabric as well as alternating Shaft 1 and Shaft 2 to create the base cloth background on the top side of the fabric. At the same time, Shaft 1 and 2 threads will also tie down the pattern wefts on the back side of the fabric to create the pattern weft floats in Block A. You also need to weave two picks of weft that alternate raising Shafts 1 and 2 for to complete the plain weave. Thus, you need to have two treadles each raising Shaft 3 pattern warp threads plus one of the plain weave shafts.

	4				
	3	3	3		
2			2		
1		1			
P1	P2	A1	A2		

Figure 3: Adding the pattern shafts to the tie-up for Block A

Time to tie up for Block B. Block B pattern is threaded on Shaft 4, and once again, you have to complete both picks of the plain weave to create the background in Block B and at the same time lift all the pattern shafts assigned to Block B pattern, so the pattern weft floats are on the bottom side of the fabric.

Here's the tie-up for two blocks of pattern:

	4			4	4
	3	3	3		
2			2		2
1		1		1	
P1	P2	A1	A2	B1	B2

Figure 4: Tie-up for two blocks of pattern

What if you have more than 2 blocks of pattern? The same sequence/pairings apply. For example, here's what the tie-up would look like for four blocks of pattern.

	6							6	6
	5					5	5		
	4			4	4				
	3	3	3						
2			2		2		2		2
1		1		1		1		1	
P1	P2	A1	A2	B1	B2	C1	C2	D1	D2

Figure 5: Tie-up for four blocks of pattern

And what happens to the pattern weft in the other blocks when you treadle for pattern in a particular block? The pattern wefts in all the other blocks will be on the top side of the fabric! Because the pattern wefts dominate that side of the fabric, this is the "winter" side of the fabric.

When you flip the fabric over, the pattern floats will be in the individual blocks, surrounded by background in all the other blocks. This is the "summer" side of the fabric. (If you skipped the introduction to the chapter, the Summer vs. Winter sides is explained there.)

TREADLING

Summer and Winter uses two wefts so 2 shuttles are required—one shuttle for the pattern weft and the second shuttle for the base cloth weft.

You need to alternate a pick of base cloth weft and pick of pattern weft to get a stable fabric. Both pattern picks and base cloth picks are woven in pairs. This means that each colored-in square on the profile draft treadling represents a minimum of 4 picks of weft—2 picks with pattern weft and 2 picks of base cloth weft. Weaving some patterns to "square" may require more pairs of weft picks.

For a 4 shaft/2 Block Pattern:

The treadling sequence for Block A is:
Treadle 1 tied to Shafts 1 and 2: Base cloth weft pick
Treadle 3 tied to Shafts 1 and 3: Pattern weft pick
Treadle 2 tied to Shafts 3 and 4: Base cloth weft pick
Treadle 4 tied to Shafts 2 and 3: Pattern weft pick
The whole sequence is treadled: 1-3-2-3.

The treadling sequence for Block B is:
Treadle 1 (Base weft)
Treadle 4 (Pattern weft)
Treadle 2 (Base weft)
Treadle 4 (Pattern weft)
The whole Block B sequence is treadled: 1-4-2-4.

Notice that the treadling sequence is the same as the threading sequence for each block due to the tie-up created. Since Treadles 1 and 2 are tied up for plain weave, you weave with the plain weave weft when you press those treadles. Treadles 3 and 4 are tied up for pattern, so you use pattern weft when you press those treadles.

KEEPING TRACK OF TREADLING IN THE BLOCKS

To help me keep track of my treadling, I set up the treadles in pairs.

- Plain weave on Treadles 1 and 2 are pressed with my left foot.
- Pattern treadles for Block A on Treadles 3 and 4 and Block B on Treadles 5 and 6. I press the pattern weft treadles with my right foot.

I start weaving with my shuttle entering the shed from the right-hand selvedge. Then I can say, "going left, press the left" and "going right, press the right" to keep track of which treadle to press in each pair of treadles.

For example, if I'm treadling for Block A.

- Going left base weft = Treadle 1, pick of base weft—Treadle 1 is on the left side of the base cloth pairs
- Going left pattern weft = Treadle 3—first pattern weft using treadle on the left in the pair of Block A treadles
- Going right base weft = Treadle 2, pick of base weft—Treadle 2 is on the right-hand side of the base cloth pair
- Going right pattern weft = Treadle 4 (Block A second pattern pick is on the right in the pair of treadles)

I do the same for Block B, using the treadles assigned to Block B.

Summer and Winter works in pairs of weft thread picks. Label your treadles with the letters of the Block the treadle weaves and add the number for first or second treadle in treadle pair.

Here's a tip to help keep track of your treadles: Label the treadles with the block designation plus the number for which plain weave shaft is being used for the pattern weft tie-down. Here are the treadles on my Glimarkra countermarche loom tied up and labeled. A 1 is block A pattern/raises Shaft 1 for pattern tie-downs and A2 for Block A pattern/raises Shaft 2 for tie-down. T1 and T2 are the plain weave/tabby treadles for hems and base cloth picks.

SKELETON TIE-UP

Referring back to the 4-block design in the tie-up section earlier, to weave 4 blocks of pattern requires 6 shafts. But I need 10 treadles—two treadles for the plain weave picks and eight treadles for the pattern picks (2 treadles per block of pattern). My 8-shaft loom has 10 treadles, so four blocks is easily done.

But what if I want to maximize the number of blocks on 8 shafts? With an 8-shaft loom, it's possible to weave 6 blocks of pattern. However, I would need 14 treadles—2 treadles for the plain weave base cloth and 2 treadles for each block of pattern. 6 blocks times 2 treadles per block = 12 treadles plus the 2 treadles for plain weave equals 14 total treadles.

But it can be done using a skeleton tie-up! If I'm using an 8-shaft jack loom, I have 10 treadles available. Treadles 1 and 2 are tied up for the plain weave picks, just like in earlier tie-ups, with Treadle 1 tied up to the tie-down / plain weave shafts and Treadle 2 tied up to all the pattern shafts. We still need to alternate these two treadles for a plain weave picks of weft. I have labeled these treadles P1 and P2.

For a skeleton tie-up, we also need to add the tie-down shafts (Shafts 1 and 2) individually. I have labeled these treadles T1 andT2. We alternate these two treadles no matter what block of pattern you are weaving.

The remaining 6 treadles are each tied up to one shaft for pattern (6 blocks) for a total of 10 treadles.

To weave our blocks, we need to press two treadles at the same time, alternating the treadles T1 and T2 assigned to Shaft 1 and Shaft 2, while at the same time also pressing the corresponding treadle assigned for the pattern shaft in the block you are weaving.

Figure 6 shows the skeleton tie-up for six blocks of pattern.

	8								8
	7							7	
	6						6		
	5					5			
	4				4				
	3			3					
2			2						
1		1							
P1	P2	T1	T2	A	B	C	D	E	F

Figure 6: Skeleton tie-up for 6 blocks on an 8-shaft loom

Treadles 1 and 2 weave plain weave across the fabric for hems. Treadles 3 and 4 are the alternating tie-down/plain weave treadles on Shafts 1 and 2 that are usually included in the pairs of treadles per block. Treadles 5 through 10 are the pattern shafts.

Here's what the treadling for each block is pressing two treadles at the same time (figure 7). The plain weave across the fabric treadles is marked as black boxes, the block tie-down shafts are blue boxes, and the pattern shafts for each block are yellow.

	8								8	
	7							7		
	6						6			
	5					5				
	4				4					
	3			3						
2			2							
1		1								
■										Plain weave across fabric pick 1
	■									Plain weave across fabric pick 2
		3		5						Block A pattern plus tie-down 1
			4	5						Block A pattern plus tie-down 2
		3			6					Block B pattern plus tie-down 1
			4		6					Block B pattern plus tie-down 2
		3				7				Block C pattern plus tie-down 1
			4			7				Block C pattern plus tie-down 2
		3					8			Block D pattern plus tie-down 1
			4				8			Block D pattern plus tie-down 2
		3						9		Block E pattern plus tie-down 1
			4					9		Block E pattern plus tie-down 2
		3							10	Block F pattern plus tie-down 1
			4						10	Block F pattern plus tie-down 2

Figure 7: Skeleton tie-up treadling sequences per block

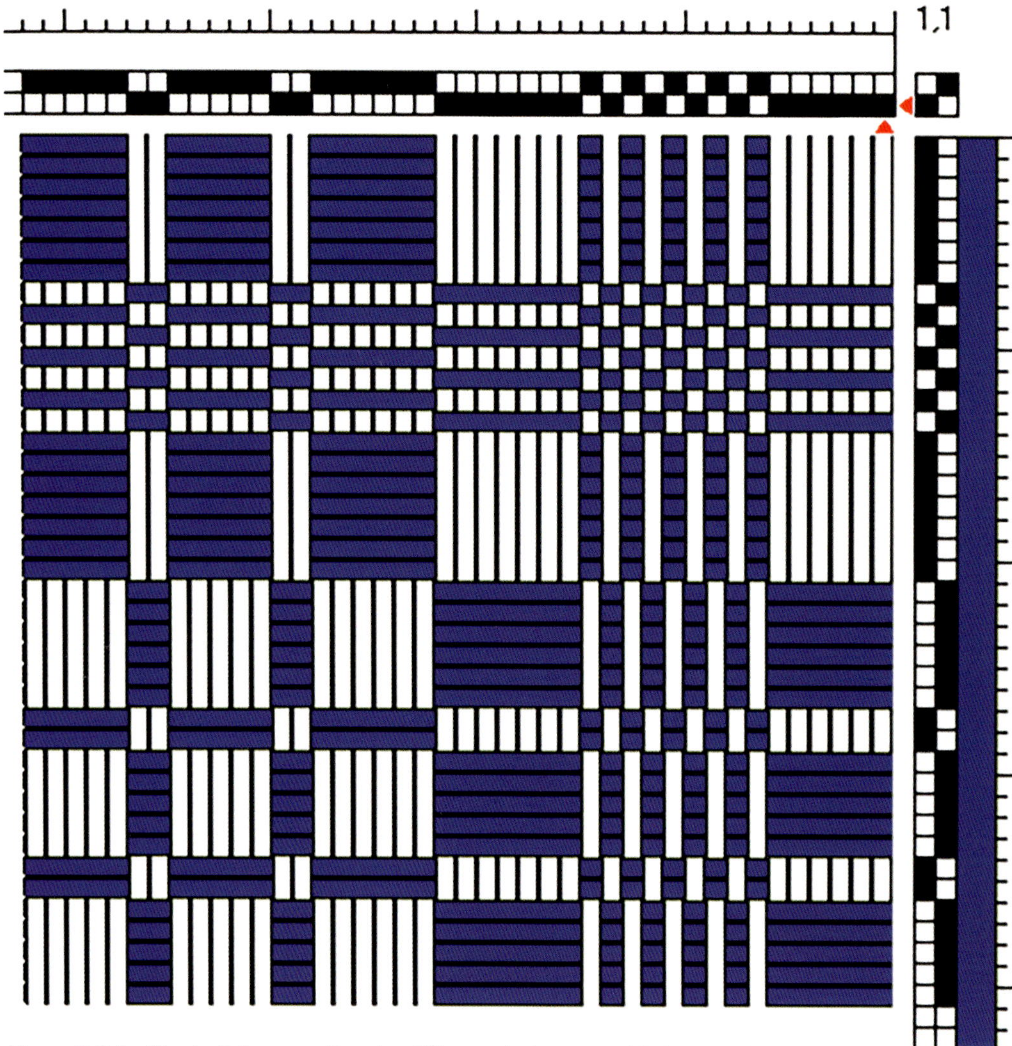

Figure 8: 2 Profile draft for sampling the different designs possible by simply changing the treadling sequences for Summer and Winter.

Could we do even more blocks on 8 shafts? Sadly, no, because each block of pattern requires one shaft, and we have maxed out on our 10 treadles. If you have more shafts available on your loom, then yes, you can weave more blocks of pattern!

Can you do more than two blocks on a 4-shaft loom? Sadly, no, because you need one pattern shaft per block of pattern and you only have 4 shafts available after tying up the plain weave shafts. However, there's more fun to come!

Now the real fun begins. Play with pattern with a design reference sample.

What I truly love about Summer and Winter is you can easily change the pattern interlacement and change the overall block patterns simply by changing how the blocks are treadled.

I've created a 2-block draft (see figure 8) for you to play with treadling options and create your own reference sample while examining how blocks play together. Note that I have attached paper price tags (available at office supply stores) to the selvedges that have notes about the sample. The large tag tells me the yarns used/colors and sett on one side and tie-up/treadling for the blocks on the other side. The small tags tell me what pattern/treadles I used in each section. It's a simple, inexpensive way to make sure all the information on the sample stays with the sample.

The sample blocks are threaded using the 1:1 ratio. Reminder: You need to alternate the P1 and P2 plain weave treadles between each pattern treadle. The plain weave/base cloth weft picks are not noted on the treadling sequences.

Treadling Option 1: Alternates (also called "bricks" in some books): This is the classic Summer and Winter pattern using alternating pattern weft tie-downs. The profile draft starts with 7 treadling squares colored in for Block A. Each square equals 4 picks of weft yarn—2 picks of base cloth and 2 picks of pattern weft. Start with Treadle A1 and alternate treadling between Treadle A1 (tied to Shaft 1 and 3) and Treadle A2 (tied to Shaft 2 and 3) for the first block of treadling in Block A. For Block B treadling, you alternate Treadle B1 with Treadle B2.

Treadling Option 2: Bird's eye or "O"s pattern: Start your treadling sequence for a block with the treadle tied to Shaft 2 for one pick, followed by two picks of Treadle 1 tied to Shaft 1, then 2 picks of Treadle tied to Shaft 2. End the block changes with 1 pick of the Treadle 2 tie-up.

Block A treadling sequence: A2-A1-A1-A2, repeat
Block B treadling sequence: B2-B1-B1-B2, repeat

Treadling Option 3: "X" pattern: The intersections between the blocks will form an "X." Treadle one pick of the treadle tied to Shaft 1, followed by 2 pattern picks, using the treadle that is tied up to Shaft 2.

Block A treadling sequence: A1-A2-A2-A1
Block B treadling sequence: B1-B2-B2-B1

Treadling Option 4: Columns (sometimes called ribs): Treadle the same pattern treadle over and over. For example: for Block A, treadle the same block over and over until the length you want is achieved—either the treadle tied to Shaft 1 or Shaft 2.

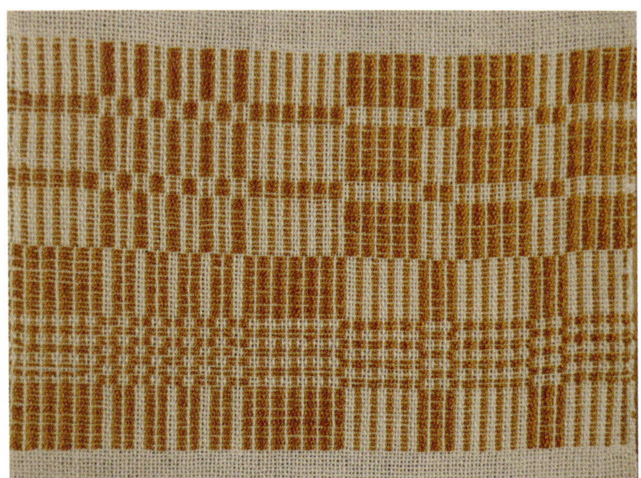

Block A: treadle A1-A1-A1 or A2-A2-A2
Block B: treadle B1-B1-B-1 or B2-B2-B2

Treadling Option 5: Mix and match the different treadling sequences. You can also create new designs by combining the different treadling sequences in the blocks. For example, start with a pattern section woven in columns. For the next pattern section, start with columns then the next section in "O's" followed by columns. Or start with columns and treadle the middle section in "X" style, then back to columns.

Let your imagination go wild on a sample. Make sure you label each section of woven fabric with what treadling sequence you used, or you will be frustrated when you refer back to it later! I like the little paper price tags on a string that you can purchase at office supply stores.

Try the following additional options on your own sample to explore more possibilities.

Treadling Option 6: Combine blocks of pattern by pressing two or more treadles. For example, if you have a four-blocks pattern, you can create a larger block by pressing treadles assigned to different blocks at the same time.

Perhaps you want to combine Blocks A and B into one large block at some point. Then you press Treadle A1 and Treadle B1 at the same time and throw your pattern weft shuttle. Then press Treadle A2 and B2, and throw the pattern shuttle back across for your complete treadling/weave sequence. You don't have to restrict yourself to adjoining blocks either! You can press A1 and C1 vs. A2 and C2. You will get pattern in Blocks A and Blocks C across the width of the fabric.

Now it gets even better! If you want to add this combined block as a regular motif, you can do your tie-up so that when you press the treadles for the combined block, threads in both blocks are raised!

The profile tie up adding combined blocks would look like this:

Figure 8

The thread-by-thread tie-up for combining blocks looks like this. Note that I do not have a separate set of treadles for the plain weave, so you need to add treadles tied up to Shafts 1-2 and 3-4 for plain weave. This also means you need 8 treadles:

Figure 9

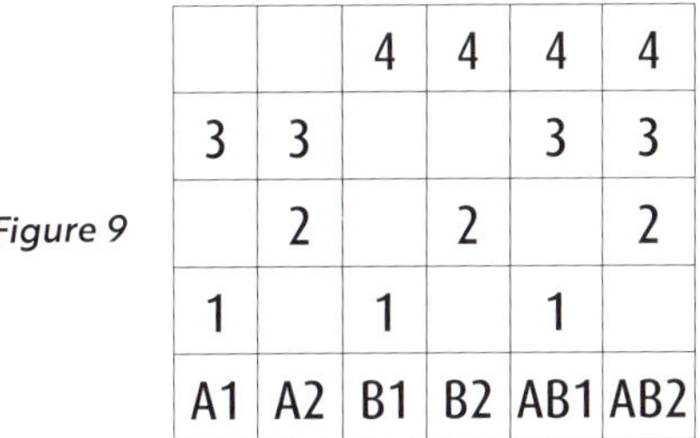

		4	4	4	4
3	3			3	3
	2		2		2
1		1		1	
A1	A2	B1	B2	AB1	AB2

Treadling Option 7: Changing the order of the blocks. When you get into more than two blocks of pattern, you can change the order that the blocks are woven (see the Summer and Winter scarf project). And blocks don't have to be woven in alphabetical sequence. You may decide to weave pattern in Block A, followed by pattern in Block C, followed by Block A again.

Treadling Option 8: You can change the size of the blocks lengthwise on the fabric. For example, Block A could be ½ inch while Block B could be 1 or 2 or 3 inches. Play around with combinations!

Put a sample warp on your loom and weave up all these combinations and any others you can think of. Keep notes when you are weaving, so you can label each section of the sample. Then file the sample in your Weaving Sample Reference Box.

◆ PROJECT ◆

SUMMER and WINTER PLACEMATS

2 BLOCKS ON 4 SHAFTS

Now it's time to practice what you've learned and create a woven piece! I have changed the treadling sequences within the blocks for each placemat for completely different designs! Pick your favorite. Or make up your own combinations of the treadling sequences/patterns.

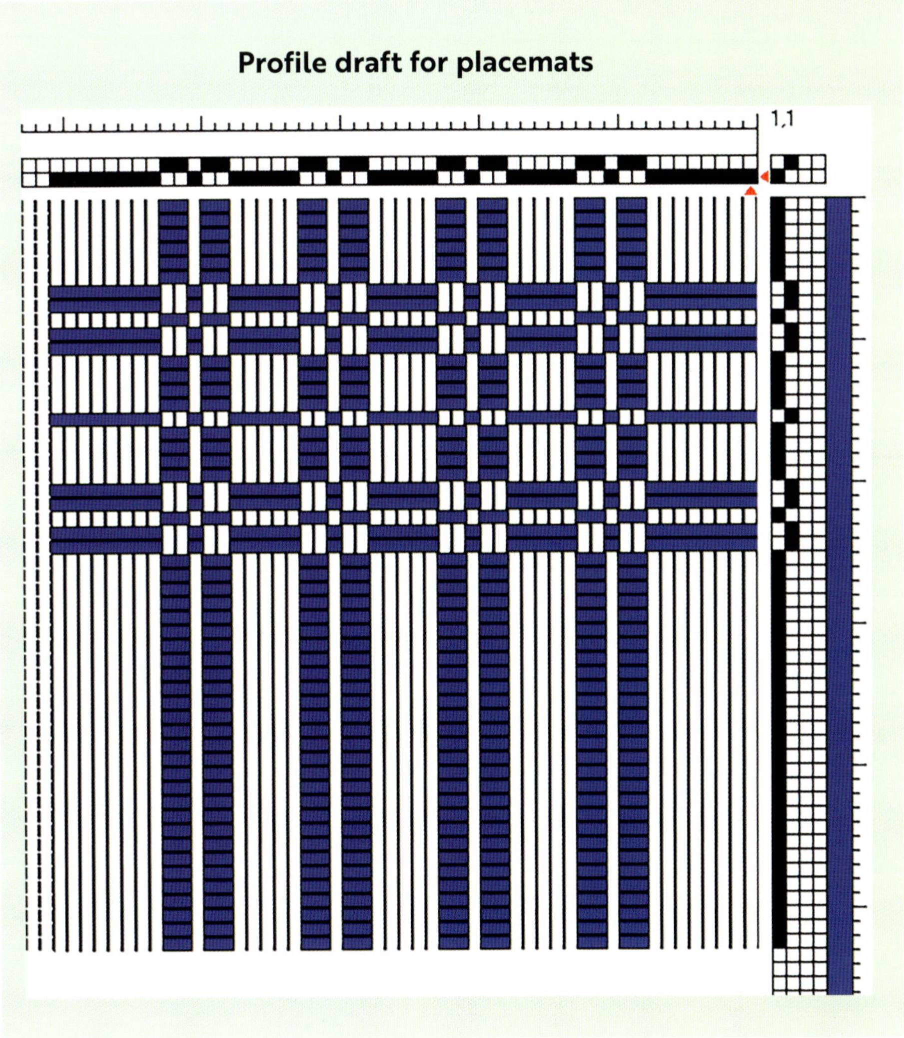

EQUIPMENT NEEDED

4-shaft loom
2 shuttles—one shuttle for the pattern weft and one shuttle for the base cloth weft
8-dent reed (sleyed 2 ends per dent)

Threading units: For Summer and Winter, each threading unit/group has 4 threads. Therefore, each colored-in square on the profile draft threading equals 4 warp threads. You can simply substitute the threading units for each colored-in square of threading—there is no need to create a thread-by-thread draft. Work off the profile draft and save time!
Block A: 1-3-2-3
Block B: 1-4-2-4

Yarns:
Lunatic Fringe Yarns 5/2 Tubular Spectrum mercerized cotton yarn
Forest
Cobalt
Copper
Teal

Warp: 5/2 mercerized cotton in forest

Sett: 16 e.p.i. This is a dense sett for 5/2 cotton. Usually, 5/2 wraps out to about 12–14 ends per inch. However, since these are placemats, I wanted a dense fabric with enough body/stiffness that the placemats lie flat.

Calculate the number of warp ends: Count the number of colored-in squares in each block of threading on the profile draft and multiply the number of threading squares times the number of threads in each threading unit. You can count the total number of threading squares and multiply by 4 threads/square, but doing each block separately gives us a head start on calculating the heddles per shaft.

Block A squares: 35 threading squares × 4 threads/square = 140 warp ends
Block B squares: 16 squares × 4 threads/square = 64 warp ends

140 + 64 = 204 warp ends + 2 floating selvedges = 206 warp ends

Calculate the heddles per shaft: Both Block A and Block B use Shafts 1 and 2 in every threading unit, so every block on the profile draft uses Shafts 1 and 2. There are 51 total threading blocks across the draft.
Shaft 1: 51 heddles
Shaft 2: 51 heddles

Block A uses Shaft 3 twice in each threading unit. There are 35 threading squares for Block A.
Shaft 3: 35 Block A squares × 2 heddles/square = 70 heddles.

Block B uses Shaft 4 twice in each threading unit. There are 16 threading squares for Block B.
Shaft 4: 16 × 2 = 32 heddles

Check your work:
Shaft 1: 51 heddles
Shaft 2: 51 heddles
Shaft 3: 70 heddles
Shaft 4: 32 heddles
Total heddles: 51 + 51 + 70 + 32 = 204 total heddles/warp threads + 2 floating selvedges

Tie-up:
Treadle 1: Shafts 1 and 2 (first base cloth plain weave pick—label as treadle P1)
Treadle 2: Shafts 3 and 4 (second base cloth plain weave pick—label as treadle P2)

Treadle 3: Shafts 1 and 3 (A1)
Treadle 4: Shafts 2 and 3 (A2)

Treadle 5: Shafts 1 and 4 (B1)
Treadle 6: Shafts 2 and 5 (B2)

Warp length: Allow 22 inches of warp length per placemat you intend to weave (includes 2-inch hems on each end, 17 inches of pattern section, and 10% for shrinkage) plus allowances for tie-on and thrum waste. For two placemats, I used a warp length of 76 inches.

Width in reed: 12.75 inches

Weft: Notice that I used the same size pattern weft as the base cloth warp/weft. This is because I'm using a dense sett for the base cloth. If you use a larger pattern weft, it needs to be very squishable so the wefts fit in the little space at the warp/weft intersections.

Note that the placemats are different colors on the same warp. This is done by changing the weft color for the blue placemat. That's all! The forest green and cobalt blend into a lovely blue-green.

Base cloth wefts:
Placemat 1 (green): 5/2 mercerized cotton in forest
Placemat 2 (blue): 5/2 mercerized cotton in cobalt

Pattern wefts:
Placemat 1: 5/2 mercerized cotton in copper
Placemat 2: 5/2 mercerized cotton in teal

Woven length of each placemat on the loom:
Pattern section only: 17 inches measured off tension on the loom.

Hem allowance: 2 inches of plain weave using only the base cloth weft for each placemat

Weaving:
Treadling sequences:
Remember! Between each pick of pattern weft, you have to alternate picks of base cloth weft using the P1 and P2 treadles. Each profile draft treadling square equals 4 pattern picks/4 base cloth picks per square on the profile draft treadling.

Placemat 1: Columns treadling:
Columns in Block A: Treadle A1 repeat
Columns in Block B: Treadle B1 repeat

Placemat 2: Birds Eye treadling:
Start treadling with the second treadle (the one tied to Shaft 2) in the pair of treadles assigned to each block.

Treadling sequence for Block A: A2-A1-A1-A2 repeat for block length desired
Treadling sequence for Block B: B2-B1-B1-B2 repeat for block length desired

Finished size after washing and hemming: Each placemat is 11.5 inches wide × 17.5 inches long including turned hems on each end.

Shrinkage: 10% in both width and length

Finishing: Machine-zigzag stitch along all raw ends of the placemats or use Fray Check™. Hand wash in warm water and lay flat to dry. I find the hand wash/dry step blocks the placemats so the shape will be retained with future machine washings. Cut the placemats apart. Turn the hems under to the length you want. Press. Now turn the raw edges under so the raw edges are sandwiched between the placemat and the turned hem. Match this fold to the beginning of the pattern area of the placemat. Press. Machine- or hand-stitch the hems.

TIP: When I weave multiple pieces on the same warp, I do 2 picks of plain weave between the end of one piece and the beginning of the next piece, using a piece of thrum in a contrasting color yarn (3/2 cottons work great). Cut the placemats apart between these two picks, and you have a perfectly straight cut. Remove the contrasting yarn after cutting placemats apart.

◆ PROJECT ◆

SUMMER and WINTER SCARF

4 BLOCKS ON 8 SHAFTS

This project has 4 blocks of Summer and Winter treadled in the ribs/columns treadling. I did a test sample, and I like the block definition best using the ribs/columns treadling. However, you are free to try any of the treadling sequences listed on page 151! That's the beauty of profile drafts!

Block A: 1-3-2-3
Block B: 1-4-2-4
Block C: 1-5-2-5
Block D: 1-6-2-6

Yarns:
WEBS Valley Yarns 8/2 Tencel for warp and base cloth picks
WEBS Valley Yarns 5/2 Bamboo for pattern picks

Warp:
8/2 Tencel in Aquamarine for center section
8/2 Tencel in Straw for the outer borders

Weft:
8/2 Tencel in Silver gray (base cloth weft)
5/2 Bamboo in Amethyst (pattern weft)

Sett: 16 e.p.i.

Calculate the number of warp ends: Count the number of colored-in squares in the threading on the profile draft and multiply the number of threading squares times the number of threads in each threading unit.

Block A: 8 squares x 4 threads/square = 32
Block B: 12 squares x 4 threads/square = 48
Block C: 12 squares x 4 threads/square = 48
Block D: 10 squares x 4 threads/square = 40
Total warp ends: 32 + 48 + 48 + 40 = 168 warp ends plus warp 2 ends for floating selvedges

EQUIPMENT NEEDED

8-shaft loom
2 shuttles—one for pattern weft and one for base cloth tabby weft
8-dent reed (sley 2 ends per inch)

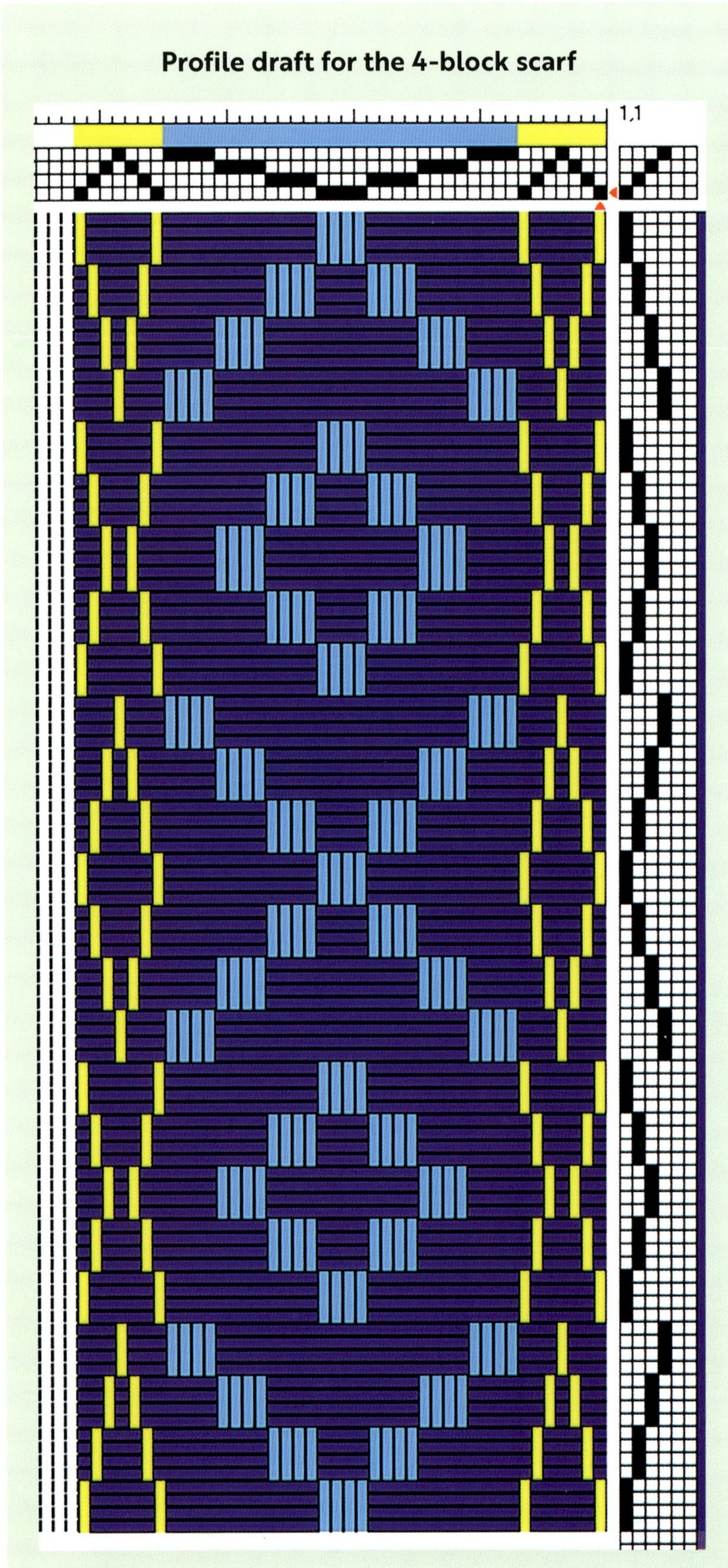

Profile draft for the 4-block scarf

Calculate the heddle count: Look at the threading units. Shafts 1 and 2 are used in every unit of 4 threads regardless of which block is being threaded. Therefore, when you count the total number of colored-in threading squares, you are also getting the number of Shaft 1 threads (one per square) and Shaft 2 threads (one per square). The total number of squares in the profile draft = the number of heddles needed on Shaft 1 and the number needed on Shaft 2. Total number of threading squares = 42

Shaft 1: 42 heddles

Shaft 2: 42 heddles

In Block A threading, you have 2 threads on Shaft 3, so for each colored-in square, you have 2 threads x total number of Block A squares = Number of heddles needed on Shaft 3.

Shaft 3: 8 squares Block A × 2 threads/square = 16 heddles

In Block B, you have 2 threads on Shaft 4, so for each colored-in square, you have 2 threads × the total number of Block B squares = Number of heddles needed on Shaft 4.

Shaft 4: 12 squares Block B × 2 threads/square = 24 heddles

In Block C, you have 2 threads, in the Block C unit on Shaft 5 so 2 threads × the total Block C squares = heddles on Shaft 5.

Shaft 5: 12 squares Block C × 2 threads/square = 24 heddles

In Block D, you have 2 threads in the Block D unit on Shaft 6. 2 × the number of Block D squares = heddles on Shaft 6.

Shaft 6: 10 squares Block D × 2 threads/square = 20 heddles

Check your work:
Shaft 1: 42 heddles
Shaft 2: 42 heddles
Shaft 3: 16 heddles
Shaft 4: 24 heddles
Shaft 5: 24 heddles
Shaft 6: 20 heddles
Total: 168 heddles matches our 168 warp ends without the floating selvedges. Add a floating selvedge to each of the gold bands.

I wound the warp in two colors: The outside bands are straw, and the middle area is aquamarine. Wind your warp: 29 warp ends of straw, 112 warp ends of aquamarine, 29 warp ends of straw. When winding a section with an odd number of warp ends, simply end on the turning peg (by the cross on my warping board), cut color 1, and tie on color 2. Then simply continue winding the warp until you reach 112 warp ends and tie on the straw for the last border.

Tie-up: I decided to weave this in the columns/ribs treadling. Thus, I only needed to tie up 6 treadles on my 8-shaft loom. However, if you decide to weave any of the other patterns, you will need to use 10 treadles adding the treadles in each block pair that are tied up to Shaft 1 and the pattern shaft for the blocks. (Refer to the options on page 151.)

Treadle 1: Shafts 1 and 2 (plain weave pick 1)
Treadle 2: Shafts 3, 4, 5, 6 (plain weave pick 2)
Treadle 3: Shaft 2 and Shaft 3 (pattern picks Block A)
Treadle 4: Shaft 2 and Shaft 4 (pattern picks Block B)
Treadle 5: Shaft 2 and Shaft 5 (pattern picks Block C)
Treadle 6: Shaft 2 and Shaft 6 (pattern picks Block D)

Treadling Sequence: I found that 4 pattern picks per treadling square made the central pattern blocks square up nicely. The treadling sequence below includes the plain weave base cloth picks.

Block A: Treadle 1-3-2-3, repeat
Block B: Treadle 4-2-4-1, repeat
Block C: Treadle 1-5-2-5, repeat
Block D: Treadle 1-6-2-6, repeat

Warp length: 94 inches (allows 65 inches weaving length, 6 inches take up, 6 inches fringe and 18 inches thrum waste)

Width in reed: 10.5 inches

Woven length on loom (measured off-tension): 64 inches

Hem allowance: Start and end the scarf with ½-inch plain weave using silver gray weft only.

Finished size after washing: 61 inches long x 9 inches wide.

Shrinkage: 10% length and width

Finishing: Tie fringe in overhand knots of 8 warp ends/knot. Soak the scarf in warm water and lay flat to dry. The scarf will feel very stiff off the loom and when wet. However, it softens up nicely once dry. Trim the fringe to your desired length.

WEAVE STRUCTURE
Taqueté

Taqueté (pronounced Tah-koo-tay) is a weft-faced weave that is basically weft-faced Summer and Winter woven, using only the pattern weft picks without the plain weave base cloth. Other names for this weave structure are a 2-tie weft-faced unit weave, weft-faced compound tabby weave, weft-faced Summer and Winter, and polychrome Summer and Winter. So many names for a weave structure that is as much fun to weave as it is to say its name!

Historically, Taqueté has been around much longer than Summer and Winter. In Egypt, textile fragments of Taqueté woven by Coptic weavers have been found dating to as early as the second to seventh centuries C.E. There is speculation that the weaving technique was created in an effort to make tapestry weaving faster. Another theory is that weft face silk textiles arrived in the Middle East from China via the Silk Road, and Taqueté grew out of attempts to replicate those fabrics. Textiles from China indicate that Chinese weavers were weaving Taqueté during the Tang dynasty in the seventh to tenth centuries C.E., so perhaps Taqueté was brought back to China along the trade route.

The unit threading for Taqueté is the same unit threading as Summer and Winter. Each square on the profile threading represents four threads. Because it is a weft-faced weave, the treadling squares tell you which pattern block is being woven for pattern. You can treadle those pattern blocks to any woven length you want by repeating the treadling for that particular block. Each square of treadling does not represent the number of weft picks. You weave with two shuttles, each with a different color of weft.

The biggest differences between Taqueté and Summer and Winter are (a) you weave pattern picks only, (b) you don't weave a plain weave pick between each pattern pick, and (c) Taqueté is a weft-faced weave.

When you treadle, the pattern weft colors travel from the top side of the fabric to the backside of the fabric, depending on which block of pattern you are treadling, just like with Summer and Winter. However, with Taqueté, you can change the weft colors between blocks and on each side of the fabric depending on which weft color is thrown first. (Put a pin in that—I will be discussing this in more detail.)

THE RULES OF TAQUETÉ

The sett for a Taqueté project is calculated for weft-faced weaving. Calculate the number of warp threads per inch for plain weave and then divide the plain weave sett by 2. For example, if a yarn wraps out to 32 wraps per inch (see "Calculating Sett" on page 10), the plain weave sett is 32 divided by 2 = 16 e.p.i. For a weft-faced weave using this warp thread, we divide 16 e.p.i. by 2 for a weft-faced sett of 8 e.p.i.

The tie-down warp threads are on Shafts 1 and 2. Shafts 1 and 2 are raised alternately in all blocks to catch the weft threads, thus tying down/securing the weft at consistent intervals. The tie-down warp threads are called the "binding" warp threads.

The pattern warp threads are threaded on Shaft 3 (Block A), Shaft 4 (Block B), Shaft 5 (Block C), and Shaft 6 (Block D), and these warp threads actually lie between the layers of weft and are covered by the weft threads between the tie-down/binding warp threads. If you have more shafts on your loom, you can weave more blocks of pattern, assigning each additional shaft to a block of pattern.

Pattern weft shafts are raised or lowered depending on which surface (top or bottom) that you want the pattern weft you are weaving with to show. (Stick a pin in that—this is important.) As with pattern weft in Summer and Winter, when the weft doesn't show on the top surface of the fabric in a block, it is showing on the bottom surface of the fabric and vice versa.

You weave with one or more colors of weft. The wefts are woven in sets of two picks. Across the warp and back with each weft is considered a pair (2 picks of each color). Two pairs of weft picks are called a pass and equal 4 picks of each color on both sides of the fabric.

Like Summer and Winter, the shafts in a block are tied up in pairs of treadles that work together. Treadle 1 in the treadle pair weaves the first pick in a block by raising the Shaft 1 tie-down and the pattern warp threads for the block you are treadling. Color 1/weft 1 weaves on the bottom in the block you are treadling for and on top in all the other blocks of threading. Treadle 2 in the treadling pair weaves the second pick for the same block by raising the Shaft 2 tie-down and the pattern warp threads in the other blocks, leaving the pattern weft for the block down. Color/weft 2 is on the top surface of the fabric.

With Taqueté, you alternate weaving with two colors of weft. The treadling/tie-up determines which side of the fabric each color will be within the blocks of threading. Weaving with one color of weft will give you the same color in all blocks across the fabric.

The first pick with color 1 weaves the back side of the block you are treadling for, and the second pick of color 2 will weave that color in. To change which color of weft shows on the top layer within a block, you simply change which color of weft you start weaving with for the blocks of treadling.

Use floating selvedges for tidy edges. Some books recommend threading the first and last warp threads for selvedges using the same shaft. I've found that doing this requires you to wrap the wefts around each other at the selvedges, and I don't find it as visually pleasing as using floating selvedges. I use the floating selvedge standard of the shuttle which enters the shed over the first floating selvedge and exits under the opposite floating selvedge. Then on the return pick, the shuttle enters over and exits under. However, I recommend that you experiment and see which technique you prefer.

THREADING THE BLOCKS OF PATTERN

The block threading units are the same as Summer and Winter. Shafts 1 and 2 are the tie-down shafts. Shafts 3 through 8 are the pattern shafts.

Block A: 1-3-2-3
Block B: 1-4-2-4
Block C: 1-5-2-5
Block D: 1-6-2-6
Block E: 1-7-2-7
Block F: 1-8-2-8

TIE-UP AND TREADLING

The following instructions are for rising shed (jack) looms or using the jack loom tie-up for countermarche looms that I discussed back in chapter 1.

First, let's look at the threading blocks again. The tie-down shafts in every block are Shafts 1 and 2. One of these shafts has to be engaged in each block with every pick of weft to secure the weft threads across the fabric at regular intervals.

Shafts 3–8 are the pattern shafts. For this weft-faced weave, the pattern warp threads do not show on either surface of the fabric, because they are encased by the weft threads. When we weave, the weft will be under the warp threads on pattern shafts that are raised and over all warp threads on pattern shafts that are left down.

The key question you have to remember is "Which color of weft do I want to show on the top vs. the bottom in the blocks of pattern threading across the fabric based on my treadling for the different blocks?"

Remember: It takes 4 picks of weft (refer to the box on page 163) to complete a full pass of weft across the fabric. We need to alternate the weft colors according to where we want a color to show in the blocks of threading—on the top or bottom sides of the fabric.

Let's start with two blocks of pattern: Block A and Block B. Because you need weft yarn on both sides of the fabric in both blocks, we need to alternate raising pattern in Block A with pattern in Block B, using the same tie-down shafts but raising the pattern shafts for the other block. Thus, you have to alternate pressing A1 with B1. It's easier to press treadles in order, so here's the tie-up for two blocks treadling in sequence:

	4		4
3		3	
		2	2
1	1		
A1	B1	A2	B2

To treadle a pair (see box) of weft:

Treadle 1: First pick of Block A (use weft color 1—color 1 on top in Block B, bottom in Block A)
Treadle 2: First pick of Block B (use weft color 2—color 2 on top in Block A, bottom in Block B)
Treadle 3: Second pick of Block A (use weft color 1—color 1 on top in Block B, bottom in Block A)
Treadle 4: Second pick of Block B (use weft color 2—color 2 on top in Block A, bottom in Block B)

Repeat the treadling sequence for a full pass of the wefts (see page 163).

Because of the threading sequence, both blocks use Shaft 1 and Shaft 2 as tie-down shafts. By alternating treadling between the blocks, the pairs of weft threads are weaving in the same warp tie-down shed, so the weft yarns slide close together and the pattern wefts stack up on top of each other in the 2 layers.

MORE THAN TWO BLOCKS OF PATTERN

You can weave two blocks of pattern on a 4-shaft loom. However, on an 8-shaft loom, you could weave 6 blocks of pattern if you have enough treadles.

We still need to alternate treadling for a particular block vs. the same tie-down shaft with all other pattern blocks. I call those other picks "Everything Else" which I've shortened to EE on the tie-up below. So, when you treadle for a block, you alternate treadling for the block for pattern vs. all the other blocks using the same tie-down shaft.

The threading for 6 blocks is:
Block A: 1-3-2-3
Block B: 1-4-2-4
Block C: 1-5-2-5
Block D: 1-6-2-6
Block E: 1-7-2-7
Block F: 1-8-2-8

	8		8		8		8		8		8		8		8		8		8	8		8	
	7		7		7		7		7		7		7		7	7		7			7		7
	6		6		6		6		6		6	6		6			6		6		6		6
	5		5		5		5	5		5			5		5		5		5		5		5
	4		4	4		4			4		4		4		4		4		4		4		4
3		3			3		3		3		3		3		3		3		3		3		3
		2	2			2	2			2	2			2	2			2	2			2	2
1	1			1	1			1	1			1	1			1	1			1	1		
A1	EE	A2	EE	B1	EE	B2	EE	C1	EE	C2	EE	D1	EE	D2	EE	E1	EE	E2	EE	F1	EE	F2	EE

Here's the tie-up for six individual blocks of pattern—it takes 24 treadles. Even 4 blocks of pattern will take 16 treadles.

However, you can create fabulous patterns by combining blocks with your treadles. The rug project uses 4 blocks of pattern that normally would take 16 treadles individually, but by combining blocks with my tie-up, I used 4 blocks of threading but only 8 treadles. Add in changing weft colors in various blocks, and the fabric pattern looks much more complicated than it is.

To start exploring the designs, I recommend starting with two blocks of threading and play with the mug rugs project! I say, "Start exploring," because I'll bet that you will run out of warp before you run out of ideas!

◆ PROJECT ◆

TAQUETÉ MUG RUGS

2 BLOCKS

When I was considering ideas for a Taqueté project, it struck me that weaving a series of mug rugs exploring different weft combinations of color would be a fun and fast way to play with the possibilities of Taqueté while practicing/observing the warp and weft interactions. Think of it as a practical sample that you can proudly display and use all the time.

The warp is an 8/4 carpet warp that has a plain weave sett of 12 e.p.i. For a weft-faced fabric, I divided the plain weave sett by 2 for a sett of 6 e.p.i. I decided to weave a test sample at 6 e.p.i. and then re-sleyed the warp to 8 e.p.i. for a second test sample. Comparing the two samples, I felt that the denser 8 e.p.i. made a better fabric for mug rugs. The dense sett and weft of cotton / wool blend yarn make good, sturdy, and absorbent mug rugs.

My only wish was that I'd put on a longer warp. So many possibilities! So much fun! Be sure to take good notes of what you weave in each section of the mug rugs so you can use the information in other projects.

EQUIPMENT NEEDED

4-shaft loom
8-dent reed sleyed 1 end per dent
2 shuttles with bobbins (When using multiple weft colors, it's nice to have a bobbin for each weft color.)

Threading units:
Block A: 1-3-2-3
Block B: 1-4-2-4

Yarns:
Warp: Maysville 8/4 carpet warp (100% cotton)
Weft: "Cotton Fleece" DK weight 80% cotton/20% merino wool by Brown Sheep Company, Inc.
Approximately 215 yards / 197 meters per skein

Sett: 8 e.p.i.

Calculate the number of warp ends: I decided the mug rug would be 4 inches square off the loom. To allow for draw-in shrinkage, I decided they should be 5 inches wide in the reed/on the loom. I have a total of 10 squares in the profile draft threading. Each square represents ½ inch of warp or 4 warp ends per square.

10 square × 4 threads/square = 40 warp ends plus 2 more warp ends for floating selvedges = 42 warp ends.
To confirm this gives me the project width desired: 40 warp ends divided by 8 e.p.i. = 5 inches warp width

Calculate the number of heddles/shaft:
Count the number of square for each block. Both threading blocks use Shafts 1 and 2, so count the total number of squares
Shaft 1: 10 squares × 1 = 10 heddles
Shaft 2: 10 squares × 2 = 10 heddles
Shaft 3: is only in Block A and 2 threads/block
4 Block A squares × 2 threads/square = 8 heddles
Shaft 4: is only in Block B and 2 warp threads/block
6 Block B squares × 2 threads/square = 12 heddles
Total heddles: 40 heddles

Warp length for 6 mug rugs: Allow at least 12 inches of warp length per mug rug. This gives you 5 inches of weaving length per mug rug plus 3.5 inches of warp on each end of the mug rug for tying knots/fringe. Add to the warp length for the number of mug rugs for tie-on to the apron rods and thrum waste. The tie-on and thrum waste will depend on what loom you are using and if you use the lashing method or tie on directly to the apron rod.

Width in reed: 5.25 inches

Profile draft for the 2-block mug rugs

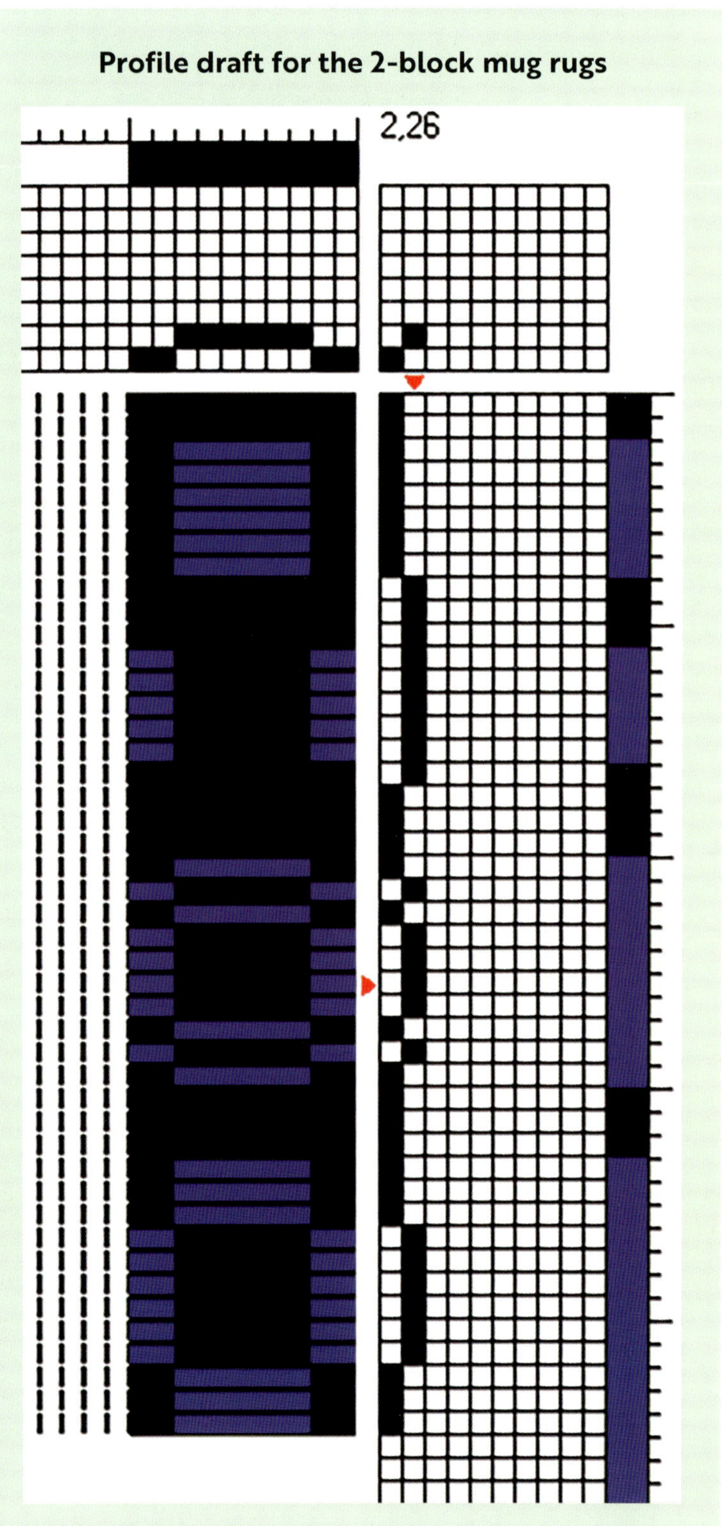

Tie-up: Use the 2 block tie up in the Taqueté chapter so you can treadle in order.
Treadle 1: Block A pick 1 tied up 1-3 (A1)
Treadle 2: Block B pick 1 tied up to 1-4 (B1)
Treadle 3: Block A pick 2 tied up to 2-3 (A2)
Treadle 4: Block B pick 2 tied up to 2-4 (B2)

To treadle a pair of weft:
Treadle 1: First pick of Block A (use weft Color 1—Color 1 on top in Block B, bottom in Block A)
Treadle 2: First pick of Block B (use weft Color 2—Color 2 on top in Block A, bottom in Block B)
Treadle 3: Second pick of Block A (use weft Color 1—Color 1 on top in Block B, bottom in Block A)
Treadle 4: Second pick of Block B (use weft Color 2—Color 2 on top in Block A, bottom in Block B)

Repeat the treadling sequence for a full pass of the wefts.

Weft:
"Cotton Fleece" DK weight in Emperor's Robe (blue); 1 skein
"Cotton Fleece" DK weight in Sunflower Gold (yellow); 1 skein
"Cotton Fleece " DK weight in Terracotta Canyon (burnt orange); 1 skein
I used about ½ skein of each color to make 6 mug rugs (5 in the photos and 1 test mug rug).

Woven length on loom:
Weave the mug rugs to square. On the loom this was about 4.5 inches per mug rug.

Hem allowance: There are no hems, but you will need to allow 7 inches between each mug rug for tying knots/fringe. I cut 1-inch-wide pieces of cardboard and wove them in between each mug rug. You can use scrap yarn as well.

Finished size: 4.5 inches wide × 4.5 inches long.

Shrinkage: Width shrinkage was about ½ inch for 10% shrinkage widthwise. You will be packing in the weft pretty densely, and I didn't find shrinkage in length/mug rug off the loom.

Weaving: I found the densest beat I could get was 28 picks per inch (counted on one side/color). This makes a very dense/stiff mug rug. If you want your mug rug to be a bit softer, beat in fewer picks/inch. You could experiment with different beats in each mug rug (being consistent within each rug) as a way of sampling for future projects.

MUG RUG 1:

Central square with borders. Make sure you do complete weft passes in each section. (Start on A1 Treadle and end on B2 treadle.)

1 • Weave 1 inch starting with the blue weft (A treadles) followed by yellow weft (B treadles).
2 • Weave 2.75 inches starting with the yellow weft (A treadles) followed by the blue weft (B treadles).
3 • Weave 1 inch starting with the blue weft (A treadles) followed by yellow weft (B treadles).

MUG RUG #2:

Wide blue borders with 2 stripes of wavy yellow lines. Remember 4 picks = 1 pass.

1 • Weave 1 inch with only the blue weft.

2 • Weave 4 picks (one full pass) in yellow.

3 • Weave 4 picks (one full pass) in blue.

4 • Alternate these 2 picks of each color for 1 inch.

5 • Weave ½ inch with only the blue weft. (Pretend your yellow weft is part of the floating selvedge thread and carry the yarn up to the next section without cutting it off. The blue weft should go over both the starting floating selvedge and the yellow weft.)

6 • Alternate the 4 picks of yellow/4 Picks of blue for 1 inch.

7 • Weave 1 inch with only the blue weft.

MUG RUG # 3:

Solid blue borders with wavy doubled lines in center

1 • Weave 1 inch with only the blue yarn. You can carry the blue up along the outer warp thread through the center section and wrap the new colors of weft around both the blue yarn and floating selvedge or cut/tuck tail.

2 • Weave 2.5 inches for the center section, alternating the weft colors of 8 picks of yellow with 8 picks of Terracotta Canyon. Cut and tuck in tails on both colors on their last picks.

3 • Weave 1 inch with only the blue yarn.

MUG RUG #4:

Yellow/blue stripes with Terracotta center

1 • Weave 8 picks using only blue yarn.

2 • Weave 4 passes (8 total picks) using blue yarn with A treadles and yellow yarn with B treadles.

3 • Weave 4 passes (8 total picks) using yellow yarn with A treadles and blue yarn with B treadles.

4 • Repeat instructions 2–3 5 times.

5 • Cut off and tuck tail on the yellow yarn.

6 • Weave 1.5 inches using the blue yarn for the A treadle picks and Terracotta Canyon yarn for the B treadle picks. Be sure to end on Treadle B2.

7 • Weave 4 passes (8 total picks) using the yellow yarn with A treadles and blue yarn with B treadles.

8 • Weave 4 passes (8 total picks) using blue yarn with A treadles and yellow yarn with B treadles.

9 • Repeat instructions 7–8 5 times.

10 • Weave 8 picks using only the blue yarn.

MUG RUG #5:

Striped center with solid blue borders. (The reverse side will have solid blue center & stacked squares borders.)

1 • Weave 1 inch using blue yarn with A treadles and yellow yarn with B treadles.

2 • Weave 1 inch using blue Yarn with A treadles and Terracotta yarn with B treadles. (Carry yellow up the edge.)

3 • Repeat 3 more times for a total of 6 colored squares on the edges.

MUG RUG #6

Do a mug rug of your own design!

◆ PROJECT ◆

TAQUETÉ RUG

3 BLOCKS ON 6 SHAFTS AND 8 TREADLES

Now that you've played with two blocks of Taqueté, you may feel the urge to weave with more blocks. As with many weave structures, more blocks means more shafts are needed. With Taqueté, more blocks also means more treadles—and therein lies the rub.

Taqueté needs four treadles per block of pattern. When working with Taqueté, I like to think in terms of pairs of treadles that work together in a block. As you discovered in the Mug Rugs project, you can do a lot of design options with just two blocks by changing which color of yarn weaves first, doing both pairs in a pass with the same color of yarn, and deciding how you can stack up the picks/passes/pairs of yarns.

Once we move on to more than two blocks, remember that, with each block, you are weaving the top layer vs. the bottom layer in all of the blocks of pattern. Two picks of each color (over and back) are called a pair, and 2 pairs of picks are called a pass. There are 4 total picks to complete one pair of pattern. Each pair weaves 2 lines of color on the top layer and 2 lines of color on the bottom layer. There are 8 total picks in a pass of pattern—4 lines of color on the top layer/4 lines of color on the bottom layer.

Some books refer to only Block A and Block B in drafts with multiple blocks of pattern;which, once I go beyond two blocks, I find repeating A and B incredibly confusing. So, I'm going to show you how I keep track of more than two blocks of pattern.

EQUIPMENT NEEDED

8-shaft loom
2 shuttles
12-dent reed (sleyed every other dent for 6 e.p.i.)

THREADING

With the profile draft for this project, I am using 4 blocks of threading. Taqueté is threaded on three shafts per threading unit.

Threading units
Block A threading: 1-3-2-3
Block B threading: 1-4-2-4
Block C threading: 1-5-2-5
Block D threading: 1-6-2-6

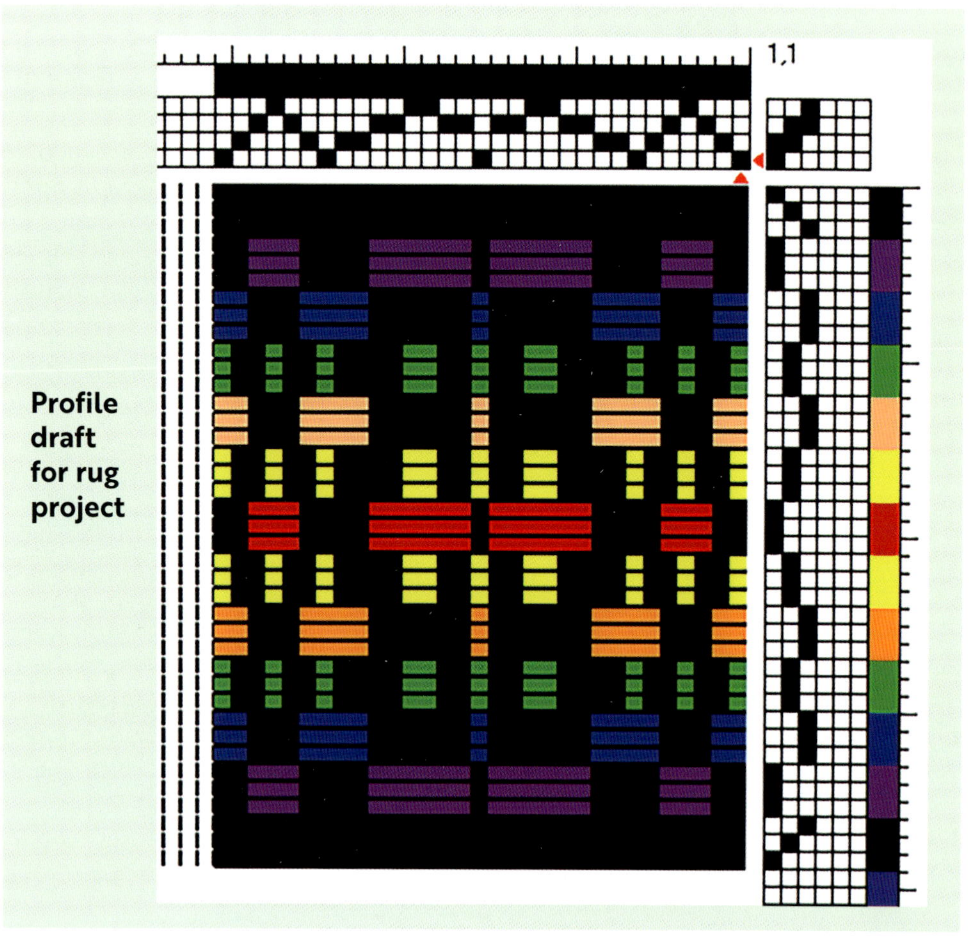

Profile draft for rug project

As with other weave structures, when you see a colored-in square on the threading for Block A, you would thread those warp threads 1-3-2-3 for Block A. If only one square is colored in, it's one repeat of the threading for that block. If there are two colored-in squares next to each other, then you repeat the threading unit twice—one threading unit for each colored-in square.

TIE-UP

As we move on to tie-up, there are two key things to remember: (1) When you alternate from the top side to the bottom side, the same tie-down shafts are engaged for both of the picks, and (2) for the second half of the treadling, you are raising all other pattern shafts plus the same tie-down shaft.

With the first 2-block mug rug, we tied up the Block A vs. Block B and used two colors of weft—one color assigned to Block A and the second color assigned to Block B. Four picks of weft equal 1 complete pass of pattern. We alternate treadling between Block A (color on backside in Block A/ top side in Block B) and Block B (color on backside in Block B and top side in Block A). To change the colors in the blocks, we changed which color yarn we weave with first.

Because we are lifting the pattern warp threads in a block, the weft will go under those threads, and the color will be on the bottom layer of fabric in the A block threading. The weft goes over the pattern warp threads in the other block so the color shows on the top layer in Block B threading because Block B pattern warp threads stay down.

Note that I am alternating between block treadles.

Treadle A1: First pick: Color 1, Shaft 1 plus the pattern shaft for Block A. Treadle is tied-up Shaft 1 and Shaft 3.
Treadle B1: Second pick: Color 2, Shaft 1 plus all the B pattern shafts. Treadle is tied-up to Shafts 1 and 4.
Treadle A2: Third pick: Color 1, Shaft 2 (the second tie down shaft), and Shaft 3
Treadle B: Fourth pick: Color 2, Shaft 2, and Shaft 4
The four picks (1 pass) are repeated for the length of my Block A treadling.

If I want to change the treadling so Color 2 is on top in Block B and Color 1 is on top in Block A, I simply change which color of weft I weave with first and keep the same treadling sequence of one pair of treadling:

Treadle A1: First pick Color 2 (Color 2 on bottom in Block A, on top in Block B)
Treadle B1: First pick Color 1 (Color 1 on bottom in Block B, on top in Block A)
Treadle A2: Second pick Color 2 (Color 2 on bottom in Block A, on top in Block B)
Treadle B2: Second pick Color 1 (Color 1 on bottom in Block B, on top in Block A)

When I move on to more than 2 blocks, I determine when I want the Color 1 pattern weft on top. I tie up to Shaft 1 and all the other pattern shafts for the other blocks.

When I want Color 2 pattern weft on the bottom, I tie up to Shaft 1 and the pattern shaft for the block.

If I have a Block C, I have to tie-up another 4 treadles:

Block C1: Shaft 1 (tie-down) and Shaft 5 (Block C pattern)
Block AB1: Shaft 1 (tie-down) and Shaft 3 and Shaft 4 (the pattern shafts in Blocks A and B)
Block C2: Shaft 2 (tie-down) and Shaft 5 (Block C pattern)
Block AB2: Shaft 2 (tie-down) and Shafts 3 and 4 (the pattern shafts in Blocks A and B)

Adding a Block D, I need another 4 treadles:

Block D1: Shafts 1 and 6
Block ABC1: Shaft 1 and Shafts 3, 4, 5 (pattern shafts for Blocks A, B, and C)
Block D3: Shafts 2 and 6
Block ABC2: Shaft 2 and Shafts 3, 4, 5 (pattern shafts for Blocks A, B and C)

I need a total of 16 treadles. And 8-shaft looms have 10! What to do? If you have a jack loom, you can press 2 treadles at a time, so you could use a skeleton tie-up and press two treadles at a time. The tie-down treadle and the pattern treadle for a block plus remember to alternate pressing Treadles 1 and 2.

Skeleton tie-up for 8 shafts/4 blocks:

Treadle 1: Shaft 1 (tie-down warp thread 1)
Treadle 2: Shaft 2 (tie-down warp thread 2)
Treadle 3: A Pattern (Shaft 3)
Treadle 4: A Shafts 4, 5, 6 (all of the pattern shafts other than Block A)
Treadle 5: B Pattern (Shaft 4)
Treadle 6: B Shafts 3, 5, 6 (all of the pattern shafts other than Block B)
Treadle 7: C Pattern (Shaft 5)
Treadle 8: C Shafts 3, 4, 6 (pattern shafts for all blocks except Block C)
Treadle 9: D Pattern (Shaft 6)
Treadle 10: D 3, 4, 5 (pattern shafts for all the blocks except Block D)

Confused? Here's another way to visualize this. I make a little chart and say to myself, "What is the pattern shaft for a specific block vs. the pattern shafts for all the other blocks?" (See figure 1.)

Tie-down 1	Tie-down 2	Blocks B, C & D Pattern	Block B Pattern Shaft	Block B Pattern Shaft	Blocks A, C & D Pattern	Block C Pattern Shaft	Blocks A, B & D Pattern	Block D Pattern Shaft	Blocks A, B & C Pattern
			6		6		6	6	
			5		5	5			5
			4	4			4		4
		3			3		3		3
	2								
1									

Figure 1: Skeleton tie-up for 8 shafts / 4 blocks

I like to think of it as setting up to treadle for the pattern shaft in a block vs. everything else (all the other pattern shafts for the other blocks). At this point, I change my designations to the block letter and the number within the treadling sequence of the of color weft for the block.

Here's the treadling sequence for the first pair of threads on each layer. Repeat for a full pass.
Block A1/Color 1: Treadle 1 PLUS Treadle 3 (tie-down Shaft 1, pattern in A)
Block A2/Color 2: Treadle 1 PLUS Treadle 4 (tie-down Shaft 1, pattern for B, C & D)
Block A3/Color 1: Treadle 2 PLUS Treadle 3 (tie-down Shaft 2, pattern in A)
Block A4/Color 2: Treadle 2 PLUS Treadle 4 (tie-down Shaft 2, pattern for B, C, and D)

Sadly, if you have a countermarche loom, you can't press 2 treadles at the same time. Thus, you are stuck with retying treadles unless you have a loom with 16 treadles. Here's the full tie-up for 4 blocks of pattern (figure 2).

Tie-Up for More than One Block of Threading
I wove this rug on my 12-shaft countermarche loom, and I was not enthusiastic about needing to re-tie treadles, so I started playing with combining blocks on one treadle.

Looking at the profile draft for the rug, you can see in the profile tie-up that there are 3 blocks of pattern that are combinations of two blocks of threading each. In other words, when I tie up my treadles for Block A1, I have to tie up for the tie-down Shaft 1 and the pattern shafts for both Block A and Block B. I call this Block AB1 because it's combining A Block and B Block of pattern into one larger pattern block where the blocks are threaded next to each other. When the A and B blocks are threaded with separation between these two blocks, then the A and B blocks are woven at the same time, but the threading creates two separate blocks of pattern. Isn't that fun?!

Looking at the chart I made for tying up 16 treadles, I made the tie-up chart in figure 3 for combined blocks. I found that combining blocks resulted in fewer treadles to tie up! Only 12 treadles, but that's still too many for most 8 shaft looms.

A1	A2	A3	A4	B1	B2	B3	B4	C1	C2	C3	C4	D1	D2	D3	D4	Pattern
	6		6		6		6		6		6	6		6		Pattern
	5		5		5		5	5		5			5		5	Pattern
	4		4	4		4			4		4		4		4	Pattern
3		3			3		3		3		3		3		3	Pattern
		2	2			2	2			2	2			2	2	Tie-down
1	1			1	1			1	1			1	1			Tie-down

Figure 2: Full 4-block tie-up for countermarche looms

AB1	AB2	AB3	AB4	BC1	BC2	BC3	BC4	CD1	CD2	CD3	CD4
	6		6		6		6	6		6	
	5		5	5		5		5		5	
4		4		4		4			4		4
3		3			3		3		3		3
		2	2			2	2			2	2
1	1			1	1			1	1		
A / B1	A / B2	A / B3	A / B4	B / C1	B / C2	B / C3	B / C4	C / D1	C / D2	C / D3	C / D4

Figure 3: Combined blocks tie-up

Then it hit me! Look at CD1 through CD4. The tie-up is the same as AB1–AB4, only in reverse order in the pairs. I need only 8 treadles by pressing the A/B treadles in reverse order when I treadle for CD Blocks. Now I'm down to 8 treadles. CD1 is the same tie-up as AB2; CD2 is the same tie-up as AB1; CD3 is the same tie-up AB4; CD4 is the same tie-up as AB3.

Therefore, when the profile treadling calls for the C/D Block, my treadling sequence using the A/B treadles is:

Treadle AB2 (Color 1)
Treadle AB1 (Color 2)
Treadle AB4 (Color 1)
Treadle AB3 (Color 2)

With this knowledge firmly in hand, it's time to do the 3-block rug! When I wrote out the profile draft, I had to "trick" my Fiberworks program to get an idea of how the blocks would line up. Yes, there is a weft-faced command, but it doesn't create as clean/nuanced intersections of the blocks in my book. It may work quite nicely for you.

I also did a bit of designing on the loom for the two borders to show the variations I could get by just changing the length I treadle a block. These variations are not on the profile draft. The first border section is ½-inch-long color sections following the sequence on the profile draft. Note that the first (purple/blue) are in the same block—because I treadled wrong and didn't catch it until I was a couple more color sections along. I decided to leave it because it demonstrates how you can change things up. The center section is blocks that are 1 inch long. For the last border, I stacked up colors in the same blocks for part of the design. Pick your favorite, create your own, and explore what lovely designs you can make!

The key? Don't overthink and make notes on what sequences you weave!

Threading units:
Block A: 1-3-2-3
Block B: 1-4-2-4
Block C: 1-5-2-5
Block D: 1-6-2-6

Warp yarns: Bockens Bomull (cotton) Smart Warp in Beige (Bockens Color #40)

Weft yarns:
Brown Sheep Company "Cotton Fleece" DK weight
Cavern (black); 4 skeins
Purple Basil; 1 skein
Bering Sea Blue; 1 skein
Jubilant Jade; 1 skein
Terracotta Canyon; 1 skein
Butter Cream; 1 skein
Salmon Berry Red; 1 skein

I used about ½ a skein of each color to weave the rug and almost 4 full skeins of black.

Sett: 6 e.p.i.

Calculate the number of warp ends: Each colored-in square on the threading = 4 warp threads. There are a total of 31 squares in the threading. 31 squares × 4 threads/square = 124 warp threads plus 2 floating selvedges is 126 warp threads.

I find that using floating selvedges makes tidier selvedges when weaving Taqueté. Do not wind the floating selvedges with the warp. Hang each floating selvedge as a separate warp thread and weight each separately. I find that wrapping the floating selvedges around the back beam and then weighting each one helps to maintain consistent tension for the floating selvedges as I weave.

Calculate the number of heddles: Count the number of threading squares for each block. Look at the threading key. Multiply the number of times a thread is used in a block times the number of blocks in that row.

Shafts 1 and 2 are each used once in every threading block. There are 31 threading squares.
Shaft 1: 31 heddles
Shaft 2: 31 heddles

In every profile square of threading, there are two pattern threads in a threading unit. Count the number of squares that are in the same threading block and multiply by 2.

Block A: 5 squares are in Block A and the pattern threads on Shaft 3.
Shaft 3: 5 squares × 2 threads in each square = 10 heddles

Block B: 8 squares and pattern threads on Shaft 4
Shaft 4: 8 squares × 2 threads per square = 16 heddles

Block C: 12 squares and pattern threads on Shaft 5
Shaft 5: 12 squares × 2 threads per square = 24 heddles

Block D: 6 squares and pattern threads on Shaft 6
Shaft 6: 6 squares × 2 threads/square = 12 heddles

Total heddle count:
Shaft 1 = 31
Shaft 2 = 31
Shaft 3 = 10
Shaft 4 = 16
Shaft 5 = 24
Shaft 6 = 12
Total heddles/warp threads = 124 warp threads

.**Warp Length:** There is very little warp length shrinkage/take-up with weft-faced weaves. I did not add plain weave hems on each end. I used 76 inches of warp length allowing 7 inches for braided fringe, 9 inches of tie-on, 40 inches of woven length, and 20 inches of thrum waste.

Width in reed: 20.75 inches

Weaving: The first weft thread in a pass (sequence of 4 picks of weft total) is always black, and the second weft thread is the color you want in the blocks. Alternate black wefts/color wefts in all pattern blocks.

Please note: I did not follow the profile draft for color placement or block proportions in the rug. I wanted to demonstrate the possibilities of playing with the colors and blocks woven. Feel free to go "off draft" in your rug. The directions below are the sequences I used to weave the project sample.

Start: Weave 3 inches using only black weft, while treadling through all blocks in the order A, B, C.

Border 1: Follow the profile treadling sequence, weaving ½ inch of color weft per block of treadling. Color order:
Block A: Purple (½ inch)
Block C: Purple ½ inch then ½ inch of Blue)
Block B: Green
Block C: Orange
Block B: Yellow
Block A: Red (center of the pattern—do not repeat when you weave in reverse)

Weave the second half of the border by treadling blocks/colors in reverse order (Block B: yellow, Block C: orange, Block B: green, Block A: ½ inch of blue followed by ½ inch of purple.

Divider: Weave 2 inches with only black weft treadling through all blocks in order.

Center: Follow treadling sequence on the draft, weaving 1 inch of weft/per block.
Block A: Purple
Block C: Blue
Block B: Green
Block C: Orange
Block B: Yellow
Block A: Red
Weave the blocks/colors in reverse order, starting with Block B after Block A in red for balance of the center section.

Divider: Weave 2 inches with only black weft treadling through all blocks in order.

Border 2:
Block A: ½ inch purple followed by ½ inch blue
Block C: ½ inch green, ½ inch orange, ½ inch yellow
Block A: ½ inch red
Block C: ½ inch yellow, ½ inch orange, ½ inch green
Block A: ½ inch blue, ½ inch purple

End: Weave 3 inches with only Bback weft treadling through all blocks in order.

TIPS:

1) Due to the size of the weft yarn, alternate which edge you start/stop each color. Otherwise, one selvedge will start distorting from turning the weft threads around the selvedge threads to trap the ends. This buildup will distort that selvedge edge. Since there are so many colors separated by a long distance before the next use of that color, I don't recommend carrying the colors up along the selvedges.

2) Split apart the weft yarn when you do a weft yarn join, so you don't have a large lump where the old weft and new weft overlap.

3) Use floating selvedges that are weighted separately from the main warp threads. Make sure they are firmly held under tension. I wrapped mine around the back beam 1 time and hung my weights. Worked like a charm.

4) Use firm warp tension when weaving.

Woven length on loom: 40 inches

Finished size: 40 inches long by 19.5 inches wide

Shrinkage: 1% in width (approximately 1 inch draw-in)

Fringe finish: 3 strand braids using 6 warp ends per braid (2 warp ends per braid strand); 2-inch-long braids.

WEAVE STRUCTURE
Beiderwand

Beiderwand (pronounced by-der-vahnd) is a double two-tie unit weave structure with its roots in northern Germany and southern Denmark in the seventeenth century. At that time, the woven fabric was commonly used for bed curtains and clothing. Beiderwand is German for "two wall." Harriet Tidball called it "double Summer and Winter" because the threading units are similar to Summer and Winter. After reading several old weaving books, I theorize that Summer and Winter developed as a weave structure after Beiderwand, possibly in North America or Europe, either by mistake or in search a of a block pattern with shorter pattern weft floats than Beiderwand. Either way, the two weave structures are "kissing cousins."

Like Summer and Winter, Beiderwand uses two tie-down warps threaded on Shafts 1 and 2 to hold the supplemental pattern wefts in place at regular intervals. The pattern weft changes sides of the fabric, depending on which block of pattern is being woven. Both structures use a smaller grist yarn for the warp and to weave the base cloth and a larger size yarn for the supplemental pattern weft. Both are woven alternating weft picks between two shuttles, one shuttle to weave the pattern wefts and a second shuttle to weave the plain weave base cloth.

Unlike Summer and Winter, Beiderwand is assigned to the doubleweave structure family called Lampas. Beiderwand pattern weft floats are long and subtly interlace within the pattern weft blocks, so it looks like a weft-faced weave on one side of the fabric and the other side in the same block shows the plain weave background with the tie-down warp threads catching the pattern wefts in a vertical line in the center of the block. With Summer and Winter, the supplemental pattern wefts do not interlace, and the tie-down warp threads are staggered within the block.

THREADING BEIDERWAND

To wrap our heads around the difference between the two weave structures, let's compare the threading units of Summer and Winter vs. Beiderwand. The tie-down threads for each unit are in orange in each threading unit. The black numbers are the shafts assigned for creating the pattern weft floats.

You may have noticed that the Summer and Winter threading units use two tie-down threads/shafts that alternate with the pattern weft shaft(s) within the same block of threading. Beiderwand has the tie-down shafts alternating between the different blocks of threading. The brackets around two Biederwand threading units indicate that Block A and Block B work together while Block C and Block D work together—although I have found that is not a hard-and-fast rule!

The hard-and-fast rule to Beiderwand is you must alternate using Shaft 1 with Shaft 2 between pattern shaft sections of threading so that these two tie-down warp threads do their job of tying down the pattern weft threads at regular intervals. You do not have to have Block A threading next to Block B threading or Block C next to Block D threading. You can combine non-consecutive blocks as long as you continue to alternate the tie-down shafts between the threading blocks next to each other.

You must have a minimum of 2 shafts assigned for pattern in each block that work together within the blocks to make the pattern weft floats. The number of pattern threads in a block can be as small as 2 threads (Block A could be 1-3-4 instead of 1-3-4-3-4), can be an odd number of threads (like 1-3-4-3), or can even repeat the same pattern shaft threading but alternate the tie down shafts between the pattern threading pairs. For example: Block A: 1-3-4-2-3-4 and Block B: 1-5-6-2-5-6. The tie-down threads are in orange, and the pattern weft warp threads are in black. All of these variations will create different interlacements of the pattern wefts to create new patterns within the blocks.

SUMMER AND WINTER THREADING UNITS

1:1 Ratio	1:2 Ratio	1:3 Ratio	1:4 Ratio
Block A: 1-3-2-3	Block A: 1-4-3-2-3-4	Block A: 1-3-4-3-2-3-4-3	Block A: 1-4-3-4-3-2-3-4-3-4
Block B: 1-4-2-4	Block B: 1-6-5-2-5-6	Block B: 1-5-6-5-2-5-6-5	Block B: 1-6-5-6-5-2-5-6-5-6
Block C: 1-5-2-5	Block C: 1-8-7-2-7-8	Block C: 1-7-8-7-2-7-8-7	Block C: 1-8-7-8-2-7-8-7-8
Block D: 1-6-2-6	Block D: 1-10-9-2-9-10	Block D: 1-9-10-9-2-9-10-9	Block D: 1-10-9-10-9-2-9-10-9-10

BIEDERWAND THREADING UNITS

Block A: [1-3-4-3-4 Block B: 2-5-6-5-6]

Block C: [1-7-8-7-8 Block D: 2-9-10-9-10]

BEIDERVAND VS. SUMMER AND WINTER

To help envision the differences between the two weave structures, here's a bit of a 2-block thread-by-thread draft for Summer and Winter in the commonly used 1:1 ratio. The tie-down threads are shaded yellow. The tie-up is on the far right after the notations column.

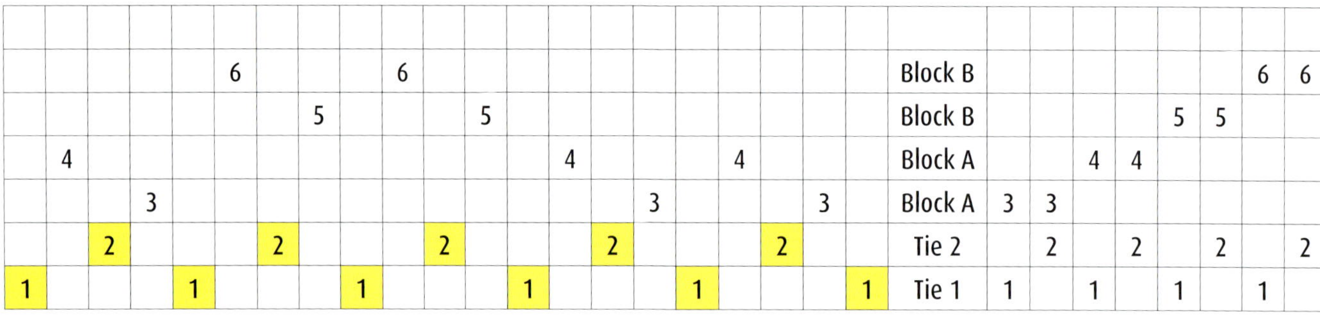

					6				6												Block B							6	6
							5				5										Block B					5	5		
	4												4				4				Block A			4	4				
			3												3				3		Block A	3	3						
		2				2				2				2				2			Tie 2		2		2		2		2
1				1				1				1				1				1	Tie 1	1		1		1		1	

Figure 1 – Summer and Winter thread-by-thread and tie-up

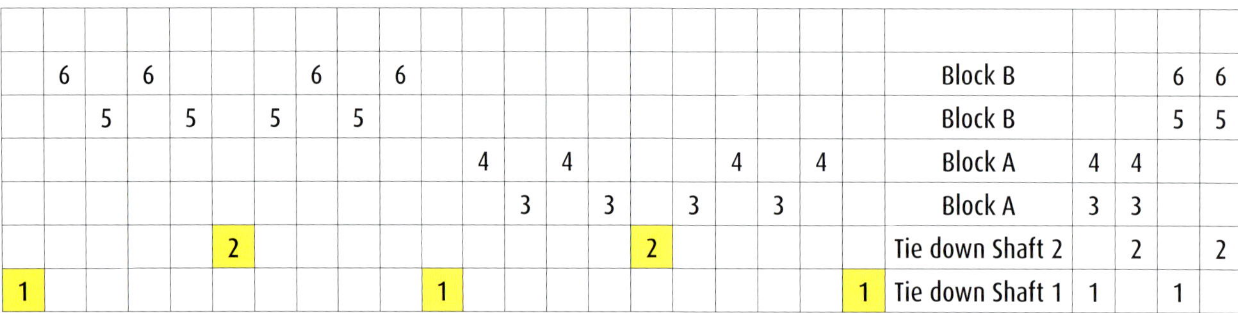

	6		6				6		6												Block B			6	6
		5		5		5		5													Block B			5	5
											4		4				4		4		Block A	4	4		
												3		3		3		3			Block A	3	3		
					2										2						Tie down Shaft 2		2		2
1										1										1	Tie down Shaft 1	1		1	

Figure 2 – Beiderwand threading and tie-up

Now let's compare that to Beiderwand threading and tie-up. Again, the tie-down shafts are yellow in the threading, and the tie-up is on the far right after the block notations column.

The drafts are similar, but not the same. Summer and Winter has the tie-down shafts alternating 1:1 with the threads on the pattern shafts. The tie-up raises each tie-down shaft with the pattern shaft for the block designation. The Beiderwand draft has the tie-down shafts between threading groups. The tie-up alternates between raising the two tie-down shafts and raising all the threads in a pattern group with each treadle. This means, when you press Treadle 1, the tie-downs on Shaft 1 are raised as well as the pattern shaft threads on Shafts 3 and 4. That means the pattern weft floats will be on the bottom side of the fabric in Block A threading. At the same time, in Block B threading, the pattern weft is tied down by Shaft 1, but the pattern weft will be on the top side of the fabric in Block B because Shafts 5 and 6 are left down.

Also note the Beiderwand threading sequences in each block are in descending order, followed by ascending order. It is important that the threads are alternating between odd- and even-numbered shaft. When you tie up for plain weave, every other thread is raised across the warp. All the odd-numbered shafts are tied up together, and all of the even-numbered shafts are tied up together. If you had two warp threads next to each other with both on even- (or odd-) numbered shafts, you would get doubled warp threads in the plain weave.

Count the number of empty squares between the tie-downs on Shaft 1 in the Beiderwand draft. The pattern weft will float over nine warp threads until the next Shaft 1 thread regardless of being on the top of the fabric or bottom of the fabric.

The next treadle raises Shaft 2 (the second tie-down shaft) plus Shafts 3 and 4 again. The pattern weft will again be on the bottom side of the fabric in Block A and the top side of the fabric in Block B, but the tie-downs on Shaft 2 will be centered in the blocks of threading. This creates another 9-thread float anchored by the Shaft 2 tie-down centered between the tie-downs in Shaft 1 in the previous pattern pick. These long pattern weft floats create weft-faced fabric in the blocks of Beiderwand.

Beiderwand

		6	6		6	Block B
		5	5	5		Block B
4	4				4	Block A
3	3			3		Block A
	2		2		2	Tie down 2
1		1		1		Tie down 1
Pattern				Plain weave		

Summer and Winter

						6	6		6	Block B
				5	5				5	Block B
		4	4						4	Block A
3	3								3	Block A
	2		2		2		2	2		Tie down 2
1		1		1		1		1		Tie down 1
Pattern								Plain weave		

Between each pick of Beiderwand pattern weft, you need a pick of plain weave to create a stable fabric, just like Summer and Winter. Here are how the two tie-ups compare side by side with two blocks of pattern threading plus the tie-up for plain weave for Beidervand vs. Summer and Winter.

The plain weave tie-ups are similar, yet different. It all hinges on the threading of the blocks! Look closely at each thread-by-thread draft. Keep two important things in mind: (1) Plain weave requires every other thread to be raised so the weft travels over 1 thread/under 1 thread across the fabric. (2) Pattern weft floats cover the plain weave base cloth on either the top or bottom of the fabric, depending on the block threading.

Beiderwand

Beiderwand alternates the tie-down shaft threading between repeated sets of warp threads in a block and between different blocks. Note that the threading alternates between an odd-numbered shaft and an even-numbered shaft in the different blocks. Thus, the tie-up for plain weave in Beiderwand raises the odd-numbered shafts together and the even-numbered shafts together. The block threading combined with the treadle tie-ups raises every other thread for plain weave. Note in the Beiderwand photo how the pattern block wefts create a weft-faced pattern in the blocks.

Summer and Winter

Summer and Winter on a 1:1 ration alternates the tie-down shaft threading between pattern warp threads within a block, and the pattern weft shafts alternate between odd and even shafts in each block. This means that when you raise the tie-down Shafts 1 and 2 at the same time, every other thread is raised. The pattern weft shafts are threaded between the tie-down shafts, so for the second pick of plain weave, we need to raise all the pattern weft shafts. Note how the pattern wefts "stack up" to create pattern.

CHOOSING YARNS FOR BEIDERVAND

Warp: Use a smooth, strong yarn for your warp. The sett of the fabric is the plain weave sett for your warp yarn. The warp yarn can be any size of yarn, but remember the larger the yarn, the fewer ends per

inch, and the pattern weft floats will still be over 9 warp ends, so those floats could be very long.

Plain weave base cloth weft: Use the same size yarn as your warp yarn. Generally, use the same yarn color/fiber content for the weft as the warp, but you can play with this.

Pattern weft: This yarn should be slightly larger in grist than your warp yarn, so you get good coverage in the pattern blocks. In the project sample, I use 10/2 cotton with a 5/2 cotton pattern weft. If you want to use a larger pattern weft, consider using wool yarn. Wool yarns have more air incorporated in the yarn, allowing for more compression of the yarn as it weaves in the tiny hole created between the intersections of the warp and weft of the plain weave base cloth. I have experimented with using the same size yarn as the base cloth warp/weft. It works, but I would suggest sampling before making a full commitment to make sure you have good coverage in the pattern weft-prominent sides of the blocks.

Technically speaking, the plain weave base cloth and the pattern weft floats create two separate layers of fabric. One layer is weft-faced; the other layer is plain weave. The two layers are connected together with the tie-down shafts.

◆ PROJECT ◆

BEIDERWAND PLACEMATS
ON 8 SHAFTS

Both placemats are woven on the same warp, but with different treadling sequences for different patterns in the placemats. Note that Beiderwand has pattern-dominant and base-cloth-dominant sides to the fabric. On the plain weave-dominant side of the blocks, the weft tie-downs create a lovely fine stripe that is technically in the center of each threading repeat of the blocks.

For each block of pattern, you need two shafts for the pattern floats plus two shafts for the tie-down warps. Thus, with a 4-shaft loom, you can only weave one block of pattern. You would have one side of the fabric completely covered by the weft floats. The other side would be plain weave with the fine stripes created by the weft tie-down. You could make a lovely fabric with a single color of weft or use multiple colors of weft to make weft-faced stripes across the fabric. I think it would be worthy of a sample and project!

With an 8-shaft loom, you can weave three blocks:
Block A threaded on Shafts 3 and 4
Block B threaded on Shafts 5 and 6
Block C threaded on Shafts 7 and 8

This project uses three blocks of pattern which requires an 8-shaft loom. If you have 10 shafts available, you can weave 4 blocks of pattern.

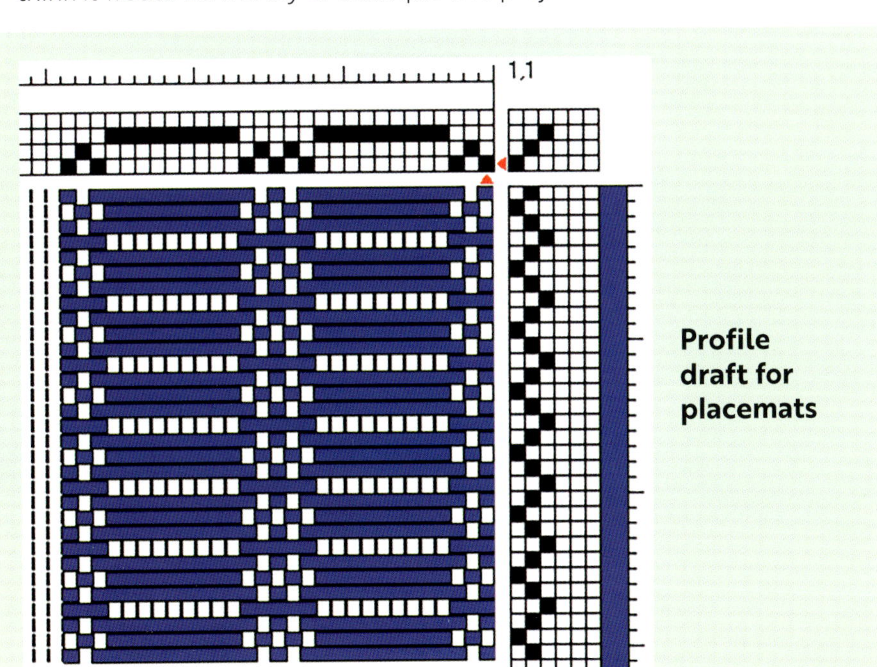

Profile draft for placemats

EQUIPMENT NEEDED

8-shaft table or floor loom

10-dent reed (sleyed 2 ends per dent)

2 shuttles

Threading units:
(tie-down shafts are colored orange)
The threading creates floats over 9 threads between the tie-down shafts. If you want smaller floats/blocks due to using a larger base cloth warp yarn, use Threading Option 2 to reduce the threading repeats between the tie-down shafts.

Note that the threading sequences in each block are in descending order followed by ascending order. This is important so that threads alternate between odd- and even-numbered shafts. When you tie up for plain weave, every other thread is raised across the warp. All the odd-numbered shafts are tied up together, and the all of the even-numbered shafts are tied up together. If you had two warp threads next to each other both on even- (or odd-) numbered shafts, you would get doubled warp threads in the plain weave!

Repeats as woven in sample:
Block A: 1-4-3-4-3-2-3-4-3-4
Block B: 1-6-5-6-5-2-5-6-5-6
Block C: 1-8-7-8-7-2-7-8-7-8
Block D: 1-10-9-10-9-2-9-10-9-10

Threading option #2 for shorter floats over 5 threads when using larger warp yarn:
Block A: 1-4-3-2-3-4
Block B: 1-6-5-2-5-6
Block C: 1-8-7-2-7-8
Block D: 1-10-9-2-9-10

Yarns:
Base cloth warp and weft: 10/2 mercerized cotton by Lunatic Fringe Yarns in periwinkle
Pattern weft: 5/2 mercerized cotton by Lunatic Fringe Yarns in cobalt

Sett: 20 e.p.i.

Calculate the number of warp ends: Each colored-in square of the threading profile represents 2 base cloth threads and 8 pattern warp threads, for a total of 10 threads per threading square.

Count the number of squares for each block and multiply by 10 threads.
Block A: 7 squares × 10 threads/square = 70 warp threads
Block B: 4 squares × 10 threads/square = 40 warp threads
Block C: 18 squares × 10 threads/square = 180 warp threads
Total warp threads: 70 (Block A) + 40 (Block B) + 180 (Block C) = 290 warp ends + 2 floating selvedges = 292

Calculate the number of heddles: Each square on the profile threading has 1 thread on Shaft 1 and 1 thread on Shaft 2 for the tie-downs.
Count the total number of squares in the threading= 29 squares.
Shaft 1: 29 squares x 1 thread per square = 29 heddles
Shaft 2: 29 squares x 1 thread per square = 29 heddles

Block A—pattern with 4 threads on Shaft 3 and 4 threads on Shaft 4 per profile square:
There are 7 squares on Block A in the profile threading.
Shaft 3 is 4 threads × 7 Block A squares = 28 heddles.
Shaft 4 is 4 threads × 7 Block A squares = 28 heddles.

Block B—pattern with 4 threads on Shaft 5 and 4 threads on Shaft 6 per profile square:
There are 4 squares on Block B in the profile threading.
Shaft 5 is 4 threads × 4 squares = 16 heddles.
Shaft 6 is 4 threads × 4 squares = 16 heddles.

Block C—pattern with 4 threads on Shaft 7 and 4 threads on Shaft 8 per profile square:
There are 18 squares on Block C in the profile threading.
Shaft 7 is 4 threads × 18 squares = 72 heddles.
Shaft 8 is 4 threads × 18 squares = 72 heddles.

You will need floating selvedges, but they are not threaded through heddles so they don't add to the heddle count.

Check your work to make sure the heddle count matches the number of warp threads:
Shaft 1 = 29 heddles
Shaft 2 = 29 heddles
Shaft 3 = 28 heddles
Shaft 4 = 28 heddles
Shaft 5 = 16 heddles
Shaft 6 = 16 heddles
Shaft 7 = 72 heddles
Shaft 8 = 72 heddles

Total = 290 heddles
Warp thread count = 290

Tie-up:
Treadle 1: 1-3-4 (Pattern Block A 1)
Treadle 2: 2-3-4 (Pattern Block A 2)
Treadle 3: 1-5-6 (Pattern Block B 1)
Treadle 4: 2-5-6 (Pattern Block B 2)
Treadle 5: 1-7-8 (Pattern Block C 1)
Treadle 6: 2-7-8 (Pattern Block C 2)
Treadle 7: 1-3-5-7 (Plain weave 1)
Treadle 8: 2-4-6-8 (Plain weave 2)

Treadling sequence: Weave blocks to square. The number of times you repeat the treadling sequence for a block depends on the size of the yarns you are using. One treadling sequence requires alternating the pattern treadles and weaving alternating picks of the plain weave treadles between each pattern pick.

For example, the profile draft starts with Block B. Block B is Treadles 3 and 4:
Treadle 3: (Pattern weft pick 1 in Block B- Shuttle 1 with pattern weft)
Treadle 7: (First plain weave base cloth pick – Shuttle 2 with base cloth weft)
Treadle 4: (Pattern weft pick 2 in Block B – Shuttle 1 with pattern weft)
Treadle 8: (Second plain weave base cloth pick – Shuttle 2 with base cloth weft)
Repeat the sequence until the block is woven to square.

Next is Block A:
Treadle 1/Shuttle 1: pattern weft
Treadle 7/Shuttle 2: base cloth weft
Treadle 2/Shuttle 1: pattern weft
Treadle 8/Shuttle 2: base cloth weft
Repeat until the block is woven to square.

Next is Block B. Repeat the treadling sequence for Block B.

Next is Block C:
Treadle 5/Shuttle 1: pattern weft
Treadle 7/Shuttle 2: base cloth weft
Treadle 6/Shuttle 1: pattern weft
Treadle 8/Shuttle 2: base cloth weft
Repeat until the block is woven to square.

Weaving:
For placemat 1, woven according to the profile draft using treadling for all three blocks
For placemat 2, woven using only Block A and Block B treadling

Warp Length: I wove 2 placemats allowing 17 inches woven length measure on the loom for pattern area only plus 2.5 inches on each end of plain weave for the hems, for a total of 22 inches per placemat. I like to weave two picks of thrum yarn between the placemats. When I'm finished weaving, I can cut the placemats apart between the two picks of thrum for a perfectly straight cut.

68 inches warp length: Allows 44 inches woven length on loom for two placemats with hems + 6 inches tie-on allowance + 18 inches thrum waste

Width in reed: 14.5 inches

Woven length on loom (measured off-tension): Per placemat, 2.5 inches plain weave for hems + 17 inches of pattern area + 2.5 inches hem

Hem allowance: 2.5 inches using only the plain weave weft on each end of each placemat

Finished size after washing: Pattern area only, 15 inches long × 12.5 inches wide

Shrinkage: 12% in length and width

Finishing: Zigzag stitch along the raw ends of each placemat. Soak in warm water and lay flat to dry to block placemats into shape. This helps reduce shrinkage in future machine wash/dry. Turn the raw ends of the hems under about ¼ inch and press. Fold over the hem allowance so the edge of the first fold matches the end of the pattern area. Press. Hand- or machine-stitch the hems.

APPENDIXES

CALCULATION FOR THE NUMBER OF WARP THREADS USING YOUR PROFILE DRAFT

Number of squares in the threading times the number of threads in each threading unit = total number of warp threads

WARP LENGTH CALCULATION:

- Desired finished length after washing + shrinkage (take-up) = woven length on the loom
- Woven length on loom + shrinkage allowance +tie-on/fringe allowance + thrum waste = warp length

Thrum waste is the amount of yarn that you just can't weave because the apron rod is too close to the back of the shafts to get a clean shed. This length can be different for every loom. To determine the amount of thrum waste needed on a loom, place your back apron rod about 6 inches away from the back of the shafts. Place your beater so it's centered between the front beam and the shafts. Place the end of a tape measure at the back of the beater and measure the distance from the back of the beater to the back apron rod through the shafts. This measurement is the amount of thrum waste needed on that particular loom. Remember, ending fringe can be taken out of the thrum waste!

CALCULATING THE NUMBER OF HEDDLES PER SHAFT USING A PROFILE DRAFT

This calculation is done for each of the projects in detail. Here are the basic steps:

- Determine the threading for each block of pattern.
- Count the number of threading squares for a particular block of pattern.
- Multiply the number of threading squares for a block of threading times the number of threads on each shaft used in each threading square.
- Add the threads on the same shafts in all the blocks where these same shafts are used.
- This gives you a total number of heddles needed per shaft.

WEFT YARDAGE CALCULATION:

Width of piece times the picks per inch equals the amount of weft needed for 1 inch of woven fabric.

- Amount of weft for 1 inch times the number of inches of woven length equals the total INCHES of weft needed
- Divide the total Inches by 36 inches in a yard = yards of weft needed to weave the piece.

If you use the metric system:

- Width of the piece times the picks per centimeter equals the amount of weft needed per centimeter of woven fabric
- Amount of weft per centimeter times the number of centimeters of woven length equals the total centimeters of weft needed
- Divide total centimeters by 100 = meters of weft needed to weave the piece.

PROJECT RECORD SHEET

Project Name ________________________________ **Date** ______________

Pattern and reference books / articles used: ______________________________

Warp length: ______________________________

________ (finished length) + ________ (take-up / shrinkage) ________ fringe+________ Loom / Thrum waste

Sett: ______________________________

Warp yarn Name / Fiber / Color(s): ______________________________

Warp Yarn supplier: ______________________________

Total number of warp threads: ______________________________

(Use floating selvedges? Yes No)

Warp yardage: ______________________________

Weft yarn Name / Fiber / Color(s): ______________________________

Weft Yarn Supplier:______________________________

Weft Yardage: ______________________________

If project uses a pattern weft:

Pattern Weft Yarn Name / Fiber / Color(s): ______________________________

Pattern Weft Yarn Supplier:______________________________

Pattern Weft Yardage: ______________________________

Weaving (write special notes on back of sheet):

Hem / header: ______________ **Fringe Finish:** ______________

Width in Reed: ______________ **Woven Length on loom:** ______________

Length off loom (unwashed): ______________ **Width off loom (unwashed):** ______________

Finished length (washed): ______________ **Finished width (washed):** ______________

RESOURCES

Here are some books for further exploration into the weave structures featured in this book. Some of these books are out of print. Look for them in your local public library or your weaving guild's library if you can't find a copy to purchase. You may be able to borrow some books through interlibrary loans at your local library.

Fabric Design and Multiple Weave Structures

Alderman, Sharon. *Mastering Weave Structures: Transforming Ideas into Great Cloth.* Interweave Press, Ft. Collins, CO, 2004

Atwater, Mary Meigs. *The Shuttle-Craft Book of American Hand-Weaving*, Macmillan Publishing Co., Inc., New York, 1973

Bress, Helene. *The Coverlet Book*, copyright Helene Bress, 2003

Collingwood, Peter. *The Techniques of Rug Weaving*, rev. ed., Faber and Faber Limited, London, 1993

Frey, Berta, *Designing and Drafting for Handweavers*, Macmillan Publishing Co., Inc., New York, 1958

Hoskins, Nancy Arthur. *Weft-Faced Pattern Weaves—Tabby to Taqueté*, Schiffer Publishing, Atglen, PA, 2011

Strickler, Carol, ed. *A Weaver's Book of 8-Shaft Patterns from the friends of* Handwoven, Interweave Press, Ft. Collins, CO, 1991

van der Hoogt, Madelyn,.*The Complete Book of Drafting for Handweavers*, Shuttle Craft Books, Basin, MT, 2000

Lace Weaves

Knisely, Tom. *Huck Lace Weaving Patterns with Color and Weave Effects*, Stackpole Books, Mechanicsburg, PA, 2019

van der Hoogt, Madelyn, ed. *The Best of Weaver's: Huck Lace*, XRX, Inc., Sioux Falls, SD, 2000

Twill Threading-Based Weaves

Brusic, Lucy M. *A Crackle Weave Companion: Exploring Four-shaft Crackle*, Kirk House Publishers, Minneapolis, MN, 2012

Moore, Jennifer. *Doubleweave*, Revised and expanded version, Interweave Press, Ft. Collins, CO, 2018

Snyder, Mary E. *The Crackle Weave*, 5th printing, Robin and Russ Handweavers, McMinnville, OR, 1989

Sullivan, Donna Lee. *Weaving Overshot: Redesigning the Tradition*, Interweave Press, Ft. Collins, CO, 1996

Tallarovic, Joanne. *The Weaver's Studio: Rep Weave and Beyond*, Interweave Press, Ft. Collins, CO, 2004

van der Hoogt, Madelyn, ed. *The Best of Weaver's: The Magic of Doubleweave*, XRX, Inc., Sioux Falls, SD, 2006

Unit Weaves

Sullivan, Donna Lee. *Summer and Winter: A Weave for All Seasons*, Interweave Press, Ft. Collins, CO, 1991

van der Hoogt, Madelyn, ed, *The Best of Weaver's: Summer and Winter Plus*, XRX, Inc., Sioux Falls, SD, 2010

INDEX

Note: Page references in italics indicate projects; references in parentheses indicate intermittent references.

R

S

T

U

W